Susannah Fullerton has been pa
for as long as she can remembe
at the University of Auckland an
degree in Victorian literature
Edinburgh. She is a well-known
speakers' circuit and gives talks regularly at the State
Library of NSW, the Art Gallery of NSW, and at WEA
and other education centres. Every year she leads popular
literary tours to the UK or to the USA.

Her first book, *Jane Austen—Antipodean Views*,
a collection of opinions about Jane Austen by famous
Australians and New Zealanders, was published in 2001.
Her second book, *Jane Austen and Crime*, was published
in 2005 and is the first-ever study of crimes such as
duelling, elopement, theft, poaching and even murder
in the writings of Jane Austen. Susannah is the president
of the Jane Austen Society of Australia.

She lives in Sydney.

Brief Encounters

Literary travellers in
Australia 1836–1939

SUSANNAH FULLERTON

PICADOR
Pan Macmillan Australia

To Ashley Wilson, the best of dads, with my love, and the hope that the chapter on Darwin will make up for my failing science at school.

Every effort has been made to contact copyright holders to obtain the necessary permission for use of copyrighted material in this book. Any person who may have been inadvertently overlooked should contact the publisher.

First published 2009 in Picador by Pan Macmillan Australia Pty Limited
1 Market Street, Sydney

National Library of Australia
Cataloguing-in-Publication data:

Fullerton, Susannah, 1960–
Brief Encounters: literary travellers in Australia 1836–1939/
Susannah Fullerton.

978 1 4050 3950 5 (pbk.)

Authors–Travel–Australia
Authors–Australia–Attitudes
Australia–Description and travel

919.4

Typeset in 13/16pt Granjon by Midland Typesetters, Australia
Printed in Australia by McPherson's Printing Group

Papers used by Pan Macmillan Australia Pty Limited are natural, recyclable products made from wood grown in sustainable forests. The manufacturing processes conform to the environmental regulations of the country of origin.

CONTENTS

FOREWORD

Susannah Fullerton brings to her writing all the attributes that have made her Sydney's most popular and engaging literary lecturer: liveliness, clarity, narrative drive, and a careful deployment of choice anecdotal detail. It is the liveliness itself, along with the narrator's infectious enthusiasm for her subjects, that sustains the reader through a sequence of disparate stories that might in other hands have collapsed into sameness. The passion for literature we are told Susannah Fullerton has had 'for as long as she can remember' is evident in every brief encounter the reader has with the famous authors in this book.

We are treated to a feast of irony, idiosyncrasy, and occasional insight, from Charles Darwin's fascination with the survival instincts of the misnamed lion-ant, through Mark Twain making light of the German language before an audience of German immigrants in Geelong and Jack London covering a bloody boxing match between a criminally mismatched Jack Johnson and Tommy Burns, to Arthur Conan Doyle's missionary spiritualism and a restless DH Lawrence, greeted on his arrival in Sydney by (of all things) a rainbow.

None of these authors could be said to have rewritten the Australian story in any spectacular or influential way, nor indeed could their experience of Australia be said to have precipitated any radical change in their own style or vision. Where Susannah Fullerton's chronological narrative sequence is most effective is as social history. Coleridge once said that watching Edmund Kean perform Shakespeare was like reading Shakespeare by flashes of lightning, and so in these peripheral episodes in the lives of a handful of famous authors we get sudden flashes of insight into the authors themselves, certainly, but also into the Australian nation and the Australian character: Anthony Trollope on our cultural cringe; Joseph Conrad's vision of Sydney's wasted, criminal 'underbelly' around The Rocks area and its wharves; Robert Louis Stevenson's histrionics over the failure of due deference; Rudyard Kipling on Australia's sad, second-hand Americanism; Arthur Conan Doyle on the 'dark stain' of white Australia's treatment of the Aboriginals.

It is not all negative, by any means, and one way or another in the hearts of each of the main players a respect for this awkward, egalitarian continent grows. The real hero of these narratives, however, is Sydney's harbour. On one thing, it seems, these illustrious occasional visitors and their excited hosts can heartily agree.

William Christie
9 February 2009

INTRODUCTION

'When I look at the map and see what an awfully ugly-looking country Australia is, I feel as if I want to go there to see if it cannot be changed into a more beautiful form.' Oscar Wilde never did get to Australia, either to change it or be changed by it. For him it remained that 'ugly-looking' shape on a map and little more. But the writers in this book *did* make the journey, not to try to change the way it looked but for a great variety of other reasons: they came for scientific research; to sort out difficult children; to make money from lecturing; to escape demanding women back home; to find themselves; to shop; to see doctors; and as part of their jobs. Two even came with a mission to convert.

Most arrived remarkably ignorant about the country. Generally, they knew about three things—kangaroos, convicts and Aboriginals. When the very first drawings of the strange marsupial, with its pouch and a tail like a fifth leg, were taken to England in the late 1700s, people were intrigued. Jane Austen's one and only reference to anything Australian is to this exotic creature, the 'Kangaroon' as she called it. Writers who visited were all anxious to see kangaroos, and most were disappointed that the countryside was not swarming with bounding 'roos. DH Lawrence was reduced to having his memorable encounter with a kangaroo not in the countryside but at the zoo.

Every writer came to Australia with a strong sense of the country's convict heritage. Most saw this as a blot on the nation's history, and yet as something deeply fascinating. Convicts were the stuff of fiction—Abel Magwitch, the unforgettable convict of Dickens' *Great Expectations* had been transported to Australia and there made a fortune. But how did convicts and their descendants fit into the social hierarchy? Visitors did not know how to categorise them, and had no idea how to treat the sons and daughters of felons. Each visiting writer searched the faces of Australians for the 'criminal stamp' which Robert Louis Stevenson's wife Fanny found so obvious, examining the society to see how convict origins may have shaped it. Charles Darwin saw chain gangs at work on the roads and gazed at them with horror and pity. Anthony Trollope, escorted around Port Arthur by old convicts, listened sympathetically to their stories and gave them tobacco. Along with many around the world, the literary visitors read Marcus Clarke's 1874 novel *For the Term of his Natural Life* to learn more of the experiences of the wretched prisoners transported to new lives at the other end of the earth.[1]

Many were just as fascinated by the 'black fellows' they encountered. Darwin observed the appearance and customs of Aboriginals from the scientific viewpoint;

---

1 American visitors read a different version of the novel. The original tragic ending was considered unsuitable for readers in the United States, so Marcus Clarke added extra, happier chapters for their edition. The novel was also published in Europe.

Trollope predicted they would soon die out; Jack London was convinced before visiting Australia that blacks were vastly inferior to whites and left without changing that opinion; but Agatha Christie loved looking at Aboriginal artefacts in the museum and wanted to learn more about those who had crafted them.

So these literary travellers arrived, naïve, unsure of what to expect, unaware of how the country and its inhabitants, human and animal, might affect them. And along with their suitcases, they brought personal baggage—their attitudes and prejudices, their convictions and problems. Often their final responses to Australia depended on how successful they were in achieving what they had come to do—whether that was to make money, solve personal problems or write books.

I include the 'brief encounters' of ten men and one woman in this book. Many more writers came and went during the century after Darwin's visit, and their experiences and reactions could have been added. I have chosen not to include them because of the inferior quality of what they wrote. They may have been well known in their day, but their fame has now, justifiably, faded. However, to whet your appetite, I'll mention a few here. William Howitt, novelist and author of travel and history books, came in 1852 and stayed for two years. His book *Land, Labour and Gold* recounted his experiences on the goldfields, while *A Boy's Adventures in the Wilds of Australia* was a popular novel that filled young Englishmen with a desire to find adventure in the outback. RH Horne came looking for gold in 1852 and stayed on for seventeen years, though he never got rich. The tale of Burke and Wills inspired his long poem 'Australian Explorers' and he also penned a lyric drama with the undramatic title of *Australian Facts and Prospects*. In 1855 Frank Fowler tried to form a Literary Association in New South Wales and wrote *Southern Lights and Shadows* in his two years in Australia. H Havelock Ellis, pioneer writer on sexual psychology, came to find his soul and resolve religious doubts. Australia helped him come to terms with his problems and inspired his novel *Kanga Creek: An Australian Idyll*. Poet and journalist Francis Adams came for five years and worked on local newspapers, but left depressed that Australian society was not more egalitarian. He gathered all his articles into *The Australians*, a book he published in 1893. JA Froude, renowned for his biography of Thomas Carlyle, visited briefly and was much criticised for the superficiality of his *Oceana or England and her Colonies*. EW Hornung, the popular creator of Raffles, the 'Gentleman Thief', spent 1884 to 1886 in Australia, and it was in the Victorian town of Yea that he had Raffles take his first steps into the world of crime. Hornung had published novels wholly or partly set in Australia even before his visit. Unusually, he sent Australian characters to London in his fiction, instead of depicting Englishmen travelling to the Antipodes, and his tales of bushrangers, station life and convict days reflect his fondness for Australia. Nat Gould is barely known today, but his works were popular during his lifetime, and he was responsible for creating an image of Australia and Australians among ordinary British readers. His enjoyment of the racing scene inspired his novel *The Double Event: A Tale of the Melbourne Cup*, a book called *On and Off the Turf in Australia* and many stories. Thomas Wood, who toured the country as a music examiner, wrote *Cobbers* about his travels and had fun tracking down the origins of 'Waltzing Matilda', a song he loved. One writer who was *not* as welcome a visitor was Czech journalist Egon Kisch. The Lyons' Government tried to deport him when he came to speak at an anti-Fascist conference in Melbourne. His book about the experience, *Landung in Australien*, was written in German.

Louisa Ann Meredith visited and wrote of the challenges of her new life in Australia in her *Notes and Sketches of New South Wales* and *My Home in Tasmania* after she came as an emigrant in 1839. A talented artist, Louisa illustrated her own works on natural history. She was a woman ahead of her time, encouraging her political husband to legislate for the conservation of countryside and wildlife. Her non-fiction works and two novels gave readers in Britain a greater knowledge of Australian flora and fauna. American temperance reformer and journalist, Jessie Ackerman, visited several times around the turn of the century and wrote *Australia from a Woman's Point of View* in 1913. She praised the role women had taken in its history: 'No words can express the part women have taken in the settlement of Australia . . . There is no kind of toil to which man has put his hand, but woman has bravely and heroically taken her share, bearing and rearing children, as well as performing unlimited and unnamed drudgery'. Jessie also contributed to the Australian suffrage movement.

Englishwoman Angela Thirkell (cousin to Rudyard Kipling) decided after her stay that Australia might be a 'wonderful country for Warrant Officers', but it was *not* the place for her! The voyage out gave her the material for *Trooper to the Southern Cross*, but her other thirty-four novels all had English settings. Fabian and political writer Beatrice Webb spent a joyless two months in Australia with her husband and fellow writer Sidney Webb as part of a round-the-world trip—she hated everything she saw and did in the 'crude and monotonous' continent. Her disapproval, irritation and contempt went into her *Australian Diary*.

Better known is John Galsworthy, creator of *The Forsyte Saga*. He formed a friendship with Joseph Conrad in South Australia, but only passed through briefly. H Rider Haggard, author of the bestselling *King Solomon's Mines*, visited for six weeks in early 1916, giving speeches and trying to persuade state governments to provide farming land for ex-soldiers and their families after the war. Australians liked his non-patronising manner and he was given a warm reception in Hobart, Melbourne, Sydney and Brisbane. Five years later W Somerset Maugham arrived from Honolulu to connect with a ship bound for Singapore. In spite of being in the country for only a very short time, he was received with 'the most gratifying enthusiasm'. He called Sydney 'the Mecca of the decrepit author' because writers whose fame had dwindled in Britain could still be made to feel courted and important there. He noted how Robert Louis Stevenson's visits some thirty years before were still remembered with excitement. Lastly, there was Zane Grey, who was attracted by stories of man-eating sharks in southern waters. More than forty million copies of his books were sold, so his tales of Australian fishing expeditions, and his belief that Australia was 'of beauty and wildness beyond the power of any pen to delineate', were carried to a vast readership around the world. He filmed *White Death* about sharks, and wrote *An American Angler in Australia*. *The Wilderness Trek* is his only novel with an Australian setting.

Many of these writers were popular in their day, but most have now sunk into obscurity. W Somerset Maugham and John Galsworthy are still recognisable names, but their visits were short, of minimal interest, and did not result in any literary works about Australia. The eleven writers included in this book, on the other hand, have enjoyed more lasting literary fame. Their works have remained in print, biographies have told and retold the stories of their lives, and their writings have been studied. Zane Grey might have felt he could never capture the country's beauty with his pen, but other writers have had greater success.

The authors in *Brief Encounters* wrote in a variety of genres during and after visiting Australia. They penned short stories for adults and children, novels and novellas, poems and memoirs, and of course travel books—Anthony Trollope's record of all he saw and did is an early version of a *Lonely Planet Guide*. What they wrote was sometimes controversial, yet always fascinating as an historical record. Some had significant literary worth and, occasionally, even literary genius. Kipling's *The Sing-Song of Old Man Kangaroo* and his poem 'Lichtenberg'; Lawrence's poem 'Kangaroo', and parts of his novel of the same name; Trollope's *John Caldigate*; Jack London's *A Piece of Steak*; and parts of Mark Twain's travel book, are all superb pieces of literature—these works exist because their authors travelled to Australia.

When Charles Darwin arrived in 1836, Australia's population was 89,417. By the time HG Wells visited, just over a century later, there were 3,538,660

Australians.[2] Darwin arrived after a long, arduous journey by sailing ship and travelled within the country by horse and cart, but HG Wells arrived on an ocean liner and complained that it didn't have all the mod-cons he expected. He took train and car trips between cities and he departed the country in an aeroplane. It was a century of enormous change, change reflected by each writer.

And yet, despite the differences wrought each decade, these writers had many reactions in common. All, except Agatha Christie, fell in love with Sydney Harbour. Only HG Wells saw it spanned by the Sydney Harbour Bridge, but the magnificent stretch of water, with its inlets, beaches and boats, impressed them all as being a view worth coming around the world to see. It is appropriate that the 'Writers' Walk' at Circular Quay is set beside the harbour they found so enchanting. Those who went there also fell in love with Tasmania, finding it more English than the rest of Australia, with a climate fresher and more temperate and, as modern visitors also discover, a place producing excellent food products. The Blue Mountains, with their stunning views, delighted all who visited them, so it is fitting that the 'Darwin Walk' is an attraction there today. Meat, its cheapness and abundance, was remarked upon by many, though some also thought the way it was cooked three times per day could be improved. And there was admiration for the pioneering spirit: the fact that early settlers had rapidly and efficiently established prosperous cities, built roads and transport systems, set up schools and libraries and other institutions. Darwin's grandfather

---

2   These population figures come from the website of the Australian Bureau of Statistics.

had written a poem and made a pottery medallion to commemorate the first landing by the British at Sydney Cove. HG Wells, when he arrived a hundred years later, found his books for sale in bookshops and his words quoted in newspapers; he could talk on the phone in Perth to someone in Sydney, and he could address a variety of cultural and political societies. Australians, with their resourcefulness and determination, had certainly achieved a great deal in a short time.

But there were things which irritated the writers as well. They were forced to change trains at Albury because of the different rail gauges between states, and were often roused from sleep to do so. It was a system they regarded as positively medieval. Many of their trips were disrupted by strikes: Robert Louis Stevenson had difficulty leaving because of maritime disputes, while Conrad's shipping work was disrupted by union stop-works. The Melbourne Cup, it was thought by many, should *not* 'stop the nation', and there was disapproval of the money wasted on betting and gambling. In theory, visiting authors approved of Australians' relaxed attitude to life and their lack of class-consciousness, but in practice it wasn't always quite so admirable. Several writers were irritated by servants who regarded themselves as 'equal' to those they served. There was a general feeling that Australians took informality too far, that there was not quite enough tugging of forelocks or doffing of caps. The Americans were less worried by this, being used to a more egalitarian society, but the British struggled to let go of the view that 'colonials' should display more deference.

Many also thought that Australians needed to be more modest and not enthusiastically praise their country to every tourist who arrived. Trollope called this 'blowing' and it irritated him intensely, but he was far from being the only one to get cross about it. During the one hundred years covered in this book there was an emerging sense of national pride as Australia forged an identity, nationally and internationally, separate from that of Britain (or 'Home' as it was called by many). But there was still a sense of inferiority, the 'cultural cringe', an awareness of being 'only colonials', which made many Australians acutely sensitive to criticism, overly touchy, a little too ready to ask for reassurance and to demand instant impressions of Australia.

Interestingly, another thing these literary travellers had in common was that the majority of them had given up religion. Only Trollope, Kipling and Agatha Christie were conventional churchgoers—the others were either atheists, agnostics or (as in Darwin's case) serious doubters. This high proportion of non-believers was unusual in the nineteenth and early twentieth centuries. Perhaps abandoning religion made them, as travellers, more ready to explore faraway places, to move out of comfort zones, to open their minds to the new and the challenging. Sir Arthur Conan Doyle and HG Wells arrived desperate to 'convert' as many Australians as they could, but they were not conventional missionaries—it was not the Bible they pushed, but Spiritualism and pacifism. Both managed to upset Australian Christians during their visits.

With so many different motivations for travelling to Australia, the authors inevitably encountered a range of reactions and achieved their aims with varying degrees of success. Some did what they set out to do, and went home happy. Others failed in their purpose, or were unrealistic in their aims, and so left dissatisfied. Some blamed Australia for not fixing their problems: others thanked Australia for sorting them out.

Australia's landscape is unique, its animals exotic and strange. All the literary travellers experienced culture shock and responded to the land in different ways. Darwin noted how the leaves of gum trees refused to behave like the leaves of an English tree; Kipling was frightened by the vast open spaces and whether or not the 'Yellow Peril' might arrive to fill them; DH Lawrence discovered the spirituality of the bush; and Agatha Christie found it sublimely artistic. Some rejoiced in the climate, others found the heat unbearable. HG Wells, visiting during a record-breaking heatwave, thought the bushfires so memorable that he wrote of them at length when he went home. Coming from densely populated Britain and America, they puzzled over the fact that most Australians lived around the edges of their land, leaving the middle empty. They found it too dry, too hot, too different. Whether they responded positively or negatively to those differences of landscape and of nationality, and how their personal responses influenced what they went on to write, is the story of this book.

⁂

Any traveller, literary or otherwise, walking today in Sydney's Domain (where Stevenson, Kipling, Lawrence and Jack London all once walked) can stop and pause in front of a statue of one of the greatest writers of all time. Robert Burns stands there in bronze with the plough that turned up a mouse and inspired one of his finest poems about man's relationship with the world around him. Burns never visited Australia in his short life, but his words made the journey for him, travelling from Scotland and making such an impact that statues have been erected in several Australian cities in his memory. In his 'To a Louse' he wrote the famous lines:

> O Wad some Pow'r the giftie gie us
> To see oursels as others see us.

Through their brilliant way with words, their powers of observation and their literary genius, Darwin, Trollope, Conrad, Stevenson, Kipling, Twain, London, Conan Doyle, Christie, Lawrence and Wells have given all Australians the 'pow'r' to see themselves as others saw them during one hundred years of their colourful and fascinating history. Thanks to these wonderful writers, the wish of Robert Burns has been fulfilled.

CHAPTER ONE

Charles Darwin

In January 1836 Charles Darwin lay on a sunny bank of the Cox's River, not far from Bathurst in NSW, and watched with interest as a life and death struggle took place nearby. It was happening in the little burrow of an antlion. A fly had fallen into the burrow and disappeared, providing the antlion with lunch. But an unwary ant came along soon after and it was this creature's desperate fight for life which fascinated Darwin. Sand flew up around the insect as it resisted its attacker and, finally, after violent efforts, the little ant was able to escape being turned into dessert.

To a young botanist, geologist and scientist like Darwin, the whole tiny episode raised so many interesting questions. Why had one insect been eaten, while another 'fitter' insect had managed to escape? Why were the creatures of this country so different from those he had observed back in England? What was the

Portrait of Charles Darwin by Richmond, painted just after Darwin visited Australia.

origin of these differences? How and why had they been created and who or what had created them? His mind tossed these questions around and he wondered and speculated about the creation of an ant that appeared to belong to the 'same genus' as the European ant, but at the same time had so many vital differences: 'An unbeliever in everything beyond his own reason, might exclaim, "Surely two distinct Creators must have been [at] work; their object however has been the same and certainly in each case the end is complete"'. How could God or 'any two workmen ever hit on so beautiful, so simple and yet so artificial a contrivance?' Were these different ants the result of 'periods of Creation . . . distinct and remote'? Had there been more than one Creator? Or, audacious thought, perhaps there had been no Creator at all?

It would be nice to regard this moment on an Australian riverbank as Charles Darwin's 'Eureka!' moment, the instant when his theory of the origin of species flashed upon him, ready formed and complete. In reality, Darwin's musings on that Australian riverbank would be just one of the many thousands of thinking sessions that would lead him to the full development of his evolutionary theory. Eight years later he was ready to write a 230-page 'sketch' of his ideas, but only in 1859, twenty-three years after watching those ants, was Darwin ready to present his full theories to the world in *The Origin of Species*. They were years of clarifying, studying, postulating and questioning, trying to find answers to the questions he had raised in Australia and elsewhere, until Darwin was so certain of his evidence that it couldn't be disputed. The result was a book that created a furore, both academic and religious, and which launched a debate about science and religion that, even today, remains unresolved.

It's ironic that the literary visitor who underwent the longest and most arduous voyage to Australia should be the one who least liked to travel. Getting to Australia was far from easy for Darwin. He suffered chronic seasickness and weeks and weeks aboard the *Beagle* were spent battling nausea, lying wretched in his bunk. No wonder he could state with conviction, 'I hate every wave of the ocean'. He avoided ships for the rest of his life after he returned to England—nothing would induce him to go through that dreadful nausea ever again. A trip to Paris as a young man would remain his only experience of the Continent, and the last forty years of his life were passed quietly at Down House in Kent, with only occasional excursions to London, or to Shrewsbury, his birthplace. 'Certainly I never was intended for a traveller', Darwin wrote from Sydney to his friend and mentor Professor Henslow. And yet, it was his epic five years of travel with HMS *Beagle* that made him famous and which turned him into a writer whose books would change the world.

Darwin was excited about seeing Australia well before his arrival in January 1836, an excitement caused not only by his usual longing to be on dry land once more. 'I am looking forward with more pleasure to seeing Sydney, than to any other part of the voyage', he wrote to his sister Caroline. She would certainly have understood his anticipation, knowing of the Darwin family connection with the place. Their remarkable grandfather, Erasmus Darwin, naturalist, doctor and writer, had written what was probably the very first published poem about Australia. It was inspired by a lump of Sydney clay picked up in Sydney Cove by Captain Arthur Phillip and sent by Phillip to Darwin's other grandfather, Josiah Wedgwood. Wedgwood was already a famous potter, and in his workshops he turned this chunk of clay into a medallion. The medallion depicted personifications of 'Hope' encouraging 'Labour' and 'Art' to bring joy and security to the new white settlement of Sydney Cove. 'Peace' looks on benignly. Several copies were made of the medallion (one of which is now in Sydney's Powerhouse Museum) but it

Drawing by Owen Stanley of HMS Beagle *in 1841, in Sydney Harbour on a return voyage after the voyage which Darwin made.*

The Sydney Cove Wedgwood medallion, made by Darwin's grandfather Josiah Wedgwood, for which Erasmus Darwin, his other grandfather, wrote a poem —probably the first published poem about Australia.

was the original shown by Wedgwood to his good friend Erasmus Darwin which prompted the poem. Entitled 'Visit of Hope to Sydney Cove near Botany Bay' and published in 1789, it begins:

> Where Sydney Cove her lucid bosom swells,
> Courts her young navies and the storm repels,
> High on a rock, amid the troubled air,
> Hope stood sublime, and wav'd her golden hair.

And it continues in many more dull and sentimental lines, predicting that one day Sydney Cove would have 'broad streets and crescents', 'cities o'er the cultur'd land', 'solid roads', 'Embellish'd villas', farms and orchards, piers and quays. Charles Darwin knew both the poem and the medallion and was keen to see if his grandfather's prophecies for Sydney, made nearly fifty years before, had been fulfilled.

His other reason for wanting to see Australia was social. He had friends to visit and people to meet. Conrad Martens had joined the *Beagle* as ship's artist from Rio de Janeiro, two months after the voyage began, until leaving it in 1834 in Valparaiso. Armed with a letter of introduction to Captain King, an influential Sydney citizen, from the *Beagle*'s captain Robert FitzRoy, Martens had sailed to New South Wales with a sketchbook full of travel paintings, in the hope that new Australians would be avid to buy them. Darwin and Martens had got on well, so Darwin was looking forward to seeing him again and buying some pictorial souvenirs from Marten's Bridge Street studio.

He also wanted to see Captain Philip Parker King, last seen when King waved goodbye to the *Beagle* from

Conrad Martens (by Maurice Felton), Darwin's shipmate on board the Beagle *and the artist whose paintings of Sydney hung in Darwin's study for the rest of his life.*

the Plymouth docks. King had himself commanded the *Beagle* expedition when the little ship made its first great surveys of the southern coasts of South America; but after seeing the ship off on its next big voyage, King had retired to a farm (between Parramatta and Emu Ferry) established by his father Governor Philip King. Darwin planned to visit him there. When he did, the two men had a great time talking over 'the Natural History of T[ierra] del Fuego'.

But more than anything else he wanted contact with his family and he approached Sydney hoping that letters from home would be waiting there. Charles Darwin was one of six children. His mother Susannah died when he was only eight years old, but his three older sisters brought him up and had been more like mothers than sisters to him. With his brother Erasmus, young Charles had collected beetles, trawled nets, conducted laboratory experiments and learned to be a naturalist. The brothers were very close. He was also close to a large number of Wedgwood cousins, and he had Cambridge friends and scientific colleagues he was likewise anxious to hear from. For family news he was more than anxious; he was almost desperate. He'd been away from those he loved for over four years and the last family letter he'd received was in the Galapagos seven months earlier. It had been posted March 1835 so he had been cut off from up-to-date home news for nearly a year. It's easy to understand how getting letters was starting to obsess him. Everyone on board was in like condition: 'There never was a ship so full of home-sick heroes as the Beagle'.

With excitement mounting on board, HMS *Beagle* approached Sydney Harbour on 11 January 1836. The lighthouse at South Head came into view at ten past eleven that night, so it was dark when they arrived. Darwin, however, was up early to get his first proper view of Australia: 'Early in the morning, a light air carried us towards the entrance of Port Jackson: instead of beholding a verdant country, a straight line of white cliffs brought to our minds the shores of Patagonia. A solitary light-house, built of white stone, alone told us,

Sydney in 1836, the year of Darwin's visit, in a painting by William Romaine Govett.

we were near to a great and populous city'.[1] The ship entered the harbour and Darwin, ever the naturalist, took note first of the geology and flora before observing human habitation. The harbour he thought fine and spacious, but 'the level country, showing on the cliff-formed shores, bare and horizontal strata of sandstone, was covered by woods of thin scrubby trees that bespoke useless sterility'. Also in view were two- to three-storey houses, several windmills and a little fort.

Darwin never fell in love with Sydney. Perhaps his view of the city (which then had a population of twenty-three thousand) was coloured by what happened next—'not a single letter' awaited him, or any other man on the *Beagle*. He was devastated. Certain that his family had been writing, he feared that his post would follow him around the world without ever catching up with him: 'The same fate will follow us to the

---

1   This was the Macquarie Light, designed by ex-convict Francis Greenway and built in 1818. A replica of it still stands today.

C. of Good Hope; & probably when we reach England, I shall not have received a letter dated within the last 18 months', he wrote despairingly. It was a melancholy prospect, especially for a man who loved letters as much as Darwin did (nearly 14,500 of his letters are known to exist). No wonder he felt 'much inclined to sit down and have a good cry'.

Darwin spent three full days in Sydney. Just as his grandfather had predicted in the poem, Darwin found its streets 'broad' and its roads 'solid'. 'Gigs, Phaetons & Carriages with livery Servants' took people from 'Embellish'd villas' to shops, farms and businesses. Interestingly, the prosperity and development he observed made him think of England and left him feeling proud to be English: 'It is a most magnificent testimony of the power of the British nation: here, in a less promising country, scores of years have effected many times over, more than centuries in South America—My first feeling was to congratulate myself, that I was born an Englishman'.

He discovered that the Sydney obsession with real estate was alive and well in 1836: 'everyone complains of the high rents and difficulty in procuring a house'. Sydney, he felt, was a city of business and money-making. Even ex-convicts, he was intrigued to see, were making fortunes. He heard of one who was planning to return to England taking with him one hundred thousand pounds, made from auctioneering.[2] Darwin disapprovingly noted that everyone seemed 'bent on acquiring wealth'.

---

2 According to *Charles Darwin in Australia* this was probably Abraham Polack, who made his fortune 'in less than 10 years'.

His friend and disciple Thomas Huxley would later remark: 'I know no finer field of exertion for any naturalist than Sydney harbour', but Darwin was keen to do his botanising elsewhere. There's no record as to whether the 'pleasant walks' he took in the Botanic Gardens and Domain yielded specimens for his collection. What he really wanted was to get into the interior: 'Large towns, all over the world are nearly similar, & it is only by such excursions that the characteristic features can be perceived'. So he hired two horses and a guide to take him on the 120-mile trip to Bathurst, at that time the second-biggest settlement in the colony. The name of Darwin's companion isn't known, but it is known that he left his servant Syms Covington behind. Syms had accompanied his master on many collecting expeditions, but this time he stayed in Sydney. Perhaps during the nine days of Darwin's absence Syms found his own attractions because he would return there a few years later and make New South Wales his permanent home.

In Darwin's pocket, when he set off for Bathurst, was a new notebook. On all his field expeditions he carried a memorandum book and a metallic pencil so he could jot down the impressions, types of rocks and the curious plants or creatures he saw. Later he would write up these notes more fully for his *Beagle Diary*. Fourteen of these notebooks had been filled by the time he reached Sydney, so a brand new one was needed for the next stage of his journey. It provides a wonderful record of his first fresh impressions of the Australian countryside.[3]

3 This notebook, known as the Sydney–Mauritius Notebook, is now in the Darwin Museum at Down House, Kent.

Darwin's route was not the one that a traveller driving from Sydney to Bathurst would take today. If he had a map with him it would probably have been that created by Major Mitchell just two years before, for it was the major's route that he followed. (Later Darwin and Mitchell would correspond when Darwin had questions to ask about the geology of the Blue Mountains.) The first stage took him to Parramatta where he stopped for a pub lunch, then on to Emu Ferry during the afternoon. The night of 16 January was spent there. Early on the 17th he crossed the Nepean River in a ferry boat (which cost 2s.8d for the two men and the horses), and then began the ascent up Mitchell's new road, Mitchell's Pass. This new road, only opened in March 1834, is further north than the road in use today, but the arched stone bridge Darwin used is once again open to traffic after restoration. Lunch was eaten at the 'Weatherboard' (no longer there). The position of the little inn, which began as a storage hut, is today marked by the Darwin Tree, planted on the centenary of Charles Darwin's stop there.

Darwin then left his driver and set off alone on a walk to see Wentworth Falls. As any tourist can discover today, the Blue Mountains is a place full of surprises. A walker can be strolling along and then, on rounding a corner, discover that a magnificent view has, without warning, opened out beneath him. This is exactly what Darwin found: 'suddenly & without any preparation, through the trees, which border the pathway, an immense gulf is seen at the depth of perhaps 1500 ft. . . . Below is the grand bay or gulf, for I know not what other name to give it, thickly covered with forest'. This too has been commemorated for the modern hiker. 'The Darwin Walk' is a two-kilometre stretch that follows his path, and a plaque marks the spot near where he saw the

> **WENTWORTH FALLS 1836**
>
> IN THE MIDDLE OF THE DAY WE BAITED OUR HORSES AT A LITTLE INN, CALLED THE WEATHERBOARD. THE COUNTRY HERE IS ELEVATED 2,800 FEET ABOVE THE SEA. ABOUT A MILE AND A HALF FROM THIS PLACE, THERE IS A VIEW EXCEEDINGLY WELL WORTH VISITING. BY FOLLOWING DOWN A LITTLE VALLEY AND ITS TINY RILL OF WATER, AN IMMENSE GULF IS UNEXPECTEDLY SEEN THROUGH THE TREES, WHICH BORDER THE PATHWAY, AT THE DEPTH OF PERHAPS 1,500 FEET. WLKING ON A FEW YARDS ONE STANDS ON THE BRINK OF A VAST PRECIPICE, AND BELOW IS THE GRAND BAY OR GULF (FOR I KNOW NOT WHAT OTHER NAME TO GIVE IT), THICKLY COVERED WITH FOREST. THE POINT OF VIEW IS SITUATED AS IF AT THE HEAD OF A BAY, THE LINE OF CLIFF DIVERGING ON EACH SIDE, AND SHOWING HEADLAND BEHIND HEADLAND, AS ON A BOLD SEA-COAST. THESE CLIFFS ARE COMPOSED OF HORIZONTAL STRATA OF WHITISH SANDSTONE, AND SO ABSOLUTELY VERTICAL ARE THEY, THAT IN MANY PLACES, A PERSON STANDING ON THE EDGE, AND THROWING DOWN A TONE, CAN SEE IT STRIKE THE TREES IN THE ABYSS BELOW. SO UNBROKEN IS THE LINE, THAT IT IS SAID, IN ORDER TO REACH THE FOOT OF THE WATERFALL, FORMED BY THIS LITTLE STREAM, IT IS NECESSARY TO GO A DISTANCE OF SIXTEEN MILES ROUND. ABOUT FIVE MILES DISTANT IN FRONT, ANOTHER LINE OF CLIFF EXTENDS, WHICH THUS APPEARS COMPLETELY TO ENCIRCLE THE VALLEY, AND HENCE THE NAME OF BAY IS JUSTIFIED, AS APPLIED TO THIS GRAND AMPHITHEATRICAL DEPRESSION. IF WE IMAGINE A WINDING HARBOUR, WITH ITS DEEP WATER SURROUNDED BY BOLD CLIFF-LIKE SHORES, LAID DRY, AND A FOREST SPRUNG UP ON ITS SANDY BOTTOM, WE SHOULD THEN HAVE THE APPEARANCE AND STRUCTURE HERE EXHIBITED. THIS KIND OF VIEW WAS TO ME QUITE NOVEL, AND EXTREMELY MAGNIFICENT
>
> EXTRACT FROM THE JOURNALS OF CHARLES DARWIN JANUARY 17TH, 1838

The plaque on the Darwin Tree in the Blue Mountains, commemorating the place where Darwin stayed a night.

view that so impressed him, a view that has not changed since he stood there, admiring.

The night was spent at Blackheath in the 'very comfortable' Scotch Thistle Inn (now gone, although some of its sandstone blocks make up a commemorative cairn opposite Blackheath Railway Station). January 18 began with an early morning constitutional stroll of three miles to see Govett's Leap, 'a view of a similar, but even perhaps more stupendous, character' than the view of the day before, though perhaps not as surprising as he'd already seen the view in two pictures made by his friend Conrad Martens. After that he set off for the Victoria Pass and Old Bowenfels.

Here Darwin took a detour. He had a letter of introduction to a Mr Andrew Brown, superintendent of Wallerawang Station. He stayed two nights on the station, along with its fifteen thousand sheep. In his youth, Darwin had been so fond of hunting that his father had had to warn him about becoming addicted to it, he had not yet grown out of the compulsion to shoot everything that moved. So he was delighted when Mr Brown offered to give him an Australian experience of hunting, and they rode out into the bush together. Every tourist who comes to Australia wants to see a kangaroo. Charles Darwin was no exception, but unlike the modern tourist, he wanted to shoot one when he saw it. His diary records his disappointment at not seeing this strange and enchanting animal. A kangaroo rat was hunted out of a tree, but Darwin never did get to see (or kill) a kangaroo during his time in Australia. He wrote with regret in his notebook that kangaroos were 'scarce' and later predicted that they would soon be extinct. Their ride took them north to the Wolgan Valley and it was while resting by the Cox's River that Darwin watched the antlion and began to ponder the creation and origins of Australian species.

This was no easy journey that Darwin had embarked upon. January 20 saw him taking 'a long day's ride to Bathurst', as he crossed the Great Dividing Range at its highest point. The temperature reached 48°C. Not surprisingly, he felt 'half roasted with the intense heat' and was relieved to reach Bathurst where he was to stay at the military barracks (he had another letter of introduction to Captain Chetwode, the troop commander there).

No other literary visitor to Australia has brought with him such a highly trained naturalist's eye. Darwin was an obsessive observer of the world around him. As a small boy he'd sat by Shrewsbury's Severn River noting plants and insects. In the Galapagos he had observed the finches and how they differed from one island to the next.

At the end of his life he lay on his sickbed watching an Australian climbing plant, trying to discover what made its tendrils climb in the manner and direction they did. He was a born naturalist, with an intense curiosity about his environment. So what did he see in the Australian landscape and what did he make of it?

Darwin was not enamoured of gum trees. It must be remembered that he was a Shropshire lad, from a lush part of England where the variety and rich foliage of the trees had given him endless pleasure. Australian flora failed to match up: 'The trees nearly all belong to one peculiar family; the foliage is scanty & of a rather peculiar light green tint'. He found the trees messy: 'the bark of some kinds annually falls or hangs dead in long shreds, which swing about with the wind: & hence the woods look desolate and untidy—Nowhere is there an appearance of verdure or fertility, but rather that of arid sterility'. He found the millions of eucalypts 'scrubby', too 'uniform' and 'exceedingly monotonous' and pitied Australians because they could not see these trees change with the seasons: 'The inhabitants of this hemisphere ... thus lose perhaps one of the most glorious, though to our eyes common, spectacles in the world—the first bursting into full foliage of the leafless tree'. The botanist in him noted that the gum's leaves hung vertically, rather than 'nearly horizontal' as did those of most European trees, so that they were less scorched by the sun. But he missed the shade that a flatter canopy of leaves would have provided. Generally Australian trees proved a disappointment to him and crops didn't fare much better in his opinion. They seemed sparse and shrivelled, and with the lack of a reliable water supply to nourish them, could not, he felt, ever 'succeed on a very extended scale'.

He looked at parched fruit orchards and was saddened to see everywhere the scorching of bushfires. On his return from Bathurst he actually walked unconcernedly through smoke from fires raging nearby.

Darwin was more impressed with the wildlife than he was with the plants. Although disappointed not to see a kangaroo or emu, he did have an experience that many Australians have not shared. He saw a platypus. In fact, he saw several 'diving and playing in the water' and was intrigued by this 'most extraordinary animal' that looks like a mixture of a duck and an otter. Mr Brown, his hunting companion, shot one and although Darwin had just been watching with delight as it frolicked in the stream, he still considered it 'a great feat, to be in at the death of so wonderful an animal'. Not words to please any modern naturalist! The birds he saw, 'Coccatoos', parrots and currawongs impressed him. Darwin was critical of the lack of imagination shown by settlers in the naming of many of the animals and insects of their new land: 'animals are called tigers and Hyaenas, simply because they are Carnivorous', and complained that the 'lion-ant' bore no resemblance to a lion. Such criticism was a bit rich coming from a man whose own family had re-used names with a monotonous lack of imagination; Erasmus, Josiah and Charles having been recycled with each generation.

The geology of the Blue Mountains fascinated Darwin. Like most every tourist to the area, he was overwhelmed by the views once he got over his initial surprise at finding that the 'mountains' were not the sort of tall protruding hills he'd been used to. The 'whitish Sandstone' of the cliffs, the deep valleys like arms of the sea, the stratifications of rock were quite novel to him and left him wondering how 'the enormous amount of stone' had been so formed. Was it erosion 'by the action of water'? Had the area once been beneath the sea? How long had it all taken? For the rest of his life he would puzzle over possible answers to these questions.

Human beings were never quite as intriguing to Charles Darwin as rocks, but still he took an interest in the people he encountered on his journey to Bathurst. There were two new 'species' for him to study and he came across both on the first day. 'The most novel and not very pleasing object are the Iron gangs; or parties of Convicts'. Dressed in yellow and grey, labouring convict gangs were a common sight in and around Sydney in 1836. Wallerawang Station had forty convicts as labourers. They were 'hardened profligate men' in Darwin's view, after he heard stories of their drinking and violence from Andrew Brown. His Wedgwood family had been fighters in the campaign to abolish the slave trade and Darwin compared the convicts he saw to 'the slaves from Africa', but also seemed to feel that they'd brought their misfortune upon themselves through crime and therefore lacked a slave's 'claim for compassion'.

More worthy of compassion, in his view, were the Aboriginals. He had the 'good fortune' to see 'a score of the Aboriginal Blacks [pass] by, each carrying ... a bundle of Spears & other weapons'. For a shilling they put on a spear-throwing display for him. Darwin found their faces 'good-humoured & pleasant', but ranked them as 'savages' on the scale of human civilisation. He did pity them for the ravages that alcohol, European diseases and loss of hunting grounds were making on their numbers. Later, in Tasmania, he considered that 'Van Diemen's Land enjoys the great advantage of being free from a native population', but still regarded as 'cruel' the process of hunting down and exterminating that had brought about this freedom. What he saw made him speculate about the implications of competition between racial groups: 'Wherever the European had trod, death seems to pursue the aboriginal . . . the varieties of man seem to act one on each other; in the same way as different species of animals—the stronger always extirpating the weaker'.

The prosperity of the white settlers surprised him. The roads were excellent, the inns were comfortable, the pubs were plentiful (too plentiful, he felt, after passing seventeen pot-houses between Sydney and Parramatta), the food was tasty, and the locals civil. Bathurst, however, did not please him. It was 'a place of exile' and 'not very inviting'. He had been told *not* to form *too good* an impression of the town, but never felt 'in the least danger' of doing so. Even its church, Holy Trinity, now an historic monument, he thought 'hideous'.[4] To be fair, Bathurst was in the grip of drought, with hot winds and dust storms, but by January 22 Darwin was delighted to leave the place behind him.

He took a different route back to Sydney, south of the way he'd come, via O'Connell, Tarana and Lithgow. One day's journey included thirty-seven kilometres of riding, and then on reaching Wentworth Falls he took a five-kilometre walk through the bush to have another look at the view. He and his guide averaged forty-five kilometres a day, plus the extra sightseeing trips he did on his own. No mean feat on bad roads in a hot Australian summer. By January 24 he was sick, and

4 Only opened for business the previous year, Holy Trinity has, since Darwin's visit, been extended and improved. When it was new, many shared Darwin's opinion of its ugliness.

spent a day in bed, and then on the 26th descended from the mountains to Dunheved, home of his friend Captain King. There, chatting to King, he recovered and had a chance to enjoy some colonial social life. King took him to Parramatta to visit Hannibal and Ann Macarthur at their home 'Vineyards' across the river from Elizabeth Farm. After all the dust, heat and scorched trees of the past week, the colonnaded house must have seemed like a little piece of English heaven. There were lush gardens, a well-stocked cellar, hordes of servants, a ballroom and four pretty daughters of the house to flirt with. Later, two of his *Beagle* shipmates would marry two of these girls, but Darwin left no record as to whether he was tempted himself. Reluctantly he had to leave this 'most English-like house' and ride on alone into Sydney.

He had two days before the *Beagle* sailed to gain final impressions of Sydney. They were not good ones. The bookshops were empty and inferior (a serious problem for a lifelong reader of scientific books, travel, poetry and novels), the lower classes were dissolute, the society was too divided into factions, there were too many convicts ('being surrounded by convict servants, must be dreadful'), prices were 'villainously dear' and everyone was obsessed with making money. He was glad to go beetle-hunting for a few hours to escape the rancour and jealousy of Sydney society. As the authors of *Charles Darwin in Australia* have noted, 'of the ninety-two species [he] collected in Sydney, thirty-one were previously unknown'. At least the specimen collecting was worthwhile, even if the rest of the Sydney visit was disappointing. 'Nothing', he concluded, 'but rather severe necessity should compel me to emigrate'. While he felt proud that Britain had established such a colony, he foresaw no great future for Sydney and he decided that 'On the whole I do not like new South Wales'.

No sailor in the Sydney to Hobart yacht race could have hoped for a better run down the east coast than the *Beagle* had from January 30 to February 4. As they neared Tasmania, however, the weather turned nasty—cold and squally, and as they 'entered the mouth of Storm Bay: the weather justified this awful name'. Once again, the first things to strike Darwin were the rock formations at the mouth of the Derwent River: 'extensive Basaltic platforms, the sides of which show fine facades of columns'. Then he noticed the 'fine & broad' streets, the fort, warehouses and, brooding over all, Mount Wellington, which he did not think picturesque.

Tasmania at the time of Darwin's visit had a population of 36,505 people, 13,826 of whom lived in Hobart. He spent twelve days there and although his homesickness was daily increasing and he never saw a ship 'start for England, without a most dangerous inclination to bolt', he was happy there—much happier than he had been in New South Wales. It was a good place to spend his twenty-seventh birthday on February 12, though he appears to have had no special celebration for what would be the last birthday he ever spent out of England.

Dung beetles and weevils helped keep him happy. Darwin did a lot of walking and botanising in Tasmania. With Syms Covington he spent five and a half hours climbing Mount Wellington (it was always his custom in a new place to climb the nearest hill to learn the lie of the land), he took 'long pleasant walks', caught a ferry to Kangaroo Point and was taken on rides through the bush by George Frankland, the Surveyor General. Every excursion resulted in interesting specimens—of the 119 species that he took back on board ship, sixty-three were unknown to science. He found wasps and ladybirds, bees and beetles, and the dung beetle that especially fascinated him because it raised important issues of local adaptation. It's amusing to picture Darwin rooting about in cow pats trying to extract the specimens he needed and writing in his new notebook about the exact quality of the dung. He was a contented man as he did so, and happy also in concluding that dung beetles which had lived on kangaroo dung until thirty-three years before, had adapted remarkably quickly and successfully to cow dung when that animal was introduced.[5]

Shells, barnacles (Darwin would later spend eight years of his life writing the definitive book on barnacles), lizards, worms and skinks were all gathered into his nets and bags, to be taken back to England where they would be categorised by the foremost experts of the day. One has to wonder what his ship's cabin smelt like on the return voyage with all these specimens on board. Darwin also tried to add a snake to his collection. As he caught it, the snake's abdomen burst open and 'a small snake appeared from the disrupted egg'; it was a live-bearing rather than

5 *Charles Darwin in Australia* explains that 'This rapid adaptation is still regarded as quite remarkable especially in view of recent evidence showing that among the *Onthophagus* dung beetles observed by Darwin, only the Tasmanian members of the species have such catholic tastes in dung: on mainland Australia, three of the four species are associated solely with the dung of native animals'. *Charles Darwin in Australia*, p 126.

an egg-laying snake. He examined it with interest and with absolutely no concern for his safety, but the creature he held so casually was either a copperhead or a black tiger snake. One bite from either variety would have killed him, so the world came awfully close to never knowing *The Origin of Species*.

In 1844 Darwin published a geological work called *Volcanic Islands*. A section of this book gives an account of Tasmanian geology and is the result of his wanderings around Hobart. Once again the notebook was in use—he made extensive jottings, which he wrote up (when seasickness would allow) on the return voyage to England, and he took back with him samples of sandstone, greenstone, basalt, mudstone, travertine, quartz, lime-stone and nine different sorts of fossil. At Long Beach near Battery Point he became the first person to realise that the area he was exploring was once the crater of a volcano. George Frankland, his guide on some of these collecting walks, soon became a friend. The two men had much in common as Frankland had founded the Van Diemen's Land Society which aimed at scientific discoveries and publications. Frankland proved his friendship by recommending to Darwin the best places for field research, providing him with a horse to ride, and discussing with him his findings at the end of the day.

It was also thanks to Frankland that Charles Darwin had his 'most agreeable evening since leaving England'. George Frankland was thirty-five years old and had been nine years resident in Tasmania. 'Secheron', his home, still stands today at Battery Point, and it was there that Darwin ate his birthday dinner. A few nights later he dined with the Attorney General, Alfred Stephen, at his house in

Macquarie Street. This was a musical evening and Darwin greatly enjoyed the 'first rate Italian' performances in the elegantly furnished home. He gained the impression that Hobart had 'a good deal of Society' which was 'much pleasanter than that of Sydney'. He heard talk of private balls and fancy dress parties that were well attended, he walked in gardens that 'delightfully resemble England', saw attractive and flourishing farms and a prosperous settlement when he rode the twenty-two miles to New Norfolk, and saw fewer rich convicts parading ostentatiously in their carriages. All this made him feel that if 'obliged to emigrate [he] should prefer this place' to any other in Australia or to what he had seen of New Zealand.[6] Tasmania reminded all the homesick *Beagle* men of England and they all preferred Tasmania to New South Wales.

With rocks, shells, beetles and crew back on board, the *Beagle* set sail in a fair wind on February 17. This was a few days later than planned because poor weather had prevented Captain FitzRoy from taking the sextant readings that were an essential part of their surveys, but at last the little ship set off bravely along the southern coast of Australia. Poor Darwin, seasick again, spent the ensuing weeks in a state of misery until they weighed anchor in King George Sound, on the south-west coast where Albany is today, on March 6.

---

6 New Zealand, which Darwin visited for nine days before arriving in Australia, was not a place that impressed him at all. He only saw the Bay of Islands, but there he found the Maoris dirty and uncivilised and the whole population 'addicted to drunkenness and all kinds of vice'. He felt the white people there were 'the refuse of society' and was happy to leave: 'I believe we were all glad to leave New Zealand. It is not a pleasant place'.

The settlement in which Charles Darwin spent his last week in Australia was a new one, barely a decade old. It was a dreary little place. Captain FitzRoy was so unimpressed by its straggling homes, cheerless setting and bare hills, that he was tempted to sail away there and then. Darwin 'formed a very low opinion of the place' and could 'not remember since leaving England, having passed a more dull, uninteresting time'.

However, he didn't waste his time. Once again he hurried off the ship and was soon out geologising and botanising. His collecting excursions took him out around the shores of Princess Royal Harbour and he was lucky to find a previously unknown species of rodent, the Australian bush rat, which he tempted into a trap with cheese. Another find was the southern frog, known only to that part of Australia. He and his shipmates went fishing and of the twenty types that were caught, four turned out to be new species. To some of the insects he netted and trapped, Darwin's name has since been given—*Haplodelphax darwinii* and *Alleloplasis darwinii* are planthoppers; *Hydroporus darwinii* is a diving beetle; *Ogcodes darwinii* is a seed bug and *Anipo darwinii* is a parasitic wasp. Not a bad quantity of nomenclature for one naturalist to leave behind him. Indeed, it's odd that Darwin found King George Sound as boring as he did, when it yielded so many intriguing specimens and so many detailed geological notes and samples. The area is today noted for its botanical richness and diversity; it should have been a paradise for Darwin.

There were also matters of human interest to be observed. An Aboriginal tribe 'called the White Coccatoo men' had come to town to stare at the new arrivals and were bribed by 'tubs of boiled rice and sugar' to 'hold a "Corrobery" or dancing party'. Darwin was fascinated by the entertainment and wrote a detailed account in his *Diary*:

> As soon as it grew dark they lighted small fires & commenced their toilet which consisted in painting themselves in spots & lines, with a white colour.—As soon as the dance commenced, large fires were kept blazing, round which the women & children were collected as spectators.—
>
> The Coccatoo & King George's men [formed] two distinct parties & danced generally in answer to each other. The dancing consisted in the whole set running either sideways or in Indian file into an open space & stamping the ground all together & with great force.—These were accompanied each time with a kind of grunt or sigh, & by beating of their clubs & weapons & various gesticulations, such as extending their arms or wriggling their bodies.
>
> It was a most rude barbarous scene & to our ideas without any sort of meaning; but we observed that the women & children watched the whole proceeding with much interest.—Perhaps these dances originally represented some scenes such as wars & victories; there was one called the Emu dance where the set extended one arm in a bent manner: so as to imitate the movements of the neck of a flock of Emus. [In] Another dance a man took off all the motions of a Kangaroo grazing in the woods, whilst another man crawled

up & pretended to spear it.—When both tribes
mingled in one dance, the ground trembled with
the heaviness of their steps & the air resounded
with their wild cries.

Leaving Australia proved more difficult than arriving.
The weather was bad and strong winds and rain kept
the *Beagle* in port from March 10 to 14. Even after
setting out, she ran aground and had to be pulled off
by cable and a schooner. Darwin began to think they
would never get away. Finally, however, the little ship
was free and sailed out of the harbour to the oceans that
must be crossed and the thousands of nautical miles to
be traversed before home waters were reached.

For the desperately homesick men on board, any
delay caused by the weather was frustrating, so it was
a relief to them all to depart and be at least heading in
the direction of England. Darwin was longing to be
back there, with his father and siblings, with the experts
who could analyse and categorise what he'd collected,
and with the cousins of whom he was so fond. One of
those cousins, Emma Wedgwood, soon became his
beloved wife and the mother of their ten children. His
collections became the basis of the many papers and
books Darwin wrote over the next forty-five years of
his life. The voyage of the *Beagle* became the starting
point of his fame and notoriety. With that in mind, it's
disappointing that the last words he wrote in Australia
were so negative: 'Farewell Australia, you are a rising
infant and doubtless some day will reign a great princess
in the South. But you are too great and ambitious for
affection, yet not great enough for respect; I leave your
shores without sorrow or regret'.

While the master was delighted to be home, the servant was not so happy. As Syms Covington[7] sorted the extraordinary collection of rocks and insects, birds and plants Darwin had brought home, and laboriously copied manuscripts, he pondered his own future. He'd taken a fancy to Australia and couldn't get it out of his mind. For a young, single, lower-class man like Syms, Australia appeared a golden land of opportunity. Two and a half years after returning to England, he decided to emigrate.

Syms Covington, Darwin's servant and assistant, who settled in Australia and who helpfully sent Darwin barnacle specimens.

Darwin, although sorry to lose a good servant, was happy to give all the help he could. Letters of introduction were written recommending Syms as 'a most useful assistant', honest and hard-working. These letters were addressed to William Macleay (a zoologist colleague who had gone to Sydney in 1839 to help his father, former Colonial Secretary Alexander Macleay), to Captain PP King and to Major Mitchell. He also helpfully arranged for Syms to work his passage as a ship's cook. With this assistance, Syms Covington left England in late 1839. Australia was good to Syms—he appears to have soon found work as a clerk (helped by Captain King) and within a year was married.

He was grateful to Darwin and wrote to tell him how he'd prospered. Much of the original correspondence has been lost, but some of the letters were published in a

---

7   The name 'Syms' is probably an abbreviation of Simon, but there is no printed record of him by that name.

Sydney newspaper in 1884 and they reveal something of the unusual epistolary relationship between the two men. Darwin always showed great interest in the fortunes of his former servant, kindly enquiring about his health, congratulating him on being settled in 'a country in which your children are sure to get on if industrious' (Darwin, who at the time had seven children of his own, was worried about finding careers for his sons), and keeping him informed as to news of their *Beagle* shipmates. He was delighted at how speedily Covington's letters reached him. A letter posted in Australia on 25 May reached Down House in Kent on 11 October and Darwin thought this a credit to the postal service between the two countries.

It wasn't only letters that passed between them. In 1843 Darwin posted off an ear-trumpet. Syms had poor hearing even when he left for Australia, and it soon got worse. Darwin thought an ear-trumpet, the only form of hearing aid then available, might be of assistance. Syms wrote asking Darwin if he knew of any good remedies for preventing further hearing loss, but there Darwin was unable to help. In return, Covington posted off to Darwin a curious range of 'presents'. In 1850 his box of barnacles proved useful to Darwin in his great barnacle study. 'I have received a vast number of collections from different places but never one so rich from one locality', he wrote gratefully. 'One of the kinds is most curious. It is a new species of a genus of which only one specimen is known . . . The collection must have caused you much time and labour, and I again thank you very sincerely'. It's a testament to what a good employer and friend Darwin had been to Syms, that his former servant was happy to spend so much time collecting and dispatching samples.

In Darwin's book about barnacles he was able, thanks to Syms and a few other Australian friends who sent specimens, to describe thirty-one species of Australian barnacles. In 1856, hard at work on his 'species' book, he asked Syms to send him the skins of 'any odd breeds of poultry, or pigeon, or duck', but there is no record of whether Syms obliged in this respect. However, Syms Covington's contribution of collecting and organising specimens during and after the voyage of the *Beagle* was never publicly acknowledged in *The Origin of Species*.

Syms Covington finally settled with his family in Pambula, on the south coast of New South Wales.[8] He became a postmaster and made enough money to buy a house there, a building that was not only home to his family of eight children but a post office and a hotel as well. Today it's a National Trust building and has become a restaurant, not an inappropriate fate for the home of a man who once worked as ship's cook. Syms Covington's life in Australia was not a long one and he was only forty-seven when he died in Pambula in 1861, as a result of paralysis. His grave can be seen today in Pambula Cemetery. But his story is fascinating, and inspired Australian novelist Roger McDonald to fictionalise it in *Mr Darwin's Shooter* (1998).

Syms was not the only person in Australia with whom Darwin remained in contact. Conrad Martens settled in Sydney, profitably teaching art and painting landscapes. Martens and Darwin also corresponded and Martens was able to tell Darwin of the notoriety his 'species' book was achieving in Australia. Such notoriety,

---

8   The diary that Syms Covington kept while on board
HMS *Beagle* has survived and is now in the Mitchell
Library, Sydney.

in fact, that Martens himself was 'afraid' to read it as he did not 'want to think [he had] an origin in common with toads and tadpoles'. He was delighted to hear that the two pictures Darwin had purchased from him in Sydney were still hanging on his study walls at Down House, and posted another picture off to him, *View of Brisbane, 1862*, which Darwin's son eventually presented to the Queensland Art Gallery.

His shipmate Philip Gidley King[9] also recieved letters from Darwin and, unlike Martens, King did read *The Origin of Species* 'with much interest', though was alarmed at the thought of where Darwin's deductions might lead. Darwin sent King a photograph of himself, and in their old age the two men enjoyed reminiscing in their letters about evenings spent 'sitting on [the] booms' of the *Beagle*, with tropical breezes wafting the sails above them. King wrote a manuscript that was never published about his great voyage with Charles Darwin, and he assisted Darwin's son with copies of letters when he collected material for a volume of his father's correspondence. Of the 14,500 letters written by Darwin which have survived, 174 of them relate either directly or indirectly to Australia.

For the rest of his life Darwin remained interested in the people he knew in Australia and in the country itself. Indeed, now that he was safely away from it and from the dreaded ocean with all its memories of seasickness, Darwin seemed to grow fonder of Australia than he'd ever been when he was actually there. 'I feel a great interest about Australia, and read every book I can get hold of', he told Syms Covington. He read

---

9 Son of the Captain King with whom Darwin stayed at Dunheved.

newspaper reports about the gold rush and hoped his former servant would turn up a big nugget; he dined in London with Sir William Macarthur and enjoyed hearing of Australia's growing prosperity from him as he 'drank some admirable Australian wine'; and he was delighted when old shipmates who had settled in Australia paid return visits to England and came to call. The more he heard about the colony, the more he revised his previous opinion, coming to view it as a 'fine country' which would, before long, become 'a very great one'. But it is not a country he ever thought of travelling to again. Darwin's travelling days were well and truly over.

Few Australians today know why the city of Darwin was so named. Darwin never lived to know that a city, capital of the Northern Territory, had been named after him—a city that did not exist when he visited Australia and which he went nowhere near even when he was here. However, the naming was a compliment and one eminently suited to his interests and personality. On board the *Beagle* with Charles Darwin was a young man called John Wickham. He was first lieutenant and became a good friend of Darwin's. After the voyage they shared, the *Beagle* was commissioned once again for a surveying voyage and it set off in July 1837. Captain FitzRoy had married and didn't want to undertake another long journey,[10] so Wickham got the job of commander in his

10 FitzRoy's new wife was ardently evangelical and converted her husband with the result that in time FitzRoy would be amongst the strongest and most vocal opponents to Darwin's 'species' theory. FitzRoy later travelled to New Zealand and became Governor there. He also became a pioneer of modern meteorology.

place. He sailed the little ship to the north-west coast of Australia, to Torres Strait and Bass Strait, on an even longer voyage lasting six years and three months. Wickham married an Australian girl, great-niece to John Macarthur, and one of the girls Charles Darwin had met at Hannibal Macarthur's home 'Vineyard'.

While surveying the northern coasts in 1839 Wickham sailed the *Beagle* into a 'wide bay appearing between the two white cliffy heads'. One of those 'cliffy heads' had an interesting geological feature, 'fine-grained sandstone' which he had not seen before in that part of Australia. Rocks always made Wickham think of his former shipmate, Charles Darwin, who noticed geological formations before he noticed anything else. Happy to have 'an appropriate opportunity of convincing an old shipmate and friend' that he hadn't been forgotten, Wickham 'accordingly named this sheet of water Port Darwin'. So Darwin knew that a tiny port on the northern coast of Australia had been named in his honour. Thirty years later a small settlement was established there and was called 'Palmerston' for the British Prime Minister who'd recently died. But in 1911 it was felt more appropriate to name the town for its port, and so 'Palmerston' became 'Darwin' and grew into a city. Other places in the world have been named for Charles Darwin. Tierra del Fuego's highest peak was named Mt Darwin by Captain FitzRoy on his naturalist's twenty-fifth birthday, and nearby is a sheet of water called 'Darwin Sound'. In Zimbabwe an African village has been called Mt Darwin. Other capitals were named for politicians (Sydney, Melbourne and Brisbane) or for places (Perth)—Darwin is the only writer and the only scientist to be so honoured.

Before setting out on the *Beagle* voyage, Charles Darwin had intended to become a clergyman, for which his degree at Cambridge had qualified him. All he needed to do on his return was to take orders and settle down in the sort of nice clerical living that he liked to read about in a Jane Austen novel. But the great voyage changed his mind. Instead of dedicating his life to a God whose existence he was beginning to question, he knew he must dedicate himself to a life of science. This decision permanently enriched the world. Darwin's contribution to scientific knowledge and to man's intellectual progress is almost impossible to evaluate.

In the stream of books that came from his pen, Australia had its part to play. In 1838 he published *The Zoology of the Voyage of HMS Beagle, under the command of Captain FitzRoy, R.N., during the years 1832 to 1836.* This refers to Australian fish, reptiles and mammals. His 1838 *Journal of Researches* contains the passage from his diary about the antlion (though, interestingly, in the second edition of 1845 his speculation about how the insect's behaviour had evolved was taken out of the main text and reduced to a footnote as Darwin grew more aware of the implications and of the probable reactions to his developing evolutionary theory). His *Geology of Volcanic Islands* of 1844 discusses the rocks of New South Wales, Tasmania and King George Sound as well as 'Palaeozoic Shells from Van Diemen's Land' and different types of Australian coral. As it was some time since he had been there, Darwin made sure to check his facts with those on the scene. Letters were sent off to the Reverend WB Clarke to confirm the effects of glacial action, to Sir Thomas Mitchell on the forming of the Blue Mountains valleys and to Gerard Krefft, at one time curator of Sydney's Australian Museum. There was great curiosity on the part of the reading public to hear about the exotic parts of the world that the *Beagle* had visited. Darwin's journal of the voyage, first published in 1839, was a bestseller in England, sold well in many other countries, and of course carried Darwin's mixed opinions of Australia to readers around the world.

Charles Darwin might have made his fame with these and other scientific works, but notoriety and intense publicity came with *The Origin of Species by Means of Natural Selection or the Preservation of Favoured Races in the Struggle for Life.* The book exploded into public controversy in 1859 and remains one of the most influential and controversial books ever written. Once again, Australia has a place in that vitally important work. Darwin writes of 'the process of diversification in an early and incomplete stage of development' in Australian mammals. He ponders the fact that marsupials exist only in Australia when once 'in ancient times' Europe had numerous marsupials too, and he mentions fossilised mammals found in Australian caves and their similarity to living marsupials. Darwin's 'origin' interests were wide ranging—fossils and marsupials, Australian plant varieties which 'are either the same species or varieties of the same species' as European plants, and even dingoes and their differences and similarities from the domesticated dogs of England—were topics which intrigued him and which featured in his groundbreaking book.

The Origin of Species immediately entered the realm of public debate. Clergymen preached against it and its atheistic connotations. Men discussed it in the clubs, and the newspapers were barraged with letters ridiculing or praising it. Scientists began to alter their own theories in the light of Darwin's conclusions. A few years after publication, the book was the subject of the famous Oxford debate, when Reverend Samuel Wilberforce ridiculed Darwin's theory and Thomas Huxley staunchly defended it.[11] The debate started by a great Victorian scientist 150 years ago is not over yet.

Darwin knew that his journey on HMS *Beagle* was the most important event of his life. He wrote in his 1879 *Autobiography*: 'I have always felt that I owe to the voyage the first real training or education of my mind'. And what a mind it was—ever curious, questioning, unafraid of testing waters that others thought too deep, far-reaching in its interests and in its scope. It is gratifying to think that the two months he spent in Australia played a vital part in forming one of the world's finest scientific minds.

---

11 Huxley came to be known by the nickname 'Darwin's Bulldog' as a result of the tenacity and courage he showed in this debate.

*The plaque for
Charles Darwin
at Sydney's
Circular Quay.*

CHAPTER TWO

Anthony Trollope

On 24 May 1871, Anthony Trollope and his wife Rose sailed for Australia on board the SS *Great Britain*. Trollope was not entirely satisfied with Isambard Kingdom Brunel's design of the great ship and asked the ship's carpenter to make some changes to his cabin and build in a desk so that he could write on the voyage. This was done and, as soon as the ship was out on the ocean, Trollope began work on a new two-volume novel. The story he wrote, *Lady Anna*, was specially arranged to fit the duration of the voyage and Trollope knew exactly the number of pages he needed to write each day. These allotted pages were duly written. On July 27, after just over two months at sea, the SS *Great Britain* docked at Port Melbourne. As it did so, Anthony Trollope wrote 'Finis' at the end of his manuscript and laid down his pen. This makes him the only writer in history

Photograph of Trollope taken in 1868, a few years before his first visit to Australia.

The SS Great Britain, *Isambard Kingdom Brunel's great ship which brought Trollope to Australia, and on which he wrote the whole of his novel,* Lady Anna, *in a painting by Keith A. Griffin, 1843.*

to have completed an entire novel on a journey from England to Australia.

The novel's eponymous heroine is the poverty-stricken granddaughter of an earl. During the story she is courted by a handsome aristocrat and by a radical tailor who was very kind to her in her childhood. She chooses the tailor for her husband, a decision that revolted the reading public when the book was published. Trollope knew he would arouse Victorian class prejudice by creating such an unequal marriage, so deliberately ended his tale with the young couple travelling to Australia, just as he himself was doing, in the hope they would find there a more egalitarian home. Trollope virtually promises his readers a sequel: 'Of the further doings of Mr Daniel Thwaite and his wife Lady Anna,—of how they travelled and saw many things; and how he became perhaps a wiser man,—the present writer may, he hopes, live to tell'. So as Trollope stepped off the SS *Great Britain* to see something of Australia, he must have had his heroine very much in mind. Would Australia be a suitable future home for her? How would her prickly, oversensitive husband get on in a land of convicts and soldiers? What would their Australian future be? If he did decide on answers to these questions, he never shared them with his readers. *Lady Anna in Australia* was never written.

The busy activity of Trollope's voyage would characterise the time he spent in Australia, just as it had characterised his life so far. He was fifty-six years old, recently retired from a successful career in the Post Office, which had included his invention of the pillar postbox. Thirty novels bore his name, as did three non-fiction works, two plays, and several volumes of short stories. He had worked as an editor for prestigious journals, and had written travel books on the West Indies and North America after journeys to those parts of the world. He enjoyed memberships of various London clubs, and was a passionate and regular hunter, chasing the fox at least three times per week. He and Rose had raised two sons and had helped bring up a niece who lived with them. Trollope had a large circle of friends with whom he socialised and corresponded. He regularly rose at five in the morning to fit as much as he could into each day. He might have retired, but that made little difference—each day was still packed with constant activity. He wrote once to his son, Henry, 'Nothing really frightens me but the idea of enforced idleness'.

Holidays held no appeal, and the visit to Australia would be no rest-cure. Before leaving England he had negotiated a contract with his publishers for a travel book on Australia and New Zealand—he started writing this soon after arriving and completed it a month after his return to England. He begins by setting out clearly what he plans to do:

> I have attempted in these volumes to describe the Australian colonies as they at present exist; and to tell, in very brief fashion, the manner in which they were first created. In doing so, it has been impossible to avoid speculations as to their future prospects—in which is involved the happiness of millions to come of English-speaking men and women. As a group, they are probably the most important of our colonial possession, and they are certainly the most interesting.

No matter where he travelled, Trollope dipped his pen in ink and continued to write. He was used to writing in carriages and carts using a portable desk, he had written in trains and on ships. In Australia he would write in the bush and in the towns, in hotels and while camping. And he would do much else besides.

The Trollopes came to Australia to see their youngest son Frederic, who had not flourished in England. 'Boys less than himself in stature got above him at school, and he had not liked it' so, at the age of seventeen, Fred left England to try life in Australia. For three years he worked on sheep stations in New South Wales and Victoria, then a promise to his parents brought him back to England when he turned twenty-one. His mother hoped he'd got the colonies out of his system and would settle in Britain, but Fred loved Australia's freedom and outdoor lifestyle. He wanted to call it home and apart from one trip to England late in his life, in 1903, Frederic Trollope spent the rest of his life in Australia. By 1871 he had purchased 'Mortray', a small station carrying 10,000 sheep near Grenfell in New South Wales. Trollope had put up most of the purchase money, so had a financial interest, as well as an emotional one, in visiting 'Mortray'. And there was a future daughter-in-law to meet—Susannah Farrand, child of a Forbes police magistrate, who married Fred that year and eventually gave him eight children.

But work had to come before the pleasure of seeing offspring. In fact, few visitors to Australia have ever worked so hard at seeing everything, learning about Australian institutions and customs, observing locals at work and at play, and covering so much ground, as did Anthony Trollope. His publishers had asked him to write a book that would be useful to an Englishman thinking of emigrating to Australia, a book providing information on wages and rents, housing and schools, agriculture, industry and politics. His aim was to benefit 'many in England who have to learn whether Australia is becoming a fitting home for them and their children'. Conscientiously, and with his characteristic energy, Trollope set about his research. The result of this would be a early version of a *Lonely Planet Guide to Australia*.

At the time of his visit, Australia had six separate colonies, each with its own legislature and its own governor sent out from England. Customs barriers between each meant that internal trade was limited, and that crossing from one colony to another was almost like passing into a foreign country. Trollope actually needed a certificate allowing him to travel freely, and stating that he was not a convict and never had been a convict. As he crossed borders, Trollope compared one colony with another, and each one with England, so that his reader could work out which part of Australia might suit him best. As a researcher, Trollope was indefatigable—he inspected hospitals and schools, prisons and convict settlements; he reported on housing and the state of the roads; he collected figures and statistics on exports, imports, sales, wages, rents, cost of food, and he speculated on changes that the coming years might bring. He did all this in an unfamiliar, often harsh, environment, but he did it with never-failing enthusiasm.

He also did much of it alone. Rose, Trollope's wife of almost thirty years, is a shadowy figure in his life. None of their correspondence has survived, he barely mentions her in his *An Autobiography*, and friends have left few records of her personality or tastes. After a short stay in Melbourne with Anthony, Rose left him to go to

'Mortray' and see her dear boy. She had no research to
keep her away from Fred. Anthony left for Queensland,
chosen as the first colony he would explore because it was
winter and he hated heat. He was determined to save
cooler areas such as Tasmania for the summer months.
Notebook in hand, he set off north to start learning all
about Australia.

It is not possible to follow Trollope's Australian travels in
detail here. He provides a long (very long!) description
in *Australia and New Zealand* of every town he visited,
with explanations as to what he did there. Nearly
two hundred pages packed with information cover
Brisbane, Maryborough, Gladstone, Rockhampton,
Ipswich, Gympie, Fraser Island, and all the many little
Queensland settlements he passed through. Squatters
were hospitable and opened their homes to him, local
worthies were only too happy to escort the famous
novelist around goldfields and over sheep stations. He
inspected sugar plantations and learned about cattle-
stealing. He appears to have met a considerable proportion of Queensland's 120,000 inhabitants and had
questions for them all.

But what did he think of them after seven weeks
in their company? On the whole, he was impressed.
Australians, he felt, were energetic, friendly and helpful.
They lacked ostentation, shared willingly what they had,
were adaptable and versatile. They did, however, suffer
from a sense of being second-rate in comparison with
England: 'Colonists are usually fond of their adopted
homes,—but are at the same time pervaded by a certain
sense of inferiority which is for the most part very

unnecessary . . . this feeling produces a reaction which shows itself in boasting of what they can do'. Australians called this boasting 'blowing' and Trollope became very weary of blowing before his travels were over: 'Now if I was sending a young man to the Australian colonies the last word of advice I should give him would be against this practice'.

Nathaniel Hawthorne once commented that Trollope's novels were written 'on the strength of beef and through the inspiration of ale'. Certainly food features often in them and throughout his life Trollope took a great interest in what was on his plate. In Australia he was keen to sample new gastronomic delights. He thought the meat excellent and wonderfully cheap and again and again his book stresses that the Australian labourer could eat three meat meals per day at little cost. As Australia had a surplus of meat, he was particularly interested in how that surplus could be sent to England. There were preserved, tinned meats in existence. Before leaving England he 'bought some Australian preserved meat as an experiment' and paid sixpence a pound for it. 'It was sweet and by no means unpalatable, but was utterly tasteless as meat'. Artificial freezing was being considered, and meat was also being boiled down to its essence, an 'unsavoury' activity which he saw in action. Trollope sampled this essence and 'felt as though [he] were pervaded by meatiness for many hours', yet he looked forward confidently to a day when 'palatable and nutritive' Australian mutton and beef would be sold in English shops.

One unusual meat meal he ate was 'stewed wallabi' (*sic*) which he found 'not nice to eat even when stewed to the utmost with wine and spices'. Vegetables never excited Trollope. He firmly believed carrots should be boiled for at least thirty minutes before they were fit for consumption, so probably all vegetables tasted alike to him, and he fails to comment on those he ate in Australia; but he liked fruit and enjoyed Queensland's pineapples and New South Wales' oranges. Local wines were a disappointment, even though the wine producers he met did much blowing about their products, so he stuck to brandy and water as his drink of choice while in Australia.

※

From late September to mid-December Trollope was in New South Wales, and a month of that time was spent with Fred. But after travelling from Brisbane to Sydney on a three-day boat trip, he felt he must first see something of Sydney before going to 'Mortray'. What he saw impressed him. No other body of water he had seen possessed 'such a world of loveliness of water as lies within Sydney Heads'. Sydneysiders, he admitted, had a right to blow as much as they liked about 'the beauty of Sydney Harbour'. In his book, he struggled to describe it:

> I can say that it is lovely, but I cannot paint its loveliness. The sea runs up in various bays or coves, indenting the land all around the city, so as to give a thousand different aspects of the water,—and not of water, broad, unbroken, and unrelieved,—but of water always with jutting corners of land beyond it, and then again of water and then again of land.

He loved the public gardens ('unrivalled by any that I have ever seen') and went there to lie on the grass and look at the sea, or to enjoy an after-dinner cigar and a stroll. He was impressed by seabaths, he thought the Harbour fortifications surprising when he inspected them ('I had previously no idea that the people of New South Wales were either so suspicious of enemies, or so pugnacious in their nature'), he liked the cathedral, loved the villa of Woollahra and predicted that real estate in that part of Sydney would one day be worth millions. He approved of the interesting layout of city streets, and he was impressed by the standard of teaching at Fort Street School. There were only forty-one students enrolled at Sydney University when he visited, but he realised that the institution had 'not yet had time for success'.

Sydney's population had been taken by a census that very year; it had 503,981 inhabitants. As in Queensland, Trollope met as many of them as he could, visited their parliament, churches, post offices, shops, hospitals and quays. He would return to Sydney later in his journey, but each time he left it with regret: 'Sydney is one of those places which, when a man leaves it knowing that he will never return, he cannot leave without a pang and a tear. Such is its loveliness'.

Less attractive were the country towns of New South Wales—Newcastle, Maitland, Parramatta and Bathurst. 'I cannot say that as yet these communities possess many beauties to recommend them to the eye, or have much to please a stranger'. To him these straggling little towns exuded 'an apparent mixture of pretension and failure ... which creates a feeling of melancholy sadness in the mind of a stranger'. And yet banks, churches, mechanics' institutes, schools and pubs were being built at a great rate. Roads were being constructed, railways laid, Cobb & Co. were conveying people between the towns, ships were taking coal, wheat and other goods to Sydney. Trollope could report to the reader of *Australia and New Zealand* that this was a land of promise, with exciting opportunities for anyone prepared to work.

And then, finally, he took a month off to visit Fred. 'Mortray' was 250 miles west of Sydney and very remote. Trollope travelled first by rail, and then for three days in a buggy through the bush to get there. He found a simple house by a creek, a home-paddock, a woolshed and endless bush. Homestead life was lived on a twelve-foot verandah and there Trollope was forced to slow down. And, as soon as he did, he was bored. Fred and his few employees and neighbours talked endlessly of sheep and there was little social life: the men were too busy to issue dinner invitations, or dress for formal meals. Anthony began to long for his London clubs. In desperation he tried to get the men playing whist, but their minds were too full of wool prices to remember which card was highest in the suit. When back in 'Mortray' the following year, Trollope did have one interesting visitor—Alfred Dickens, son of his great rival Charles Dickens (with whom he was not at that time on speaking terms)—but generally this sociable man was left to his own company and that of his wife.

Fred was preoccupied with his sheep. Rose kept herself busy with domestic arrangements and trying to vary the monotonous station diet of mutton and tea at every meal. The food-loving Trollopes had travelled to Australia with their cook, who would have been invaluable 'had she not found a husband for herself when she had been about a month in the bush', and had gone off to cook for her husband instead.

Trollope began work on *Australia and New Zealand* at 'Mortray'. As he reported to his friend Millais, the artist: 'I write for four hours a day, then ride after sheep or chop wood or roam about in the endless forest up to my knees in mud. I eat a great deal of mutton, smoke a great deal of tobacco, and drink a moderate amount of brandy and water'. The bush seemed to close in upon him and 'there arose at last a feeling that go where one might through the forest, one was never going anywhere'.

Trollope's despondency while at 'Mortray' may also have arisen from a feeling that he had not invested wisely. Fred worked from dawn till dusk, but the place was not making money and his father could see this early on. Altogether he would lose 4600 pounds on the enterprise and for a man who worked so hard to make an income from the Post Office and from writing, this must have been exceedingly depressing.

There could well have been other worries, too. Parenthood had not been easy for Trollope because of his problematic relationship with his own parents. His father Thomas had been a manic depressive, impossible to live with, and was a poor provider. Fanny, his mother, had worked tirelessly at writing novels to bring in money while she also nursed her dying children (five of her seven children perished young), and she favoured her eldest boy Tom in preference to Anthony. His childhood had been marked by parental neglect, in fact he had been so miserable he'd been close to suicide on at least one occasion. His mother died eight years before the Australian journey, but his relationship with her had never been easy. And now he had his own son, who was causing him financial anxiety and who had settled in this remote, inhospitable place. As Anthony sat on Fred's verandah, sipping his brandy and water, he must have reflected on their relationship. When, soon after, he created a fictional portrait of Fred as young Harry Heathcote on a station called 'Gangoil', Trollope left all parents totally out of the picture—Harry was deliberately orphaned. His own father–son relationship was emotional territory he had no wish to explore in his work.

On 14 December 1881, Frederic Trollope married Susannah Farrand, but his parents were not there to witness the ceremony; they were on their way to Melbourne. It seems extraordinary that having travelled halfway round the world to see Fred and meet Susie, they were not then present on the day of the marriage. Trollope family tradition among Fred's descendents has it that Rose never liked her daughter-in-law, but that Trollope was fond of her. (When he visited Australia for the second time, he came without Rose.) Weddings were simpler affairs in those days; perhaps the Trollopes just felt their schedule should not be disrupted for a small family event? But why was the date not brought forward so they could take part before leaving? Was Fred so prosaic that he didn't care if he had the sort of marriage his father could describe for a young squatter: he 'simply goes out in his buggy and brings home the daughter of some other squatter,—after a little ceremony performed in the nearest church'? Did Rose not want to witness her darling son being forever shackled to an Australian girl when she'd hoped he'd marry a nice English one? Did they want to give the newlyweds, who would move straight into the 'Mortray' homestead after the wedding, a bit of marital privacy? Or was Anthony, having had more than enough of his 'holiday', so desperate to return to the hectic schedule he loved that even a son's wedding couldn't hold him back?

And so the frantic sightseeing and information-gathering began again. In Melbourne, 'the undoubted capital, not only of Victoria but of all Australia', the Trollopes made the Menzies Hotel their base. From there Trollope walked the 'noble streets', visited the gardens (not a patch on Sydney's, in his opinion), called in at the Houses of Parliament, and went out to the suburbs. He even inspected the gutters, which in hot weather overflowed with such deep water from the reservoirs that children drowned in them. He was tremendously impressed with Melbourne's public buildings, especially the library, which allowed anyone who wanted to sit and read the right to do so, and also provided a separate room for female readers who wished to be alone, but also the university, the post office, benevolent asylums for the destitute, the lunatic asylum, the prison and the new Government House. In his view, Melburnians had a lot to be proud of, but the irritating blowing was worse there than in all the other colonies he visited. Perhaps he got his revenge and did a bit of blowing of his own when he gave a lecture in Melbourne on December 18. His subject was 'English Prose Fiction' and on this topic he could blow with impunity.

It's surprising that he found breath enough to give a lecture, for his frantic pace had not lessened. Before Christmas he was off on the train to Geelong and Ballarat. There he descended 450 feet down a goldmine (a procedure he found quite terrifying), watched quartz-crushers at work, popped into a Chinese miners' opium den, then hurried off to see Sandhurst (later Bendigo), Mornington, Gipps Land, Sale, Walhalla, Edwards' Reef, Wood's Point and Jericho. Train, coach, buggy and the horse's back got him from place to place, and

The Melbourne Post Office, visited by Trollope so he could learn about Australian postal routes. The Australian postal system plays an important role in his novel John Caldigate.

every night he sat down to write up his book and record first impressions. He even read the local newspapers and thought *The Argus* and *The Sydney Morning Herald* were 'the best daily papers I have seen out of England'.

The condition of the Australian indigenous peoples, how they lived and what their future would be, occupied every literary visitor, and Anthony Trollope was no exception. Adept at seeing the other man's point of view, he felt that the Australian Aboriginal had had it very tough: 'We have taken away their land, have destroyed their food, have made them subject to our laws which are antagonistic to their habits and traditions, have endeavoured to make them subject to our tastes, which they hate, have massacred them when they defended themselves'. But he also felt that there was little alternative if 'civilisations' were to be spread around the world. Even in New Zealand, where he thought the Maori to be more progressive and less ugly than the

Aboriginal (though he was intrigued and revolted by the Maori cannibalism that had ceased only fifty years before his visit), he felt that the natives were the better for English culture being introduced to their land. Both peoples, he was sure, were doomed to extinction and were already 'melting' away: 'Of the Australian black man we may certainly say that he has to go. That he should perish without unnecessary suffering should be the aim of all who are concerned in the matter'. So while the 'melting' must be as painless as possible, what he saw of Aboriginals in missionary schools, in city slums, in prisons and in reservations, convinced him that 'melting' was a necessary procedure.

Trollope also shared the fascination of all literary visitors for Australia's convict origins. He reached Tasmania in January 1872 and hurried to the convict settlement at Port Arthur to hear stories of escapes and punishments, though he was 'troubled by many reflections as to the future destiny of so remarkable a place'. He met some of the 506 convicts still incarcerated—Ahern, who had tried to murder his wife; Doherty, the 'Irishman with one eye' who had mutinied as a boy and whose regular attempts to escape during forty-two years of imprisonment had left his back crisscrossed with the nearly three thousand lashes he'd received; Barron, who lived alone on a tiny island off Port Arthur, where he dug the graves in which fellow convicts were buried; and Fisher, who finally escaped confinement by dying. Trollope was sympathetic, listened to their stories, gave them tobacco, and immortalised their sad histories in his book.

Tasmania delighted him—its cooler temperature, its citizens still so loyal to the mother country, its marvellous jam ('Tasmania ought to make jam for all the world'), attractive Hobart, the Chudleigh Caves through which he waded in icy water, banging his head as he went, and lovely sea views everywhere he looked. He rightly predicted that one day Tasmania would be famed for its food products. The colony was, however, in decline— the population was dropping, exports decreasing each year, the customs barriers he so detested were crippling trade, and there was a pervading air of depression and hopelessness. However, he did 'not in the least doubt that sooner or later she will emerge from her troubles' and decided that 'were it my lot to take up residence in Australia, and could I choose the colony in which I was to live, I would pitch my staff in Tasmania'.

Albany in Western Australia, which Charles Darwin had found so dismal, had improved greatly in thirty-five years. Trollope, who arrived there by ship from Melbourne in March, thought it 'a very pretty little town', with a delightful climate. From there he set off to see something of Western Australia, riding for four days to reach Perth, camping out at night, eating bacon and potatoes, and brewing billy tea. (Rose had remained in Melbourne with friends.) 'No man perhaps ever travelled two hundred and sixty miles with less to see. The road goes eternally through wood,—which in Australia is always called bush . . . But the bush in these parts never develops itself into scenery.' He liked Perth, which had some 6000 inhabitants at the time, visited Fremantle and went across to Rottnest Island. He took the mail cart north to Northam, Toodyay and Newcastle, with his usual collecting of facts and figures en route. But his book did not recommend Western Australia as a home for future immigrants as highly as it did the eastern colonies; he felt it was too isolated, internal trade was too difficult, the convict stain still too recent. The Western Australia section is the shortest in his book.

⁂

Trollope's fifty-seventh birthday on April 24 was spent in Adelaide, but if being one year older gave him any thought of slowing down, he showed no sign of it. Throughout April and May he explored South Australia, a colony he felt was superior through never having received convicts. As always, he enquired about local government and sat in on parliamentary sessions whenever he could. Trollope believed there was no higher honour for an Englishman than to represent his country in the House of Commons. He had once stood, unsuccessfully, as a Liberal candidate. His failure to get in left him writing his political urges into his superb Palliser—or political—series of novels. He may not have enriched the House of Commons, but his political failure hugely enriched English literature. Sadly, his political obsession did not enrich anyone through the pages of *Australia and New Zealand*, where the political pages are dull and dated. However, he left any likely migrant in no doubt as to how one colony differed politically from another.

Adelaide was just planting out its parks with trees when Trollope was there and he could see what an asset they would be to the city. He admired the many churches, yet was delighted that the grandest building in town was in fact the post office. He travelled north to Kadina, Port Wallaroo and Moonta; south to Strathalbyn,

54

Poltalloch Station and Lake Albert; and by ship to Port Macdonell, Mt Gambier and Penola. Once again, he found the landscape, with 'the everlasting gum' tree, far from picturesque. True, there was the odd kangaroo jumping past and he even participated in a kangaroo hunt (on a horse too small for his weight, which threw him!), but disappointingly he never saw an emu running wild, and the South Australian saltbush country came close to his idea of hell. The towns, though, were more to his taste—pretty, clean and English-looking. The beef he ate at Poltalloch was the best he'd ever eaten in his life, and the people were hospitable and friendly.

Physically Trollope showed no sign of tiring, but emotionally he was drained. He was weary, as he wrote to his friend George Eliot, of trying to be at ease with 'all the new people and all the new things', and playing the role of 'famous author' in every town he went to. He missed hunting foxes, good coffee and cigars, his club, and a society where everyone knew their place. The man who had written so perceptively of English class distinctions in his fiction found it hard to cope with the maidservant in an Australian inn who 'has the pertness, the independence, the mode of asserting by her manner that though she brings you up your hot water, she is just as good as you'. Trollope was not always a tactful man, offending many Australians with his brusqueness and his class expectations. Because he tried to travel with as little luggage as possible, he was often wrongly dressed for formal occasions, which also raised Australian hackles. Did the famous author think so little of them that he turned up in a casual blue shirt instead of a dinner jacket, audiences wondered? Occasionally he could be amused by class difficulties in this new land, as when he heard

Anthony Trollope with notebook in a photograph taken in the early 1870s, soon after his visit to Australia.

that a postmistress refused to attend a local ball unless the barmaids were excluded: 'The barmaids—I think very properly,—were admitted and the postmistress . . . remained at home'. But for all his amusement and interest he was missing England and took a coach out of South Australia and back into Victoria with relief that his long Australian journey was nearing its end.

❧

His departure was drawing near, but there were many more miles yet to cover. The Trollopes, united again, boarded a coach from Melbourne to Bontherambo,

Wangaratta, Beechworth and Albury. Then on to Wagga Wagga and Grenfell, and finally he and Rose were back with their son and his pregnant wife. In *An Autobiography* Trollope wrote that he had travelled to Australia 'to see [his] son among his sheep'. This is hardly true. Only one month of the twelve he spent in the country had been spent at 'Mortray' with Fred, and on this last visit they were there only four days. Were Rose and Susie fighting? Could Anthony not bear another minute of doing so little in such a remote place? Could it really have been more important to go rushing off to see the Blue Mountains, admiring the same view at Govett's Leap as had Darwin, on to Sydney, back to Melbourne by ship, then more coach travel to Deniliquin and Echuca, instead of staying a few more weeks with his son? Could they not have waited to see baby Frank, who was born that year? Was the dull travel book he was writing (and Anthony knew it was dull) so vital that family had to come second? Anthony and Rose Trollope left no answers to any of those questions.

On July 29 they sailed for New Zealand, where they would traipse for two more exhausting months over South Island mountain passes in mid-winter, through towns and cities, doing all the usual research and visiting, yet feeling that although they'd crossed half the world to get there, they 'had not at all succeeded in getting away from England'. In New Zealand's inns and hotels, Trollope wrote up the last pages of the Australian section of his book and started to write about New Zealand. The book ends with a delightful picture of the author sitting naked in one of the shell-like pools of the already famous pink and white terraces at Lake Rotomahana, near Rotorua, wallowing in the warm thermal water and predicting that soon tourists would come from around the world to wallow likewise. Alas, the eruption of Mt Tarawera fourteen years later put an end to all such activity by obliterating the geological marvel, considered the eighth wonder of the world.

But what were his predictions for Australia? On the whole, they were positive. Australia, in his opinion, had a great future before it. Rich in minerals and wool, rich in its energetic people, it was a land of opportunity, especially for the British working classes. He'd found Australians to be friendly and generous, hardworking and democratic, and he commended their resource in rapidly constructing new cities and institutions. Perhaps his real opinion is best summed up by Coral Lansbury in *Arcady in Australia*, who wrote: 'His attitude was that of a member of the royal family inspecting a block of settlement flats. He approves the design and general principles, takes tea and admires the view—but would be appalled if forced to live there'.

'Of all the needs a book has, the chief need is that it be readable', Trollope once wrote. *Australia and New Zealand*, published in February 1873 just after his return to England, fails to meet its author's own criteria. It is barely readable.[1] This is partly because of its topical nature (potential emigrants would have been fascinated by all the facts and figures, but these soon dated), but also because of its flat style. Trollope tried to apologise for this by insisting that at least it had the merit of containing

---

1   The manuscript of the book is now in the National
     Library of Australia in Canberra.

fresh, on-the-spot impressions, but even he had to admit 'the pages drag with me'. The economist John Kenneth Galbraith once described Trollope's writing as a 'narcotic' because of the soothing, peaceful quality of his prose. *Australia and New Zealand* is indeed a narcotic which can be recommended to anyone with sleeping problems! It is rambling, too full of statistics and desperately in need of a good editor. But Trollope was certainly correct when he described it in *An Autobiography* as 'a thoroughly honest book . . . the result of unflagging labour for a period of fifteen months. I spared myself no trouble in inquiry, no trouble in seeing, and no trouble in listening'. The book made him thirteen hundred pounds and sold well.

Trollope was a great novelist, not a great writer of non-fiction. The moment he turned to creating a story about men and women, his pen once again moved with inspired ease. In mid-1873 he was approached by *Graphic* magazine with a request for a long Christmas story. Unlike Charles Dickens, who adored writing seasonal fare, Trollope hated such requests. Giving 'a relish of Christmas' to what he wrote did not come naturally to a novelist who tried to avoid the sentimental. But it was a commission that paid, so he sat down and, in four weeks, wrote *Harry Heathcote of Gangoil: A Tale of Australian Bush Life*. The story, or short novel, appeared in *Graphic* in December and was published in book form the following year.

For English readers, this tale of Harry and his wife Mary eating their mutton on a hot Christmas Day in Queensland had great novelty. The story is lively and vivid. When in Queensland, Trollope had been much interested in the squabbles between squatters and free-selectors. As a result of Selection Acts, animosity had arisen between these two groups concerning rights to land. Harry Heathcote, like Fred on whom he is based, is a squatter, owner of thirty thousand sheep, and a magistrate. He fails to understand why free-selectors 'should have been introduced into the arrangements of the world', and is on bad terms with any that come near him. Giles Medlicot is a free-selector who courts Harry's sister-in-law Kate. The tussle over land and over relatives, with a bushfire thrown in for added excitement, form the slight plot of the novel. Trollope had listened carefully to both sides of the argument and believed the future lay with the free-selectors, but is typically even-handed and diplomatic in his tale.

Harry Heathcote of Gangoil is not one of his better works, but is a fascinating example of an Australian story told by an English novelist. In it he depicts English middle-class values in the teeth of the levelling influence of Aussie bush life. He provides a striking portrait of the 'Gangoil' homestead, its creek, its dinner table and furnishings. Harry, an orphan from England, and Mary, an orphan from Sydney, are vividly depicted, from his moleskin trousers, flannel shirt and battered hat, to her domestic difficulties with Sing Sing, the Chinese cook. Australian pioneering life is captured with humour and exactness in a story that has historic interest as well as literary merit.

Meanwhile the real 'Harry', Fred Trollope, was struggling on at 'Mortray'. Wool prices had plummeted and the property was just too small to survive both that and extended drought. Trollope decided to return to Australia to sort out the financial mess. No travel book would finance this journey, but he did make arrangements with the Liverpool *Mercury* to write a series of travel letters for fifteen pounds per letter. These are funnier and freer in style than his *Australia and New Zealand* book. Rose decided not to accompany him, so after first visiting his brother in Italy, Trollope set sail alone. Once again he wrote in his cabin, finishing *Is He Popenjoy?*, an intriguing novel about inheritance, one of his favourite topics, as he journeyed to sort out the inheritance of his son. The ink bottle broke in his desk, ruining shirts and cigars—a bad beginning to a bad trip.

He reached Melbourne on 4 May 1875 to find he was no longer the welcome visitor he'd been before. *Australia and New Zealand* had been much read and discussed and Trollope was not forgiven his accusations of blowing. Even the customs officer who inspected his luggage on arrival was 'very courteous, but full of wrath'. Everywhere he went, he found himself 'to be regarded as rather a bad man, in having come a second time among people whom I had so grossly maligned. No good word that I had said was held in any remembrance, but any hint conveying censure was treasured up and quoted against me with indignation'.

Whatever the private feelings of the locals, publicly Trollope was again treated as a visiting celebrity. After all, another four novels has been published since he was last in Australia, including the brilliant *The Way We Live Now*. In Sydney he attended a grand official luncheon aboard the *Coonanbara* to farewell William Macleay's scientific expedition to New Guinea. He accompanied the Governor General to a military parade on the Queen's birthday. In August he was guest of honour at a picnic near Warragamba. The Premier and Chief Justice were of the party that travelled from Penrith up the Nepean River on a steam launch. The press might criticise and customs officials reproach, but politicians still wanted to be seen with one of England's greatest authors.

Trollope knew this would be his last visit. He'd turned sixty on the voyage and 'at that age a man has no right to look forward to making many more voyages round the world'.[2] So this time he spent half his visit at 'Mortray'. There were small grandsons to play with and a new novel to get under way. *The American Senator*, the book he began on Fred's verandah, has some of the slowest, most confused first chapters he ever wrote. It improves markedly later on, but 'Mortray' and grandchildren were clearly not conducive to Trollope's writing style. And there was the worry of Fred's financial mess. A decision to sell 'Mortray' was taken, Fred found a job as inspector in the Lands Department and became a magistrate (his father asked Henry Parkes to help arrange this). Fred's life was never a particularly happy one. He moved from job to job, suffered poor health, complained frequently, and always seemed in need of parental assistance to support his eight children. Never fully at home in Australia, Fred seems to have been an irritable and ultimately disappointed man. The goodbyes Anthony and Fred said in August 1875 were final. On August 28, Trollope sailed from Sydney on the *City of Melbourne*, en route for New Zealand, then America, then home. He never saw his son again.

⁂

2 Nevertheless, in 1877 Trollope made an extensive trip
   to South Africa, and wrote a book about those travels.

On both trips to Australia Trollope had been much interested in goldmines. He visited several. His trembling seventeen-stone bulk was even lowered down into a couple of them so he could inspect the internal workings. A shaft was named the 'Anthony Trollope' in his honour. In his opinion goldmines were depressing places, but also puzzling. Why, he wondered, would young men come from around the world, leaving good jobs, in the slight hope of golden gain? He could not share this lust for metal. In Currajong, 'the most hopelessly disappointing place' he ever went to in Australia, he had come across a young man whom he'd known as a boy in England. Gently bred and well educated the man might have been, but Trollope found him sitting in front of his tent 'eating a nauseous lump of beef out of a greasy frying-pan with his pocket-knife'. All comfort had been left behind in the desire for gold. The sight planted the germ of an idea for a novel in Trollope's mind.

In 1877 he began that novel, *John Caldigate*, and four of its chapters are set on Australian goldfields. John, the hero, finds life in the Cambridgeshire fens dull and sets sail for Australia to experience a life of adventure: 'there was gold being found at this moment among the mountains of New South Wales, in quantities which captivated his imagination'. On the sea voyage John flirts with Euphemia Smith, a lady of dubious reputation, and the relationship continues after they arrive in Sydney. Ahalala, the mine he goes to, is a huge disappointment—dirty, depressing and hopeless. The place soon drives Caldigate's friend to drink. Trollope describes the goldfields with an authenticity and vividness unmatched by any other English novel of the period. The plot hinges on the fact that morals are undermined there. John is in love with a virtuous young lady back in England, but while at Ahalala he lives with Euphemia as his common-law wife. When he gives up on goldmining and returns to England, Euphemia claims that a legal wedding ceremony took place. On his return he had married Hester Bolton, so he is charged with bigamy.

The plot of *John Caldigate* capitalised on public interest in the Tichborne Affair. The ancient Hampshire estates of Sir Roger Tichborne were up for grabs when the baronet disappeared in 1854. Ten years later a man named Arthur Orton claimed to be the missing Sir Roger. He was actually a butcher from Wagga Wagga. His trial for perjury was one of the longest in English legal history and kept the public riveted. Trollope has his hero, John Caldigate, pass through Wagga Wagga, and Euphemia likens herself to the 'claimant' of the Tichborne estate. The case reinforced the English belief that Australia was an immoral place. Trollope reflects this in his novel by writing of the widespread opinion at the time of Caldigate's trial that 'anything done in the wilds of Australia ought not to "count" here at home in England'. Intriguingly (especially for a Victorian novelist) Trollope never reproaches his hero for living with a woman out of wedlock, nor for lying about the relationship afterwards. When John finally does tell Hester the truth, she immediately forgives him. Trollope's publisher, Blackwoods, was deeply disturbed by John Caldigate's lack of repentance; but for many English readers, such behaviour was only what one must expect of a man who had lived in Australia!

The four chapters set in the goldfields are vital to this novel, not only for furthering the plot, but for their symbolism. Digging for money can be done in more than one way—John is blackmailed for twenty thousand pounds by Timothy Crinkett, his ex-partner in the mine; Euphemia tries to dig herself back into his riches; the sleazy past John tries to bury is dug up and raked over by the press; a character called Mr Bagwax tries to dig out the truth; and John returns to England to commence 'mining operations' on the heart of Hester Bolton. Images of mining and digging run through the novel like a seam of gold through the earth.

After a career of thirty-five years with the Post Office, Trollope could never walk past a post office without going in. Australian postal officials must have been driven crazy by this scruffy man (Trollope always looked scruffy!) with the big beard who popped in off the street to question them on their methods, suggest more efficient ones, enquire about routes, times taken for delivery and the general management of Australian postbags. As a novelist, he was almost incapable of allowing any letter to be posted or delivered in his stories without adding commentary on the route it had to take and how long it took to get there.

In *John Caldigate* he twists his plot upon all this acquired knowledge. The most damning evidence against John at his trial is an envelope addressed, in his handwriting, to Euphemia as 'Mrs Caldigate'. John maintains the letter was written on the goldfields when he had promised to marry her and was calling her by that name merely as a form of reassurance. She points to a Sydney postmark and stamp on the envelope as evidence that he had publicly acknowledged her as his wife. On this evidence, Caldigate is found guilty and imprisoned. But lurking in the background is a postal worker, Mr Bagwax, who is so determined to uncover the truth that he travels to Australia to check all the details. There he finds that the stamp had not even been issued at the time when the letter was supposed to have been sent, and that the Sydney postmark was fraudulent, stamped on the envelope at a later date than the one it bore. Euphemia Smith gets three years in prison, but Mr Bagwax is held up by Trollope as a model of dedication and skill for any post office employee. Perhaps remembering all those Australian postmasters he had hassled, Trollope added the footnote: 'I hope my friends in the Sydney post-office will take no offence should this story reach their ears. I know how well the duties are done in that office, and, between ourselves, I think that Mr Bagwax's journey was quite unnecessary'.

English readers of *John Caldigate* could only have had their negative opinions of Australia reinforced by this novel. It depicts Australia as a rough, wild place, where morals are soon corrupted, and where women are loose and men are weak. Its goldfields are harsh, unattractive, and unrewarding places that drive men to drink. Civilised Englishmen, according to Trollope, should get away from such places as soon as possible. Those readers who had picked up Trollope's *Australia and New Zealand* must have been puzzled by the contrast between that book's generally positive picture of Australia as a good home for migrants, and the picture in *John Caldigate* of Australia as a hell on earth. As so often with Trollope, it all comes down to social class. He genuinely believed that for the lower classes, who could work with their hands, Australia was ideal. But the well-educated, gently reared English gentleman should stay comfortably at home.

One of Trollope's last novels makes a highly unusual return to Australasia. *The Fixed Period* is set in an imaginary island called Britannula in the South Pacific, halfway between Australia and New Zealand. Written in 1880, it is set in 1980, and Trollope has fun inventing futuristic technology and behaviour. 'Hair-telephones' which enable talking across the miles, 'steam bicycles' which travel six miles in fourteen minutes, and guns that wipe out entire cities with a single shot are part of the Britannulan world. The novel focuses on the island's obsession with euthanasia. Its inhabitants have made a law which determines that every citizen will undergo compulsory euthanasia some time between the ages of sixty-seven and sixty-eight. This 'fixed period' policy states that at sixty-seven, a citizen will be 'deposited' in 'Necropolis' to live out his last months away from society, and then a combination of morphine, opened veins and a warm bath will peacefully terminate his existence. Cremation will follow (Trollope was an enthusiastic member of the Cremation Society in England).

While in Australia Trollope noted the national obsession with cricket. He was not fond of ball games—fox-hunting was the only 'sport' that ever interested him, but an 1877 test match between Australia and England, held in Melbourne, had attracted thousands of spectators and the Aussies had thrashed the visiting team. This victory inspired 'The Cricket Match' chapter in Trollope's novel. Charles Bannerman had made 165 runs for Australia, but in *The Fixed Period* a device called a 'steam-bowler' and protective paraphernalia for the cricketers (Trollope accurately anticipates the sort of protective gear worn by today's cricketers) allow young Jack Neverbend to make 1275 runs for his team.

The novel is told through first-person narration. Trollope distances himself from the euthanasia policy by putting all the enthusiasm for it into the mouth of his hero, President Neverbend. It's an ironic tale and a perceptive study of monomania, with some amusing characters, but it fails as a work of literature. Few critics regard Trollope's last fictional return to Australasia as a success.

❦

On his first visit to Australia Anthony Trollope enjoyed an excursion to the Hawkesbury River district in New South Wales. He had barely heard of the river, but was taken by boat from Sackville, past Wiseman's Ferry to Broken Bay and out to Sydney Harbour. It was a VIP outing, with the NSW Premier Sir James Martin and other leading politicians on board. Initially, Trollope found the journey rather dull, but when the boat chugged into Wiseman's Ferry, with its 'bluffs and high banks', he was hugely impressed. It astonished him that the area had not filled with hotels to accommodate the hordes of tourists he thought should be there. He declared that the Hawkesbury was second only to the Rhine among the world's rivers, and was vastly superior to the Mississippi.

He never forgot the church of St Mary Magdalen at Wiseman's Ferry. Originally built in the 1840s, by the time of Trollope's visit, it was in disrepair as a result of floods and the theft of its lead. In 1882 a decision was taken to demolish the building and recycle its stones for a new church. Trollope headed the subscription list to pay for its construction.

His enthusiasm, his donation, and his glowing descriptions of the Hawkesbury in *Australia and New Zealand* make it appropriate that the stretch of river flowing round the bend of Wiseman's Ferry and past the church is named 'Trollope's Reach' in memory of his visit. Australia has the honour of being the only country in the world to name a place after the author.

Trollope's direct descendants are Australian.[3] A family baronetcy which had bypassed Trollope himself, descended to Fred's son. The present baronet, Sir Anthony Trollope, is Anthony Trollope's great-grandson, and lives in New South Wales.

Trollope's visits to Australia are marked by a plaque at Circular Quay, with a quote recording his delight in Sydney's harbour. But his name is now best known to Australians through television. *Barchester Towers* is one of the most loved series ever shown in Australia, and *The Pallisers*, *The Way We Live Now* and *He Knew He was Right*, all dramatised and filmed, have also been popular with Australian viewers. Trollope, at his best, is a brilliant novelist and the issues he discusses are surprisingly modern. He is superb at depicting women, extraordinarily good on the subject of money, funny, tender and one of the most sympathetic and humane of all novelists, as members of The Anthony Trollope Appreciation group of Australia well know.

The energy and drive that saw Trollope traipse all around Australia, sightseeing, writing and questioning as he went, stayed with him until the last weeks of his

---

3   Trollope's eldest son Henry had two children, but no grandchildren.

Wiseman's Ferry church in the ruined state it was in at the time of Trollope's visit to the Hawkesbury.

Wiseman's Ferry church as it is today. Trollope donated money for its repair.

life. He then overdid it. Three huge dinners out in a row proved too much and he collapsed with a stroke. The man who had produced so many millions of words in his writing, was deprived of words for a month—he was paralysed and without the power of speech. But he left a rich legacy when he died in December 1882 having, ironically, reached his own 'fixed period' at the age of sixty-seven and a half.

The section of the Hawkesbury River at Wiseman's Ferry known as 'Trollope's Reach', in an 1879 photograph. The building centre left is probably that which Trollope described as 'the only house of any pretence'. It was the home of Solomon Wiseman and is now the Wiseman's Ferry Hotel. 'Trollope's Reach' was named in honour of the picnic the author had there with local dignitaries.

The postbox that sits in the Sydney garden of one of Trollope's direct descendants and commemorates his invention of the pillar postbox.

The plaque for Anthony Trollope at Sydney's Circular Quay.

CHAPTER THREE

Joseph Conrad

In 1867 a rather frail little boy gazed out on the ocean for the first time in his life. His uncle had taken him to Odessa, the Black Sea resort town, hoping a change of scene might take the child's mind off the recent death of his mother. He was only nine years old, but the sight of the vast ocean filled him with dreams of travel and escape. The sea would come to symbolise liberation from the problems of his family and his country, a route away from the past and into a new world of romance and opportunity. Even at the age of nine, the boy knew the sea offered adventure—the sea-stories of Captain Marryat and James Fenimore Cooper had taught him that. Across the sea new lands awaited and he could hardly wait to see them. At present they were only coloured shapes on the globe, but he promised himself that one day he would get to visit them.

And get to see them he did. When he was sixteen he joined the French Merchant Marine and trained as an apprentice and steward in several ships. Then he joined the British Merchant Navy, though he spoke no English. And soon young Jozef Teodor Konrad Korzeniowski was fulfilling his early dreams and sailing the world, travelling to the West Indies, the Far East, around the Mediterranean, to India, Malaya and Singapore, to the heart of the Belgian Congo and, as far from Odessa as he could manage, to Australia. On six separate voyages he docked at Australian ports, then suddenly he gave up the life of a sailor altogether and went to England to pursue a very different dream. In the fulfilment of that dream, he turned himself into 'Joseph Conrad'.

⚜

By taking to the sailor's life and the oceans of the world, Jozef Korzeniowski hoped to escape several things. First there was family and crushing family pressure. His mother had died in 1865 from consumption. His grieving father then grew claustrophobic in his love for his only child, withdrawing from society and turning to mathematics lessons as consolation for them both. Close to a breakdown, and ill with the consumption that would kill him four years after his wife's death, Apollo Korzeniowski was a dismal companion for his sensitive son. Jozef would later describe him as a 'vanquished man', an idealist who had been ultimately disappointed by life.

Left to the care of his grandmother and his uncle Tadeusz Bobrowski, Jozef scraped through an education in which the only subject he loved was geography. He spent hours drawing maps, reading tales of exploration

Joseph Conrad in a photograph taken in 1883, between his second and third visits to Australia.

and dreaming of faraway lands. Uncle Tadeusz was a gentleman farmer, but his nephew had no desire to step into those shoes and work the land. Nor was he enthusiastic about living with an ailing grandmother, or an uncle who kept a strict eye on his spending and pursuits. He fought hard to get their consent to his seafaring career, and finally they agreed. When he boarded a train from Cracow to Marseilles at the age of sixteen, he set off for a new life which would rarely involve contact with members of his family.

He was also escaping politics. Both his parents were ardent Polish patriots. In 1861, his father was arrested by Russian authorities for involvement in secret Polish activities. Apollo had written journalism and poetry they regarded as seditious. The result was nocturnal interrogation, arrest, searches and exile to the Urals. Ewa Korzeniowski supported her husband's anti-Russian/pro-Polish stance, as did both of their extended families. Two of Jozef's uncles suffered imprisonment for political activity, while a third was assassinated in a trumped-up duel over political disagreements. Throughout his life Jozef would resist all pressure to draw him into Polish nationalism—he'd seen first-hand the disruption politics and patriotism could cause.

Yet still he was searching for a nation he could call home. He was born in Berdichev, a city that had been Polish from the sixteenth century until it fell to Russia in 1795 as a result of the Third Partition of Poland. By the time of his birth, Poles were an ethnic minority there. His parents were Poles and Polish was his mother tongue, but he was born into the Russian Empire. Poland, as a country, had no political existence, and his parents were patriots of a land their son could not find on any of his beloved maps. Today he would be Ukrainian by birth, as boundaries have been redrawn yet again. It's hardly surprising that his sense of nationality was confused.

He left his homeland for France, rapidly became fluent in French and immersed himself in French literature, but didn't feel totally at home there either. He was twenty when he saw England for the first time. He had no contacts, no knowledge of the language he would one day write in so fluently, and no job there, but England would become his true home. In 1886 he became a naturalised British subject (boasting that while others were British merely by an accident of birth, he was British by conscious choice) and began the process of becoming more English than the English. He preferred to create British characters in his fiction rather than Polish ones, and he travelled to British colonies such as Australia, while avoiding the land of his birth. He had found across the sea a land where he belonged.

One year after first seeing England, Joseph Conrad made his first voyage to Australia.[1] Few letters survive from this time in his life and there is no record that he was looking at Australia as a potential homeland, but for a man as rootless as Conrad, it is highly likely that a land so far from his birthplace could well have attracted him as a place to settle. In the event, he was unable to see much of Australia on his first two visits and by the time of his third he'd made the decision to become British. However, he held affectionate memories of Australia, relishing the contrast of its youth and freshness as a nation to the war-torn history and persecution of Poland, and retaining 'the warmest regard for Australians generally, for New South Wales in particular and for charming Sydney especially'. His uncle wrote to a friend to say that after this first voyage Joseph Conrad came close to making his home in Australia and working as a trader between Australia and the Far East. Probably lack of money and a commitment to return to London with his ship prevented that plan from becoming reality.

⁂

He was on the bottom rung of his career ladder when he set sail for Sydney on 15 October 1878 as 'Ordinary Seaman Jozef Korzeniowski'. His captain was Scotsman

1 Although at this time in his life he was still using his Polish name, he is referred to from this point by his English name Joseph Conrad because it is as a writer with that name that he is included in this book.

John McKay, commanding his first voyage. A wool clipper, the *Duke of Sutherland* was a three-masted and fully rigged vessel of more than a thousand tons. The pay for an ordinary seaman was one shilling a month, enough to buy Conrad perhaps two meals ashore when he reached Sydney. Conditions on board were primitive, with daily rations of one pound of bread, three quarts of water, two ounces of sugar, weak coffee and tea, and just over a pound of salt pork and beef, rice and pea soup. The crew captured any birds that flew on board (larks and starlings) to augment rations. Crew quarters were cramped and Conrad spoke very little English, so felt lonely and cut off from his crewmates, who probably looked askance at the young foreigner reading books for amusement. They all had a difficult time of it during the 109 days it took to sail from London to Sydney; heavy gales and unfavourable trade winds slowed progress. Conrad suffered from 'imperfect oilskins which let water in at every seam'. It was a relief to all on board when they rounded Tasmania and, on 31 January 1879, arrived at Sydney's Circular Quay.

No cargo could immediately be found for the return voyage so Captain McKay was forced to spend five months waiting before he could fill his ship with wool and meat exports for England. Sixteen of the crew immediately quit the ship to look for other work ('ships' crews had the trick of melting away swiftly in those days') and eighteen new men had to be hired when the *Duke of Sutherland* was finally ready to sail. Conrad, however, did not leave the ship. With life savings of only five pounds, nowhere to go and no friends to spend time with on shore, he was happy to remain on board as nightwatchman, earning his meals and accommodation in return for sitting on

The Duke of Sutherland *moored at the far end of Circular Quay in an 1871 photograph. This was the ship that first brought Joseph Conrad to Australia.*

deck all night protecting the ship from thieves. The ship was anchored at the quay at the end of George Street, so Conrad could look down on a rough part of the city, The Rocks. What he saw was often violent, but always interesting. He recorded his experiences in his 1906 book *Mirror of the Sea: Memories and Impressions* and wrote fondly of his time as watchman:

> I do not regret the experience. The night humours of the town descended from the street to the waterside in the still watches of the night: larrikins rushing down in bands to settle some quarrel by a stand-up fight, away from the police, in an indistinct ring half hidden by piles of cargo, with the sound of blows, a groan now and then, the stamping of feet, and the cry of 'Time!' rising suddenly above the sinister and excited murmurs; night-prowlers, pursued or pursuing with a stifled shriek followed by a profound silence, or slinking

stealthily alongside like ghosts, and addressing me from the quay below in mysterious tones with incomprehensible propositions.

Sometimes he held conversations with those on shore:

On one occasion I had an hour or so of most intellectual conversation with a person whom I could not see distinctly . . . I on deck and he on the quay sitting on the case of a piano (landed out of our hold that very afternoon), and smoking a cigar which smelt very good. We touched, in our discourse, upon science, politics, natural history and operatic singers . . . [before the gentleman walked off into the night].

Sometimes he listened to the cab-men, lined up by the quay waiting for passengers for their hansom cabs and filling in time by telling each other 'impolite stories in racy language, every word of which reached [Conrad] distinctly over the bulwarks'. One desperate man rushed on board on a cold, July night, begging to be allowed to hide on deck as people were after him. Conrad, forced by ship regulations to refuse, got a punch in the face and a black eye for his pains.

Not far away was the King's Head pub, a popular haunt of sailors, and the cheap eating houses kept by the Chinese ('Sun-kum-on's was not bad', he remembered).[2] There was also a pedlar selling hot saveloys and the 'monotony, the regularity, the abruptness of the recurring [sales] cry' was so exasperating to a man unable to get off his ship and buy a hot sausage, that Conrad 'wished the

---

2   A Chinese population had been established in Australia since the gold rush days of the 1850s and 1860s.

fellow would choke himself to death with a mouthful of his own infamous wares'.

Even in daylight hours he rarely left the ship. Sydneysiders took great interest in the vessels berthed at the quay and 'on Sundays and holidays the citizens trooped down, on visiting bent' to be escorted by Conrad round the cabins and staterooms. He probably earned himself a few tips from guiding them. Recollections and impressions of all these aspects of Sydney, from its prosperous citizens to the seamier side of human nature apparent in The Rocks, were stored away in Conrad's mind to emerge later in his fiction. Fellow crew member George White, a black man who pronounced his name 'Wait', would inspire the name James Wait in *The Nigger of the 'Narcissus'*. A Frenchman without hands (they had been blown off by a dynamite cartridge used for fishing), who kept a tobacco shop in lower George Street and who tried to roll cigarettes on his knee with the stumps of his arms, became a character in *Because of the Dollars*, a 1915 story of murder and attempted robbery. By attaching weights to his stumps, the Frenchman is able to club a woman to death.

The job of watchman must have had its hours of monotony, with Conrad trapped on board and forced to be a spectator rather than a participant in the life of the city. He noted that the women who came to view the ship had 'engaging manners and a well-developed sense of fun', but he had no opportunity to get to know them better. Most sailors in their early twenties would have found such imprisonment irksome, but Conrad had so much to look at with the comings and goings of the docks and 'one of the finest, most beautiful, vast, and safe bays the sun ever shone upon', that he did not mind the confinement. And when he wasn't observing, he was reading: Flaubert and De Maupassant in French, Shakespeare in English. If he was picking up his English from *Hamlet* on the one hand and Sydney cabbies on the other, it is fascinating to speculate about what Conrad's own English sounded like at this time in his life.

Then suddenly, amid this lull, the ship had a cargo to be loaded and Conrad had to help move it, 'bent almost double under a ship's deck beams, from six in the morning till six in the evening (with an hour and a half off for meals)' as he carted bags of wheat into the hold. By 5 July 1879, the *Duke of Sutherland* was ready to depart and sailed out from Sydney Harbour bound for London. The storms she encountered rounding the Horn on the homeward journey would also make their way into Conrad's future writing.[3]

Joseph Conrad returned to London even more committed to his nautical profession. He was twenty-one, eager to gain professional credentials and in May 1880 he sat, and passed, an exam for Second Mate's Certificate. With precarious finances, he needed any work he could find, so signed on with the *Loch Etive*, even though the position offered was only that of third mate. The ship was 'one of the iron wool-clippers that the Clyde had floated out in swarms upon the world' and her captain, William Stuart, had made his reputation as commander of the *Tweed*, one of the fastest clippers around. Conrad was relieved to be setting off

---

3   The *Duke of Sutherland* was wrecked three years later off the coast of New Zealand. The wreck was sold as scrap for eighty-five pounds.

to sea again, later describing his emotions in his novel, *Chance*: 'And the thought that I was done with the earth for many many months made me feel very quiet and self-contained, as it were. Sailors will understand what I mean'. Conrad was the youngest officer on board and had to adjust quickly to new responsibilities. Once again, it would not prove an easy voyage. Captain Stuart, another Scot, had a bad temper which worsened when he couldn't get the speed he wanted from the ship (which was making her third voyage to Australia). He had once made the England-to-Melbourne run in seventy-two days and when he died on board the *Loch Etive* at the age of sixty-five he had succeeded in commanding ships for forty-five years without ever having lost a mast or a man overboard, so he was clearly an able captain. But Conrad found his orders imprecise, and relations between the two men were strained from the start. Chief mate was William Purdu from Glasgow, who was almost deaf, and the second mate fell ill, which resulted in Conrad being promoted to Officer of the Watch.

The *Loch Etive*'s journey lasted ninety-four days, ending in Sydney on 24 November 1880. *The Sydney Morning Herald* reported that the vessel 'has the appearance of being a thoroughly staunch ship, and has come into port in capital order'. Conrad (who had signed on for this voyage as Conrad Korzeniowski) had his twenty-third birthday in Sydney and this time had decent earnings to spend on celebration. The summer storm he experienced during his six weeks in Sydney would later appear in *Lord Jim*. But again he had no time to explore much beyond Circular Quay and George Street—the bad weather and a few names he encountered would be the only aspects of this visit which found their way into his fiction. The *Loch Etive* was soon loaded with wool and ready to leave on January 11, reaching London after a very stormy voyage ('no sun, moon, or stars for something like seven days') on 23 April 1881.

⁂

On the eastern shore of Tasmania's Derwent River is a sad memorial of Joseph Conrad's third and fourth visits to Australia. The barque *Otago* lies there sinking slowly into the sands of the river, an inglorious end for the ship in which Conrad reached the peak of his professional career. He was thirty when he first sailed in her, he had passed his Master's Examination, and the fourteen pounds per month he was paid would be the best salary he ever received. By this time his English was fluent, though strongly accented, but his disposition was gloomy and taciturn, his finances were still precarious and, although a handsome man, he was still single. He had no close ties, no settled home, but at long last he had command of a ship. He loved the *Otago*, a 'harmonious creature . . . one of those craft that in virtue of their design and complete finish will never look old . . . she looked like a creature of high breed—an Arab steed in a string of cart-horses'. He joined this Australian-owned ship in Bangkok after her captain had died in strange circumstances. The captain had spent weeks playing the fiddle in his cabin—a 'Nero' ignoring the course of his ship and welfare of his crew—before suddenly throwing the fiddle overboard and dying. This tale, and the early days of his first command, formed the basis of Conrad's novel *The Shadow Line*.

Delighted to be a captain at last, Conrad was full

The Otago *unloading at Princess Wharf, Melbourne. This is the ship that Joseph Conrad captained and in which he made his third and fourth visits to Australia.*

of pride in his ship: 'Directly my eyes had rested on my ship, all my fear vanished . . . Yes, there she was. Her hull, her rigging filled my eye with a great content. That feeling of life-emptiness which had made me so restless for the last few months lost its bitter plausibility, its evil influence, dissolved into a flow of joyous emotion'. That joy didn't last long, dissipated by a very difficult voyage in the Gulf of Siam, quarantine in Singapore and then more storms on the way to Sydney, which he reached on 7 May 1888. The *Otago*'s arrival was reported by *The Sydney Morning Herald* as being under the command of 'Captain Conrad Konkorzentowski' (*sic*)—newspapers invariably misspelled his name—and as being anchored in Elizabeth Bay. Yet again, Conrad had no time to explore Sydney and within a fortnight was off to Melbourne. Melbourne was not making life easy for maritime traders. The port was being modernised, so all arrivals had to anchor in Hobson's Bay and offload their cargoes onto lighters that could take them up the Yarra

River—a time-wasting process involving expensive double-handling. In July he was back in Sydney, only to encounter more difficulties in the form of the Seaman's Union, then in crisis negotiations over wages. Ships were blockaded, fights broke out, the police were called in. Conrad, who had filled the *Otago* with soap, tallow and fertiliser, was lucky to escape the blockade and get her out of harbour en route for Mauritius. 'Asses', was his opinion of all unionised sailors!

Mauritius provided one of the few 'romantic' moments of Conrad's life.[4] The enchanting smiles of pretty Eugénie Renouf prompted the shy captain to propose, only to find she was already engaged. He left, vowing never to set foot in that country again, but all too aware that he was no catch for any young woman. Letters he'd received from his uncle when last in Sydney contained a list of all he owned in the world—a set of silver cutlery for twelve people, two silver-plated trays, an antique clock, an armchair, a small table, table linen and 'various knick-knacks, neither beautiful nor valuable'—a pitiful collection for a man of thirty. Later, he could turn the 'Eugénie' episode to fictional account in *A Smile of Fortune*, but at this time it was all too fresh and painful. He set sail for Melbourne, arriving there early in 1889, feeling depressed and even gloomier than usual. If *A Smile of Fortune* is to be believed, the ship was loaded with potatoes, a cargo he took on reluctantly. But it proved to be highly profitable, for Melbourne had

---

4   Joseph Conrad later married Jessie George, when
    he was in his late thirties. The marriage astonished
    his friends and appears to have been a 'comfortable'
    arrangement, rather than a romantic one. In spite of
    making 'no children' a condition of marrying, Conrad
    fathered two sons, Borys and John.

been suffering 'from an unparalleled drought' which had caused a desperate shortage of potatoes. He spent a month in Melbourne, sometimes aboard his ship, sometimes lodging at the Sailor's Home, an elegant building on the corner of Collins and Spencer Streets. However, he held himself aloof from other sailors and knew no one else in the city.

In February he was off to Minlacowie, on the Yorke Peninsula in South Australia, to load a cargo of wheat. Detained there a month, Conrad finally found time to mix with the locals: 'the farmers around were very nice to me', he remembered. He returned their hospitality by hosting 'a tea-party on board the dear old *Otago* then lying alongside the God-forsaken jetty'. It must have been a strange occasion; the dandified, good-looking captain with his foreign accent, dreamy eyes, determined chin and beautifully trimmed moustache, well acquainted with the culture and literature of Europe, travelled and urbane, was not in the usual run of ships' captains. Did he and the farmers' wives of Minlacowie discuss Flaubert or Shakespeare? He could be a good conversationalist when he tried, so perhaps Conrad exerted himself to find subjects of mutual interest.

That tea party would prove to be his swan song as captain. He delivered the wheat to Port Adelaide, the *Otago*'s home port, but was there disappointed to hear that he couldn't then sail on to the China Seas, a part of the world he'd not visited and was anxious to see. The owners, Henry Simpson & Sons, refused to be persuaded, so Conrad suddenly resigned his command. He had a history of difficult relationships with employers, but no biographer knows just why he made this decision. Was he piqued at their inflexibility, bored by the mundane work they offered, or just generally restless and unhappy and in need of a change? Whatever the cause, Captain Joseph C. Korzeniowski (as he now signed himself) abandoned good prospects and steady employment, bought a ticket as a paying passenger on the *Nürnberg*, and left for London, reaching it in mid-May 1889.

That tea party also proved to be the last glorious moment of his dear *Otago*. She was sold soon after to Huddart Parker & Co. and converted for coal haulage, working in Sydney and Hobart for some years. In 1931 she was sold to a wrecker for twenty-five dollars and towed up the Derwent to be beached at the foot of Mount Direction. She still lies there, partly dismantled and rusting away, with various bits being occasionally removed by souvenir hunters. One Joseph Conrad fan took away the steering wheel, with which Conrad had guided his ship through many storms, and presented it to the Honourable Company of Master Mariners. It can now be seen on their HQS *Wellington* on the Thames. One section of the stern went off to Los Angeles; wood was removed and made into a box now on display in the Maritime Museum of Tasmania; and the timber structure

The wreck of the Otago *as it stands today in the Derwent River, Tasmania.*

of the companion hatchway is also on display there. What remains is the stern resting in shallow water, the bow sinking into the mud and the surrounding area littered with her debris. The fate of the *Otago* is a sorry one for a ship which featured as the 'heroine' of *The Shadow Line*. Indeed, it is his ships that are the true 'heroines' of his books; Conrad was poor at creating female characters in his fiction.

The three years before Conrad next travelled to Australia were life-changing. In 1890 he set off for the Congo as an employee of a Belgian shipping company. Africa had always been the most fascinating part of the globe to young Jozef, so he could not resist an opportunity to penetrate its very heart. He knew it would be dangerous (only seven per cent of the firm's employees managed to complete their three-year contracts); but he craved adventure, a life away from everyone he knew, a total change of scene. What he got was illness and horror—corpses floating down the river, the ghastly suffering of slaves, the callousness of white men exploiting Africa for everything they could get from it. His African experiences marked him for life, leaving his nerves (not good at the best of times) shattered, his body prone to malarial attacks and gout for the rest of his life, and his mind demoralised and even more pessimistic than before. Nine years later he worked through some of his suffering in his masterpiece *Heart of Darkness*, but the damage done by Africa was irreversible.

When he did set sail for Australia once again, there was a vital addition to his luggage—the manuscript of a novel. He'd been working on it since late 1889, but it grew slowly and would become a well-travelled manuscript before finally being turned into *Almayer's Folly*. Its author was writing for the first time at any length in his new language, English.[5] The beginnings of the literary reputation he'd one day achieve were tucked away with his oilskins and the compass.

This time his ship was the *Torrens* and he served in her as first officer on a salary of eight pounds a month. This was a step down in rank for a man who had qualified to be a captain, but he accepted the drop in rank and salary because of the prestige of the ship and because he was convinced that the only cure for his recent breakdown of nerves and health was to be once more at sea. The ship embarked from Plymouth on 25 November 1891, on its ninety-five-day journey to Port Adelaide. The *Torrens* was a fine ship of 1334 tons, the last fully rigged composite passenger clipper to be launched in England, and built especially for the Australian trade route. Roomy and comfortable (there was even a cow on board to provide fresh milk), she was also one of the fastest vessels afloat, setting a record, never broken by any sailing ship, of sixty-four days from Plymouth to Adelaide. Conrad developed great affection for her and put her into his novel *Chance* as *Flora*, in memory of her floral figurehead.

Conrad was later remembered by her passengers as an excellent first mate. He calmed one passenger terrified of drowning, the ship's apprentices found him considerate and capable—'Sailors and boys all swore by him'—and fellow sailors enjoyed listening to him tell stories. In 1923 he wrote *The Torrens: A Personal Tribute*, recalling the ship with great fondness: 'for apart from

---

5 Letters that Joseph Conrad wrote to relatives were either in Polish or French.

Joseph Conrad (back row, centre) on board the Torrens *with the ship's apprentices.*

her more brilliant qualities, such as her speed and her celebrated good looks (which by themselves go a long way with a sailor), she was regarded as a "comfortable ship" in a strictly professional sense, which means that she was known to handle easily and to be a good sea boat in heavy weather'. To him, she was a contemporary, as she was 'launched in 1875, only a few months after I had managed, after lots of trouble, to launch myself on the waters of the Mediterranean'.

The *Torrens* arrived in Adelaide on the last day of

The Torrens,
*the ship that
Conrad thought
so beautiful
and in which he
made his fifth
and sixth visits
to Australia.*

February 1892, with Conrad not as well as he'd hoped to be and complaining of lassitude and torpor. His nerves were not strengthened by his only recorded professional gaffe, the loss of an anchor, which involved paying a diver to retrieve it from the bottom of Adelaide Harbour. Reading *Madame Bovary* temporarily took his mind off his problems, but the month he spent in Adelaide, before returning to England aboard the *Torrens*, was not a happy one for him.

However, he was soon back in Australia, arriving again in Adelaide with the *Torrens* on 30 January 1893, for what would prove to be his final visit. Among the sixty passengers on board was a young man who would shape Conrad's future. William Jacques, frail, literate and fresh from university, became the first reader of a Joseph Conrad story, when the shy author showed him the now yellowing nine chapters of *Almayer's Folly*. Conrad's *A Personal Record* later told of Jacques' response:

> Next day . . . Jacques entered my cabin. He had
> a thick woollen muffler round his throat, and

the M.S. was in his hand. He tendered it to me with a steady look, but without a word. I took it in silence. He sat down on the couch and still said nothing . . .

'Well, what do you say?' I asked at last. 'Is it worth finishing?' This question expressed exactly the whole of my thoughts.

'Distinctly,' he answered, in his sedate, veiled voice, and then coughed a little.

'Were you interested?' I inquired further, almost in a whisper.

'Very much!'

This was just the encouragement Conrad needed.[6]

There wasn't much else to cheer him on the voyage. His health was terrible, with 'reminders of Africa' plaguing him throughout the journey. When he arrived he needed a week in the Adelaide Hills for recuperation and to escape the February heat. Although kept busy with ship's duties until late March, he could not shake off his despondency, his sense that a grey future awaited him with unrelenting ill health and depression. Soon he would give up the sea and turn to a career of letters, but at this time his prospects seemed uncertain and bleak.

One morning in Adelaide, however, things became a little brighter. As he stowed wool on board, Conrad began chatting to a young passenger. John Galsworthy was twenty-five, handsome, blond and a recent law graduate. He was also a hopeless romantic and had fallen in love with an actress, so his wealthy parents had sent him travelling round the world, hoping that distance

---

6 Sadly, William Jacques died from tuberculosis soon after the *Torrens* reached Australia.

would make him forget his Sybil. Galsworthy's stay in Australia was a very brief one.[7] He'd landed at Albany just before Christmas, sailed on to Sydney which he left almost immediately for a jaunt to Noumea and Fiji (he'd hoped to get to Samoa to visit Robert Louis Stevenson, but that plan didn't eventuate), and to New Zealand where he'd explored the thermal regions of the North Island. He was newly arrived in Sydney to catch the *Torrens* back to England. As they chatted, Galsworthy grew intrigued by the dark-haired, bearded sailor's 'tales of ships and storms, of Polish revolution . . . of the Malay seas, and the Congo', so different from his own privileged background of Harrow and Oxford. This meeting would prove to be the beginning of a long friendship. Galsworthy found Conrad 'a capital chap, though queer to look at . . . a man of travel and experience in many parts of the world, and . . . a fund of yarns'. During the return voyage to England the friendship strengthened and, on reaching London, Galsworthy looked Conrad up.

Did he ever regret that meeting in Adelaide? Conrad would prove to be a demanding friend. When Galsworthy made a financial success of his plays and novels he was often called on to assist Conrad, ever hopeless with money, with loans and advances, and even to lend him his London home on occasion. No wonder Conrad described Galsworthy as the most steadfast, the most dependable, the most sympathetic of friends. The two men wrote very different books, with Galsworthy more interested in man as a social animal, funnier

---

7 John Galsworthy saw almost nothing of Australia, and rarely mentions the country in his novels or plays. It is for these reasons that he has not been included in this book.

(Conrad's writing is not noted for its humour), and for most of his writing life far more popular with the public. Conrad's critical reputation was slower to establish, but has proved more lasting. As friends, they were often separated by time and distance, but that intimacy first established in Adelaide endured.

After six visits to the edges of Australia, Joseph Conrad had grown very familiar with its quays and ships, but knew next to nothing of its countryside and very little of its inhabitants. The visits left him, however, with 'a great affection for that Young Continent' which would 'endure as long as . . . faculty of memory itself endures'. He sailed from Adelaide in the *Torrens* and back to London, disembarked and 'took a long look from the Quay at that last of ships I ever had under my care, and, stepping around the corner of a tall warehouse, parted from her for ever, and at the same time stepped . . . out of my sea life altogether'.[8] The new life he stepped into was that of 'Joseph Conrad, Author', with its thirteen novels, twenty-eight short stories, essays and memoirs.

In 1879 Conrad's uncle Tadeusz Bobrowski wrote to his nephew complaining that Jozef's letters from his first voyage were too full of 'the direction of the winds that brought you back' and the technical challenges of navigation. Uncle Tadeusz wanted more personal news. Two years later he encouraged the young man to write contributions for *Wedrowiec*, a Polish journal with which he was associated: 'We have few travellers,

---

8 The *Torrens* was sold for fifteen hundred pounds in 1906 to Italian shipowners, but was seriously damaged soon after and broken up for scrap in Genoa in 1910.

and even fewer genuine correspondents: the words of an eyewitness would be of great interest and in time would bring you in money . . . think about this, young man, collect some reminiscences from the voyage to Australia'. Conrad never did collect those reminiscences. As a man, he only touched the edges of the continent, so it is apt that, as a writer, he brought Australia only into the periphery of his fiction. The land and its people never stirred his creative depths in the way that Africa had done.

What he did do in his stories and novels, however, was reflect on the growing importance of Australia as a commercial base in the southern hemisphere. Australia's population was growing rapidly in the 1880s and '90s. Farmers had more sheep to shear and wool to export, with by-products such as tallow and soap. There was wheat to spare being grown and markets for it were opening up not only in England, but around the Far East. Conrad's shipping work had made him well acquainted with what sold, how quickly products could reach their buyers, and the transportation costs involved. He understood that the clippers leaving from New South Dock on the Thames 'knew the road to the Antipodes better than their own skippers' and that when they reached the ports of Sydney, Melbourne and Adelaide, they were received there like 'honoured guests'. His stories also make regular mention of trading routes between Australia and Singapore, Australia and Batavia and Australia and Malaya. Sydney is represented in his writing as an important, thriving city, sending out its goods around the world.

Australia is also shown in his fiction to be an exporter of people. The desire for an 'overseas experience' was alive and well even then. *Almayer's Folly* refers to 'those bold spirits who, fitting out schooners on the Australian coast,

96

invaded the Malay Archipelago in search of money and adventure'. Unfortunately, those who set off from Australia looking for adventure were not always the most desirable types, often having a good reason for making themselves scarce at home. An important character in *Lord Jim* is the West Australian 'Chester' (he is given no other name): 'He was a man with an immense girth of chest, a rugged, clean-shaven face of mahogany colour, and two blunt tufts of iron-grey, thick, wiry hairs on his upper lip. He had been pearler, wrecker, trader, whaler too, I believe; in his own words—anything and everything a man may be at sea, but a pirate. The Pacific, north and south, was his proper hunting ground'. At the time of his introduction into the novel, he is obsessed by a scheme to bring a cargo of guano into Queensland where, he is certain, it would be the 'making of Queensland!' but he struggles to sell the idea to anyone. Chester drinks and is extravagant of speech and gesture and not a man to be trusted. His fate is a mysterious one for, after repairing his ancient boat 'at some Australian port', he 'steamed out into the Pacific with a crew of twenty-two hands all told, and the only news having a possible bearing upon the mystery of his fate was the news of a hurricane which is supposed to have swept its course over the Walpole shoals, a month or so afterwards'.

Other rather dubious Australian characters appear in *Because of the Dollars*. Mrs Davidson, a woman with a 'superficial aspect of vapid sweetness' and a 'small, red, pretty, ungenerous mouth' is also a West Australian. An unwilling exile in the Far East, at the end of the story she leaves her husband and returns to Fremantle. And there is 'Laughing Anne', a prostitute who has a history of being dumped by the men in her life. Bamtz, another Australian, is a cadger and loafer, 'an abject sort of creature' with an impressive black beard. All these characters are almost certainly based on people Conrad encountered in The Rocks, and the implication is that Australia is much better off without them. Joseph Conrad clearly felt that Australian involvement in Asian and European commerce did not always bring out the finest individuals. It was a hard, dangerous life—any Australian taking on such trading ventures had to be tough, or corrupt, to survive.

Only two of his short stories have Australian settings. *The Brute*, one of his best stories published in December 1906, has a scene set in Sydney. It's a happy scene—a man asks his younger brother (and fellow officer) to help him choose a ring for Maggie, the woman he wants to marry. It's mid-summer and 'on that awful, blazing hot day, with clouds of dust flying about', Charley and Maggie set off for a walk. He proposed and placed the ring on her finger and 'they came back after a few hours looking very staid, but didn't seem to have the slightest idea where they had been'. The scene sounds romantic, but neither Maggie nor Sydney really come alive in it. The heroine, or rather anti-heroine, of the tale is *Apse Family*, a ship that seems to bring about someone's death on every voyage. She is 'the brute' of the title. Maggie's death occurs when she is caught in a ship's anchor round the waist, clasped 'close with a dreadful hug' and flung overboard. The *Apse Family* has a personality all her own—spiteful, vengeful, sadistic. Few of Conrad's women are memorable or especially believable creations. They tend to be seen, as in *The Brute*, as disruptive threats to the close relationship between men at sea and their ships. It is Conrad's ships that are the memorable heroines, or villainesses, of his writing.

His other story with an Australian setting is the novella *The Planter of Malata*, an odd, unsuccessful tale of a man who falls obsessively in love. The story begins in the private office of an editor of 'the only literary newspaper in the Antipodes' and also has scenes set in a private home. Sydney is not even named as the location, which is merely given as 'a great colonial city', but a reference to the hero's ship being anchored off Garden Island in the Harbour makes it clear that Sydney was the city in Conrad's mind. However, there are few details given of the physical setting—the story is too concerned with inner difficulties for the outward setting to matter.

The Planter of Malata is an examination of a man's loneliness and isolation. The planter, Geoffrey Renouard, has cut himself off from society, wanting to 'evade the small complications of existence' by living on remote Malata. When he falls in love, he struggles to cope with a normal human relationship, behaves strangely, and finally suicides. Conrad, too, had held himself apart on his visits to Australia, preferring books and his own company to that of his fellow sailors. Perhaps it was a memory of his own loneliness while there which made him place this 'loner' in Sydney?

<hr />

Joseph Conrad's current reputation in Australia can best be likened to the present state of his old ship, the *Otago*, moving deeper into the mud of the Derwent River. Now sunk from the sight of most Australians are the majority of Conrad's short stories and most of his novels. The bits still visible are his classic *Heart of Darkness* and a few filmed versions of his books. *Heart of Darkness* is occasionally studied in courses alongside *Apocalypse Now*, the 1979 Francis Ford Coppola film, which is adapted from Conrad's novel (with the setting changed from the Congo to Vietnam). Universities periodically offer courses on 'literature and politics' that include *Under Western Eyes*, or on modernism, bringing in *Nostromo*, but generally Conrad's fiction is retreating from the syllabus in schools and in higher education. Film and television versions have been made of some of Conrad's writings in recent decades: *Heart of Darkness* in 1993, *Victory* in 1995, *The Secret Agent* in 1996, *Swept from the Sea* in 1997, and a 1997 BBC television adaptation of *Nostromo* was a critical success.

There is a plaque to Joseph Conrad at Circular Quay, its position at the edge of Sydney's Harbour apt for a man who came to know the Harbour and its quays intimately but who saw little of the rest of the country. This reminder of Conrad's six visits, and the sinking remains of his adored ship in Tasmania, are now the only memorials to a sailor and writer who fell in love with the ships that carried him across the oceans, but who developed no deep relationship with Australia.

The plaque for Joseph Conrad at Sydney's Circular Quay.

CHAPTER FOUR

Robert Louis Stevenson

A reception clerk at Sydney's prestigious Victoria Hotel in King Street would long remember Robert Louis Stevenson's arrival in Australia. Not recognising the skeletal, badly dressed man in front of him as the famous author, the clerk allotted the man and his wife a small room on the fourth floor of the hotel, instead of the requested suite of rooms on the first floor. Stevenson had had problems with hotel staff before and wasn't going to put up with this indignity. He took one look at the dingy, carpetless room up too many sets of stairs, and rushed back to reception, where he treated the unfortunate clerk to one of his famous 'purples', an explosion of words and fury that rapidly attracted a crowd of staff and guests.

To be fair to the clerk, he could hardly be blamed for wanting to send this guest to a less grand part of the establishment. Stevenson looked as if he had only days to live. He was dressed in ill-fitting, creased and travel-stained clothes, with a wide-brimmed straw hat and ungroomed, over-long hair. His wife looked even stranger. She was wearing a 'holoku', a loose Pacific Island dress, and she was naturally of so dark a complexion as to almost pass as a native Samoan woman. The couple's luggage was packed into three cedarwood chests held together with rope, some 'Tokelau' buckets made from tree trunks, palm-leaf baskets, native mats, rolls of 'tapa' cloth, calabashes, and a motley collection of coconut shells tied up with fish-netting. To complete the picture, there was Ah Fu, their Chinese cook. In a genteel Sydney hotel in 1890, they were lucky not to be shown the door. Stevenson, however, disliked this reinforcement of one of his own maxims—that 'to travel hopefully [was] a better thing than to arrive'.

The author soon worked himself into a total rage, a volley of furious words pouring onto the head of the unfortunate man at the desk, the growing audience watching in fascination. The awkward situation was saved by the arrival of Belle Strong and Lloyd Osbourne, who pushed their way through the onlookers to greet their mother and stepfather. Robert Louis Stevenson was so taken aback at the sight of them that he stopped his tirade abruptly, and Belle and her mother soon calmed the whole situation. They hurried him and all the baggage away from the offensive Victoria to the less fashionable Oxford Hotel across the road.[1]

---

1 The Oxford Hotel stood on Queen Square where the Supreme Court now stands. According to a hotel advertisement, it offered 'every means of entertainment, and yet the quietude when desired of a private house; means of communicating by telegraph and telephone without leaving the premises; electric lift; prompt attendance, and a cuisine unsurpassed by any hotel in Sydney'.

The Oxford Hotel in King Street, Sydney, which treated RLS courteously after his poor reception at the more prestigious Victoria Hotel.

Next morning the Sydney papers announced the arrival of the author of *Dr Jekyll and Mr Hyde*. The clerk, gazing horrified at the photo of the ill-kempt man he had treated so cavalierly, was forced to confess to his manager. The manager went rushing off to the Oxford to apologise profusely to Stevenson and to beg him to return to the Victoria. He promised not only the first floor suite, but at half price. Stevenson took grim pleasure in refusing, and even more satisfaction in obliging the staff of the Victoria to bring over in wicker baskets every day the piles of letters addressed to him. Although he returned on three more occasions to Sydney, he never applied to stay at the Victoria Hotel.

In his delightful book *Travels with a Donkey*, his tale of a journey through the Cevennes region of France, Robert Louis Stevenson wrote: 'For my part, I travel not to go anywhere, but to go. I travel for travel's sake. The great affair is to move'. He had certainly done a great deal of 'moving' and had covered thousands of miles in his brief life, but was it solely a desire to be going somewhere that had brought Stevenson to Australia? Was it the passion for adventure and excitement which had characterised every page of *Treasure Island*? Or was it the desperate need for a location that would suit his fragile health? As Sydney had also become the nearest 'big smoke' to his remote Pacific Island, perhaps Stevenson was just in need of a bit of city sophistication. The author's motivation in visiting Australia was a mixture of all these things.

He'd always travelled; his parents had often taken their delicate son to Europe to find places where he might grow stronger, because there wasn't much chance of that happening at home. Home was Edinburgh, his birthplace, his precipitous, 'scowling town' with 'one of the vilest climates under the heaven' whose grimy spell gripped Stevenson imaginatively all his life, no matter how far away he went. His father took him round the rugged Scottish coasts inspecting the lighthouses that were the family heritage and business. Then he was packed off to England to be 'cured' of his atheism and the Bohemian dress and lifestyle that were upsetting his parents. In the 1870s he travelled so much that he joked to his mother that she had a tramp and vagabond for a son.

Even Stevenson's love life incurred travel. In France in 1876 he met Fanny Vandergrift Osbourne, an American, and fell for her totally and utterly. She had the disadvantage of a husband and children and only in 1880 was she able to get divorced and marry Louis (pronounced 'Lewis', this was the name by which he was always known). To attend his own wedding in San Francisco he had endured a horrific journey, first by ship, then by train across America (vividly described in *The Amateur Emigrant*). He and Fanny went to the

Napa Valley for a honeymoon, then to Swiss resorts for his health, to the Scottish Highlands, and finally to Bournemouth. There, in English suburbia, Stevenson made his fame and a 'hundred, jingling, tingling, golden-minted quid' with *Treasure Island*, the book he wrote for Fanny's young son Lloyd. Other masterpieces soon followed—*Kidnapped*, *The Strange Case of Dr Jekyll and Mr Hyde* and *The Child's Garden of Verses*. His fame as *RLS* was born.

Travel was expensive, but his father's death in 1887 brought with it a convenient inheritance, so after Bournemouth Louis and Fanny set off again for America. New York had too many reporters pushing and shoving to get his attention, Saranac Lake in the Adirondack Mountains was too cold, so in San Francisco they decided to turn a long-cherished dream into reality and hired a boat to take them to the South Seas. Visiting this exotic part of the world was something Stevenson had wanted to do for years. It was actually a New Zealander who had first suggested to him the idea of going there. The aptly named William Seed, Inspector of New Zealand's Marine and Customs and a distant relative, was in Edinburgh in 1875, staying at the Stevenson home in Heriot Row. His stories of tropical islands with their 'beautiful places, green forever; perfect climate, perfect shapes of men and women, with red flowers in their hair; and nothing to do but to study oratory and etiquette, sit in the sun and pick up fruits as they fall' tempted young Stevenson with their promise of peace and sunshine and left him 'sick with a desire to go there'. This seed took fifteen years to germinate, but finally brought him, on the schooner *Casco*, into the Pacific Ocean, to the Marquesas Islands, Tahiti, Honolulu and finally Samoa. There, in

December 1889, he and Fanny found a home in Apia, purchased land and started building a house. A Sydney architect was engaged by post, but his costs were too high and the Villa Vailima began to take shape without his expert opinion. Stevenson's literary friends back in Britain were horrified at the idea that such a famous writer could bury himself in the islands, but Stevenson insisted that he'd at long last found a climate that suited him and had 'had more fun and pleasure of my life these past months than ever before, and more health than any time in ten long years'.

He might have found a home, but he was still restless. This restlessness would bring him to Sydney four times between February 1890 and March 1893. Any excuse would get him up and moving again. The excuse for his first visit was builders. Anyone who has lived through renovations will appreciate that the sawing, hammering and chattering of the workers putting up his house was distracting for a man trying to write. He, Fanny and Lloyd set off in the SS *Lübeck* for Sydney on February 4 and docked at Circular Quay on 13 February 1890. Today a brass plaque on the Writers' Walk there commemorates that arrival. Lloyd hurried straight from the ship to Woolloomooloo to find his sister Belle in her dingy boarding house, while Louis and Fanny went off to experience their memorable arrival at the Victoria Hotel. [2]

It is most puzzling that a man who was so very keen on travel should have made no effort to venture outside

---

2   Belle was staying at Miss Leaney's Theatrical Boarding House in St Mary's Terrace (now the Sydney Eye Hospital).

Sydney. He had claimed that his visit was for the purpose of spying out the land, but he saw precious little of it. It's almost as if he regarded Sydney as one of his beloved Pacific Islands with nothing beyond the city itself except an expanse of ocean. He didn't even visit the Blue Mountains, an area within a day's travel of Sydney at that time, and well known as salubrious for TB patients. He certainly had no desire to see Melbourne. A map of the city was enough to repulse him: 'When I think of Melbourne, I vomit! . . . Its flatness, its streets laid out with a square rule, are certain to have a detrimental effect on those who are doomed to dwell by the yellow waters of the Yarra'. Stevenson's total experience of Australia would include Sydney and absolutely nowhere else.

However, he liked Sydney and enjoyed exploring its streets and parks and meeting the locals. Fanny, however, did not share his positive view. She was a difficult woman—bossy, self-dramatising and wild—and she took an instant dislike to Sydneysiders because of the 'criminal stamp' she detected in their faces. Perhaps they were simply shocked by her appearance—Fanny traditionally went without stockings and wore 'unwashed loose dresses'. Well-dressed Sydneysiders probably thought she looked far more 'criminal' than they did. Stevenson, on the other hand, laid himself out to be sociable, and his fame brought a stream of visitors and reporters to the Oxford: 'Several niceish people have turned up', he wrote to his mother. He found 'friends old and new, the Saturday evening salons' all 'quite a lark'. He caught up with old friends including AJ Daplyn, an English painter working as an art instructor and Dr Scot-Skirving, a friend from university days in Edinburgh. The 'new' included Bernhard Wise, 'late Attorney General here, a handsome fellow', and a colourful character called Jack Buckland, who inspired Tommy Hadden, the remittance man in *The Wrecker*, the book Stevenson was working on at the time. Another new friend was Walter Oates, a beachcomber from Liverpool who had washed up in Sydney, and who spent 'evening after evening' with Louis and Lloyd: 'he sits square on a chair, drinks . . . smokes cigars, and pours forth his old experiences'. Stevenson loved meeting such oddities who could inspire characters in his novels.

The 'whirl of work and society' he encountered in Sydney required new clothes and so he hurried to the George Street shop of William Chorley, master tailor to the city gentry, to be fitted for a dress suit. When George Mackaness wrote *Robert Louis Stevenson: His Association with Australia* in the 1930s, Chorley's still had in its records Stevenson's painfully thin measurements for that suit.

Stevenson did his best to learn something of the cultural life of Sydney. He checked out local bookshops and was disappointed not to find *The Tragic Muse*, the latest book by his friend Henry James. He was pleased, however, to find a good range of detective fiction. Murder mysteries were what he liked best for relaxation, but he also planned to read the Australian classic *For the Term of his Natural Life* by Marcus Clarke and, when he found time, to study some Australian poetry. Stevenson couldn't resist indulging in some light-hearted teasing of Sydney's intellectuals. When asked what he was reading, knowing they expected to hear of something erudite on his bedside table, he replied 'Lynch, of course', referring to a popular shilling shocker called *Lady Kate, the Dashing Female Detective* by Lawrence Lynch. The joke fell flat as the enquirers had never even heard of Lynch. He hated being treated like an intellectual author or critic. When asked to explain a poem by a Mr Brown, Stevenson replied, 'I'm damned if I know what it means. It reads like cat's meat to me'. He also delighted in being brutally frank about the city's architecture, dismissing the new GPO as 'an ungainly structure with a tower'.

Reporters came to call, among them a Madame Rose-Soley who wanted to know if he had visited 'Treasure Island'. He told her that his imagined island was 'not in the Pacific. In fact, I only wish myself that I knew where it was'. She also asked about his working methods and he replied, 'I like to have several books in hand at the same time'. He wasn't too plagued by reporters on this first visit to Australia, but when he visited in 1893 the press had become more aware of his presence and he found his 'fame much grown'.

It was not a one-sided media relationship. Before long Stevenson had initiated contact with the press and created news the media found too hot to handle. While cruising the South Seas aboard the *Casco*, Stevenson had visited the island of Molokai and there looked round the leper colony, which had been founded by Father Damien, a Belgian priest, who had himself died from leprosy not long before. He found the place horrifying. The 'butt-ends of human beings' that he saw both sickened him and filled him with deep pity. Then at a dinner party in Sydney, Stevenson was asked if he'd seen a letter written by the Reverend Dr Hyde, a Presbyterian minister in Honolulu. Hyde's letter had been published in the *Sydney Presbyterian* denigrating the late Father Damien and the work he'd done with the lepers. Leaping to his feet in another of his rages, Stevenson declared that he must smash the traducer of such a fine man who was no longer alive to defend himself.

Still fuming the next day, he sat down to write an 'Open Letter', staunchly defending Father Damien. He wanted this letter published immediately in all the local papers. *The Sydney Morning Herald* refused to touch it, fearing a libel action. Stevenson frantically sent it off to editors back home in Scotland, hoping they'd be less timid than the Australian ones. Eventually *The Australian Star* took the risk, but only after it had first appeared in Edinburgh's *Scots Observer.* Later it was printed as a thirty-two page pamphlet, with royalties from sales going to the Molokai lepers. *The Australian Star's* version came out on 24 May 1890, after Stevenson had left the country. 'In Defence of the Dead' took up most of the front page and was accompanied by a portrait of the author. The circulation of the paper was forty-five thousand, so Stevenson can truly be said to have hit the front pages as a result of his visit to Australia.

Even after leaving the country, he was worried about the consequences of his letter: 'I knew I was writing a libel: I thought he would bring on an action: I made sure I should be ruined; I asked leave of my gallant family, and the sense I was signing away all I possessed kept me up to high water mark, and made me feel every insult heroic'. But his fears were unjustified. Dr Hyde failed to live up to his evil Stevensonian namesake and ignored the publicity. The Mitchell Library in Sydney now owns a first edition of the pamphlet. In his rage over Dr Hyde's criticisms, Stevenson regarded his anger as 'justified and righteous'. Later he calmed down and regretted the violence and fury of his own words, realising he could probably have better defended Father Damien less harshly.

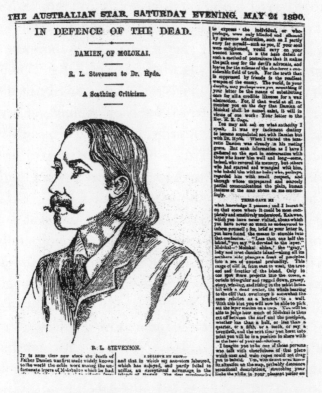

RLS's 'Damien Letter' in The Australian Star, *with which he risked a libel suit.*

Stevenson might have liked Sydney, but the city's climate never liked him. On each of his four visits he fell ill with his old enemy, 'Bluidy Jack'. Sydney's notorious February humidity brought on headaches, coughs, breathing problems and even haemorrhages. When he coughed, his sheets were splattered with blood. Fanny had him moved from the Oxford Hotel to the Union Club in Bligh Street.[3] This was a gentleman's club, so she had to go and stay with her daughter and son-in-law and

---

3 The Union Club is still in existence, but is now located in more modern premises in Bent Street. Stevenson was made an honorary member for each of his visits. The present-day club still has Stevenson's chair, a low-backed chair which the famous author particularly liked to sit in.

couldn't nurse him. As Fanny invariably (and, it must be suspected, in a bid for attention) fell ill herself whenever her husband was sick, her removal from the scene was probably a blessing in disguise. He seemed more upset that club rules prevented him playing his beloved flageolet (a rule he annoyed fellow members by breaking on several occasions) than he was at being divided from his wife. The club had a smoking room and library with all the latest journals, and Stevenson felt comfortable there. It was a Sydney base for his next three visits.

Biographers have traditionally claimed that Robert Louis Stevenson suffered from TB and certainly he was weak-chested as a child, suffered from frequent bronchial conditions and since 1875 had been coughing up blood. However, Stevenson did not die from TB, but from a stroke. He is not known to have infected any other member of his household with this highly contagious disease, even during cramped shipboard confinements, and an American doctor who analysed his sputum sample, showed it to be negative of TB. It's rare for TB patients to live as long as fifteen years after the onset of serious blood-spitting and to survive as many haemorrhages as Stevenson did. In her recent *Robert Louis Stevenson: A Biography* Claire Harman suggests that he was a victim of Osler-Rendu-Weber Syndrome, a haemorrhagic telangiectasia which brings on chronic respiratory complaints and recurrent lung haemorrhages. This is a hereditary disease and both his mother and maternal grandfather evinced similar symptoms and neither died from TB. A Sydney doctor, Fairfax Ross, consulted by Stevenson in 1893, told him he was suffering from 'exposure, malaria, worry and over-work'. Claire Harman's theory appears more convincing.

The Union Club in Bligh Street, where RLS stayed on all his visits to Sydney. Photograph by Kerry & Co.

Whatever the cause of his illness, Stevenson was indeed seriously sick by March 1890. Much to his frustration, his illnesses kept him 'a blooming prisoner' in the Club. 'This visit to Sydney has smashed me handsomely ... this is not encouraging for future ventures: Sydney winter—or I might almost say Sydney spring, for I came when the worst was over—is so small an affair, comparable to our June depression at home in Scotland'. Fanny, convinced that only her nursing would rescue him and panicking when she heard of a flu epidemic in Britain which might make its way to Australia, grew desperate to get him away and back out at sea. She set out to find a ship going to Samoa. This proved to be no easy matter. There was a seamen's strike on in Sydney at the time and she met refusals all over Circular Quay. Then she found Henderson & MacFarlane, Marine Traders, a firm which used a non-unionised crew, mostly from the Solomon Islands. At first they refused this eccentric woman, but Fanny wouldn't take no for an answer. Finally they agreed to give the Stevensons passage on the *Janet Nicholl*, a steamer setting off on a four-month Pacific cruise via Auckland. They must have regretted their decision when, on April 9, they saw their passenger being carried on board on a stretcher, wrapped in blankets and looking as if he were about to die at any moment. But Fanny had made up her mind; they would be leaving on that ship. The maritime unions wouldn't let the ship depart without a struggle and detained it in port for a day, threatening labour enquiries. The captain was so drunk he fell overboard twice, but at last Louis, Fanny and Lloyd set sail on April 11. Their Chinese cook, Ah Fu, was no longer with them. Homesickness had driven him back to China. Although he'd accepted from Stevenson a gift of fifty pounds and had promised to return, they never heard from him again.

The sea breezes worked their magic and Stevenson recovered rapidly. With 'a most agreeable ship's company', thirty-five different islands to visit, and some much-appreciated sunshine, the Pacific journey was just what he needed. The voyage included the danger and excitement of a storm that almost shipwrecked them, but on August 7 he was back in Sydney for his second visit, which lasted just under a month.

He installed himself at the Union Club, now his home away from home, but Sydney's August weather didn't suit him any better than February's had done. He was soon 'at [his] old trade—bedridden'. Even wrapped in flannels, with a blazing fire in his room, he didn't feel warm. The dreaded blood-spitting started up again. As he wrote to his friend Henry James, 'Even here, which they call sub or semi-tropical, I am come only to catch cold'. Artist Julian Ashton, visiting him at the Club, noted that 'he spent a good deal of his time in bed, his strength having been sapped by a long attack of pulmonary trouble. I often went to see him and found him hard at work lying down. His hours of work were from eight to twelve, after which, if he felt well enough he went abroad'. Stevenson was overloaded with work and, although shivering with cold and sickness, he had to get on with it.

There were family worries to plague him on this visit to Sydney as well, and he and Fanny had to make some difficult decisions. Fanny's daughter Belle was married to an American art student, Joe Strong, who had proved to be a no-hoper and a sponger. Belle and Joe, recognising a good meal ticket when they saw one, followed Stevenson from America to the Pacific. However, Joe's fondness for drink and his taste for opium and brothels had become unendurable and he and Belle had been packed off to Sydney by Stevenson. During the first Sydney visit, Louis and Fanny hoped that Sydney had improved Joe, but by this second visit it was clear they'd been overly optimistic. Joe was back to all his old tricks, spending big in the dives at The Rocks and getting into trouble with the authorities. Stevenson raged at having to finance this wastrel: 'O Christ Jesus! It is sometimes too much to have to support this creature . . . for he owes me his body, his soul and his boots, and the soup that he wipes on his moustache . . . Hard is the lot of him who has dependents'. The decision now to be made was whether Belle and her young son should return with them to Samoa, leaving Joe in Sydney. Leaving a husband behind was no small matter in the 1890s and when Belle couldn't make up her mind, Stevenson and Fanny didn't like to push her. In the end Belle insisted she needed more time to think over the future of her little family.

As solace to all these domestic worries, Stevenson read for the first time the stories of Rudyard Kipling. He loved this new young writer's exotic name and he adored his writing. 'Kipling is too clever to live', he wrote to Henry James from the Union Club. He wondered where this young author's genius would take him and generously wrote to Kipling himself, wishing him 'a long life and more power to your elbow'.

Those ongoing renovations back in Samoa were not forgotten. He rose from his sickbed to consult a Sydney architect about the Vailima house back in Apia, and was delighted with the plans produced: 'If I haven't anything else to thank Sydney for, I've got this plan. It suits me exactly; it's simply wonderful'. He and Fanny also shopped for beds that were shipped to the new house and then, on September 4, they set off on the SS *Lübeck* for their Samoan home.

Stevenson's mother, Margaret, or 'Maggie' as she preferred, was a remarkable woman. For nearly sixty years she had been a model of Victorian rectitude and propriety. A genteel child of the manse, then a dutiful daughter and devoted wife and mother, she seemed often to be on the verge of a vaporous decline, with the sofa and smelling salts never far away. But on the death of her strict husband Thomas, Maggie developed new vigour. Sofa and smelling salts went out the window.

She turned rapidly into an adventurous, enthusiastic traveller, happy to put up with extreme temperatures and great discomfort. She set off with her son and daughter-in-law when they sailed to America, helped finance travels across America for them all and, once on board the *Casco* en route for the South Pacific, she tucked into the ship's supply of champagne with a relish. She was fifty-nine years old on this first voyage and she bathed in the sea for the first time in twenty-six years. She had had to briefly visit Scotland to sort out her husband's estate, and was only able to return to the Antipodes in time to meet her son when he arrived in Sydney on 20 January 1891. He came to escort her back to Samoa and she lived there with him, apart from holidays in Melbourne, New Zealand and Scotland, until her beloved Louis' death. The Samoans adored her. Always immaculately dressed in black, with white lace caps, her back ramrod straight, Maggie mixed happily with the islanders, yet remained a picture of Victorian dignity in every situation. Fanny wrote of what must have been quite a sight—Maggie, in her Victorian dress and old lace, 'taking a moonlight promenade on the beach in the company of a gentleman dressed in a single handkerchief'.

Stevenson's voyage to meet his mother in Sydney had been a bad one. The SS *Lübeck* had broken down and been forced to revert to sail instead of using its motor, and bad weather during the trip had brought on another serious lung attack. His anxious mother brought him ashore straight to the Oxford Hotel, where she could nurse him. There he was 'laid on a bed of pain, unshaved . . . with a creditable pain in [his] side and a foolish cough'. This should have been his chance to enjoy the big smoke of Sydney without his wife keeping an eye on him (Fanny, who was becoming increasingly difficult, had remained this time in Samoa), but because he was sick Stevenson was forced to lead a quiet life in a cheap hotel with his mother:

> It is vastly annoying that I cannot go even to Sydney without an attack and heaven knows my life was anodyne; at the Club with Wise; worked all morning,—a terrible dead pull, a month only produced the imperfect embryos of 2 chapters; lunched in the boarding house; played on my pipe; went out did some of my messages; dined at a French restaurant, and returned to play draughts, whist or Van John with my family. This makes a rather cheery life after Samoa, but it isn't what you call burning the candle at both ends, is it?

The only excitements were a walk through the Domain one Sunday afternoon when he felt strong enough to listen to the orators there—hardly a thrilling outing—and reading the serialisation of his own *In the South Seas* in Sydney's *Daily Telegraph*. It was all too much to endure. On 18 February he was carried from his bed back to the *Lübeck*, to return to Samoa.

Stevenson was still travelling 'hopefully' when he came to Sydney on his final visit. This time he was hopeful that Sydney would make the whole family feel better. From the beginning of 1893, they had all suffered dreadful health. An influenza epidemic had swept through Samoa and Maggie had succumbed to it. She'd then rushed off to Scotland again as she still had affairs to sort out. Belle was 'in a terrific state of dentistry troubles' and had pleurisy on top of that. But it was Fanny's state of health that was causing the most serious concern. Neurotic, hysterical and convinced she was dying, she appeared to be turning into 'the embodiment of a female Jekyll and Hyde'. Her husband was terrified she was going mad, and had a difficult time trying to cope with her manic depression, mood swings and terrorising of their servants.

He himself was in no state to deal with such problems. Like his mother, he fell ill with flu which brought on another attack of 'Bluidy Jack'. He lost his voice, had to use sign language to communicate, and grew exhausted from worry and overwork. Quite why he thought Sydney, a place that had made him sick on every visit, would do him good on this occasion is a mystery, but to Sydney he and his three ladies (mother, wife and step-daughter) went. Their ship, the SS *Mariposa*, called first at Auckland, where Stevenson enjoyed chatting to Governor Sir George Grey about Samoan politics, and then went on to Sydney, which they reached on 28 February 1893. At least he felt better for his time at sea. *The Sydney Morning Herald* reported his arrival: 'His physique is vastly improved since his last visit ... Today he is well set-up, has the glow of health in his countenance, and altogether bears testimony to the beneficent effects of the Samoan climate'. This visit would be more public than any of the previous ones. 'People all looked at me in the streets of Sydney', he complained. He was inundated with invitations to speak.

His engagements included giving a 'delightful and witty speech' at the Thistle Club, which made him an honorary member for his pains, a speech at the Australia

RLS with his wife Fanny, her daughter Belle and his mother Maggie, photographed at the Oxford Hotel during their 1893 visit to Sydney.

Hotel in mid-March, another at a soiree at Government House, a lecture at the Cosmopolitan Club about his beloved France (with composer Henri Kowalski in the chair), a visit to the Royal Exchange where he was asked to sign the visitors' book and to the University of Sydney. He was a guest of the General Assembly of the Presbyterian Church and his speech was later printed in *The Presbyterian*. With effort, he refrained from mentioning his loathing of Scottish Sabbaths and his speech was well received. Illness prevented him from addressing the Women's Missionary Association at Quong Tart's Tearooms, but Maggie read out his 'Missions in the South Seas' paper in his place and was a success. The paper's content was a hundred years ahead of its time with advice about the need to preserve local customs and culture when introducing Christian practices to indigenous populations.

After the Father Damien affair, newspapers were wary of Stevenson. Many of his political comments were

considered 'rather too plain for publication', especially
when he spoke out against the misuse of black labour
on Queensland's sugar plantations. Nor did they want
to print his remarks about the de-civilising influence of
the white man around the world. Generally, however,
the press was kind to him:

> The personality of a famous writer is always
> interesting to his readers—and who is not a
> reader of Stevenson's enthralling books? Mr
> Stevenson may still be called a young man. He
> is tall and thin, and walks with a slight stoop of
> his shoulders. His face is refined and beautiful.
> Looking on it, one would at once say, 'This
> is a man of intellect', but looking into the full,
> glowing dark eyes, one would go further and say,
> 'This is a man of genius'.

Tighe Ryan, who interviewed Stevenson for the
Catholic Press at the Union Club, where the author sat
comfortably 'in an easy chair, one leg on the other, a book
on his knee, and a smoking cigarette in his right hand',
a glass of sherry within reach, found him a memorable
conversationalist:

> I carried away in my mind that evening a
> recollection of a soft, low, but clear voice, with
> the slight Scottish accent . . . the rare gesture; the
> thin, bronzed face, changing with every mood,
> the fine sparkling eyes, so far apart, the active
> figure, so sparse.

Stevenson was constantly on the move during the four
weeks of this visit. Staying at the Oxford Hotel in King
Street, he dined at the Union Club with his friend

Dr Scot-Skirving who 'rang him up at his hotel, for in Sydney we had telephones even then', to invite him. He spent a week as the guest of Sir Andrew Garran, editor of *The Sydney Morning Herald*, at his home 'Strathmore' in Glebe Point. Sir Andrew's son, Dr Robert Garran, was left with 'the abiding impression . . . of a picturesque figure in a velvet jacket—almost unbelievably thin and pale—with extraordinary grace and charm of manner and full of fun and cheerfulness, even when ill'.

Stevenson always favoured Bohemian-style clothing. His 'soft neck-wear and velvet jacket' and favourite white suit were remarked on by many Sydneysiders. Stevenson replenished his wardrobe while in the city, calling on Abbey the bootmaker and, once more, on Mr Chorley the tailor. It turned into quite a shopping trip—for himself, cord riding suits and velvet and serge dress suits, silk socks, ties and cravats. For Fanny he purchased a sumptuous black velvet gown with Duchesse lace as a surprise gift, hoping it might cheer her up. Books, plants, trees, boots and all their other purchases were shipped to Samoa by the Civil Service Co-op Society of NSW.

The distinguishing feature of this final visit to Sydney was chiefly artistic. The Reverend Will Burnett of Sydney's Thistle Club was, like so many who met Stevenson, magnetised by his eyes: 'Your eyes sought joy in his. No portrait or photograph portrays those eyes. Some make them flat and far apart and some make them "sleekit". The charm of them dispelled all critical faculty'. Local artists, however, were willing to take on the challenge of painting them. Stevenson's friend Julian Ashton took the author to the artists' camp at Balmoral Beach, where he met the two major proponents of the

Australian Impressionist School, Tom Roberts and Arthur Streeton.[4] Percy Spence, also there that day, did two portraits of him; the first was torn up as Fanny didn't like it, the second hangs in the National Portrait Gallery in London. Stevenson had been painted in England by John Singer Sergeant, one of the greatest British portrait painters, and had also spent time at the artists' colonies of Barbizon and Fontainebleu in France. He should have had lots to talk about with the artists that day at Balmoral but instead, Stevenson 'chummed up with the cook at the camp, "Old Ben", a stranded weather-beaten sea-dog full of reminiscences from all quarters of the world'. Clearly reminded of his own sea-dogs in *Treasure Island*, Stevenson presented the fortunate Ben with a signed copy of that novel.[5] The Balmoral visit also led to Stevenson being sculpted by a man called Leyselle. This has not survived, but Leyselle must have been an artist of dubious talent because the result was 'thought by [Stevenson's] family to be a good likeness of Mark Twain', though Stevenson did admit that the artist had very little time in which to do it.

Keen to have a more exact record of what he looked like, he endured a photographic session at Kerry & Co.'s premises in George Street. Charles Kerry was the foremost photographer of the day in Sydney, noted for his artistry and imagination, and for possessing all the latest photographic technology. He even had a multiple flash machine he'd designed himself. His scenic 'views'

---

4 It was actually at Edward's Beach which is today considered part of Balmoral Beach in Mosman.

5 Old Ben was used as the model in Julian Ashton's painting 'The Prospector' which hangs in the Art Gallery of New South Wales.

RLS in 1893,
from the
original by
Percy Spence.

of Australian landscapes, portraits of Aboriginals and of squatters, and his marketing of his photographs had afforded him a monopoly of the picture postcard business. Whether Stevenson purchased any Kerry postcards isn't known, but the photographic session ended with Stevenson delighted with the 'splendid photos'. These photos certainly do capture the magnetism of his eyes—their power remains with the viewer even when the photo has been taken away.

Louis had hoped that this Sydney holiday would sort out Fanny's mental problems. She holed up in her room at the Oxford, emerging embarrassingly on one occasion to harangue an interviewer to whom Stevenson was explaining that *Kidnapped* was his favourite work. She was depressed, began hallucinating, and was wildly wandering in her mind. Her husband tried to be sympathetic: 'Poor Fanny had very little fun on her visit, having been for most of the time on a diet of maltine and slops', but while he was well himself, he preferred 'rioting on oysters and mushrooms' and going out for 'lively sport' to remaining at her side.

*RLS met
'Old Ben',
the model for
Julian Ashton's
painting* The
Prospector,
*at Balmoral
Beach in 1893
and presented
him with a copy
of* Treasure
Island.

*Photograph
of RLS taken
in Sydney by
Kerry & Co.
He thought it a
'splendid' photo.*

And then the inevitable happened. March in Sydney that year of 1893 brought poor weather and one sudden, disastrous change drove Stevenson away from socialising to 'that inglorious spot, [his] bed', with a 'succession of genteel colds [which] succeeded in cooking up a fine pleurisy'. The doctors told him to renounce brandy and tobacco but he had 'no use for life without them', and eventually decided that he must escape and embark again for Samoa. He sailed on March 20 on SS *Mariposa*, never to see Australia again.

According to Dr Robert Garran, 'Stevenson used to say that there was material for a dozen buccaneering stories to be picked up in the hotels at Circular Quay'. It is a great pity that Stevenson never followed his own advice to write an Australian version of *Treasure Island*. Instead, he wrote *The Wrecker*. It's hard to believe that the man who created 'The Siege of the Roundhouse' chapter in *Kidnapped*, so dramatic, tense and vividly characterised, who could memorably describe Ben Gunn on Treasure Island longing hopelessly for cheese, and who was working on another masterpiece *Weir of Hermiston* on the day of his death, could write anything tedious, confusing or badly plotted. Robert Louis Stevenson managed this in *The Wrecker*, the book he worked on during his 1890 and 1891 visits to Sydney. It might have a promising title, but it is the worst book he ever wrote. Much of its failure can be blamed on Lloyd Osbourne, the co-author. Stevenson knew there was a mismatch of talents, but found it hard to say no to his spoiled step-son. The result was constant compromise, too much time spent writing it (two years), mistakes in continuity, undeveloped characters and puzzling switches of style and tone.

The Wrecker is partly set in Sydney and is the only example of an Australian setting in any of Stevenson's books.[6] His experiences in the city are given to Norris Carthew, a young remittance man. Like so many no-hoper sons in Victorian novels, Norris has been packed off to Australia by a father who wants him out of sight. Mr Carthew is determined to keep him there. The allowance of a shilling a day that he pays his son can be collected, only in person, from a Sydney lawyer: 'He was not to write. Should he fail on any quarter-day to be in Sydney he was to be held for dead, and the allowance tacitly withdrawn'. A furious Norris consequently regards the city as a prison. His allowance is soon spent and he becomes a down-and-out in the Sydney Domain, 'now on a bench, now on the grass under a Norfolk Island pine, the companion of perhaps the lowest class on earth, the Larrikins of Sydney'. His depressed state of mind focuses on the 'dingy men' and 'frowsy women' and the merciless rain that falls on him, but Stevenson does provide fascinating contrasting pictures of the Domain. By day it has 'a new society of nursery-maids and children, and fresh-dressed and (I am sorry to say) tight-laced maidens and gay people in rich traps', but with darkness 'the round of the night began again—the loitering women, the lurking men, the sudden outburst of screams, the sound of flying feet . . . Yes, it's a queer place, where the dowagers and the kids walk all day, and at night you can hear people bawling for help'.

Norris finally finds work down the coast from

---

6 *The Wrecker* was first published in serial form in *Scribner's Magazine*, between August 1891 and July 1892.

Sydney at South Clifton. He works as a navvy, blasting a new railway line, then returns to Sydney with wages in his pocket, feeling so much happier that even the streets seem 'cheerful'. 'When he came to that quarter of the city [where] the barristers were trotting in the streets in wig and gown' he bumps into Tommy Hadden and they lunch together at The Paris House, a restaurant in Phillip Street where Stevenson had himself eaten and which, he claims in the novel, provides 'the best fare in Sydney'. The men also visit a pub called 'The Currency Lass'.

Stevenson is unable to resist mimicking the Aussie accent. Hemstead, an unemployed shop assistant from Woolloomooloo, addresses Carthew in strongly accented speech:

> ' "They're a dyngerous lot of people about
> this park. My word! it doesn't do to ply with
> them," he observed, in that *rycy Austrylian* English
> which we should all make haste to imitate.'

During his four visits to Sydney, Stevenson worked on books with contemporary South Pacific settings: *The Beach at Falesa*, a novella that broke new ground in writing about the South Seas, *The Ebb-Tide* and *In the South Seas*. He also worked on Scottish books, his own family history, and a revision of *Catriona*[7] (sequel to *Kidnapped*), and the early chapters of the brilliant *Weir of Hermiston*, tragically unfinished at the time of his death. It was Scotland that really fired this young Scot's imagination—Australia just didn't provide the right impetus at all.

Stevenson died in his Vailima home in Samoa, at the age of forty-four, on 3 December 1894, less than two years after that last visit to Sydney. Had he lived longer,

---

7   Originally called *David Balfour*.

he might well have returned to dine at The Paris House, shop for clothes, see his Australian friends and search out characters in the dubious taverns of Circular Quay. 'I was not born for age', he wrote in one of his last letters. After all the illness in his short life, he was not forced to endure a protracted one at the end. Standing on the verandah while dressing a salad for dinner, he suddenly put both hands to his head, then fell backwards. He died a few hours later from a cerebral haemorrhage. On one of those hands was a little piece of Sydney—a topaz ring, his birthstone, purchased on his 1893 visit.

Today Stevenson's place in Australia is not the assured one he found on his visits in the 1890s. A plaque in Sydney's Writers' Walk records that he came here. His best books are for sale in the bookshops he liked to visit. But those books are no longer studied in schools, though they are still very popular on the school syllabus in Samoa.

Perhaps Stevenson would not have minded too much that he is no longer a household name here. 'Books are good enough in their own way', he once wrote, 'but they are a mighty bloodless substitute for life'.

*The plaque for
Robert Louis
Stevenson
at Sydney's
Circular Quay.*

CHAPTER FIVE

Rudyard Kipling

F ew writers made their fame as quickly and
at such a young age as did Rudyard Kipling.
In 1891, at the time of his visit to Australia,
he was twenty-four years old and was already seen
as the new star in the literary firmament. Two years
before, he'd arrived in London to find his reputation
had preceded him and he soon sent it soaring with
'Danny Deever', a haunting poem about a soldier
hanged by his regiment for shooting a colleague, which
was published in February 1890. Its grim subject and
tightly controlled verses, each ending with the refrain
'An' they're hanging Danny Deever in the mornin''
were acclaimed by TS Eliot, WB Yeats, by critics
and by the public. Everyone began clamouring for
more: poems, stories, novels; whatever Kipling could
produce was in demand. *The Times* devoted a leader
article to this young and exciting new writer, editors as

*Rudyard
Kipling in
1891, at the
time of his visit
to Australia.
Portrait in oil
by John Collier.*

far away as Australia offered good money for anything
he cared to write, and he was popular at London's
literary soirees.

But his adoring public did not know that behind
the glittering surface of success lurked many problems,
problems that Kipling took with him as heavy emotional
baggage on his journey to Australia.

Born in India, taken to England aged two to visit
relations, then taken back to India, then returned to
England for schooling, then India again to work as a
journalist, Kipling had grown up feeling rootless and
confused about where exactly he belonged. In India he
could be with his parents and sister, enjoying the heat

he loved and the exoticism, smells and sounds he was already capturing vividly in his writing. London, on the other hand, was the literary centre of the world, and he needed to be there for his career, but it was cold and wet and full of pressures to work. He felt that he truly belonged to neither India nor England.

But a greater problem for the young man was how to fill an emotional vacuum caused by a horrendous childhood trauma. When he was five, his parents took him and his younger sister from the family home in India. He left behind devoted ayahs, exotic pets, servants and tropical gardens. The children were deposited in a cold, grim house called Lorne Lodge in Southsea, England, there to be cared for by strangers for the next six years. Later he'd call that house 'The House of Desolation' and within its walls, the young Kipling endured appalling bullying and neglect. He later tried to recount the horrors in *Baa Baa Black Sheep*, a story that is almost too painful to read. When his mother returned to visit for the first time in six years and bent down to kiss her son, his immediate response was to flinch as if about to be hit. His sister Trix shared the ordeal—she would later be diagnosed with schizophrenia.

For six years he had felt abandoned by his mother, and the awful Mrs Holloway of Lorne Lodge was no mother substitute. Unsurprisingly, the years of his early manhood were a muddled search for a woman who could fill the emptiness inside him, and was because of one prospective candidate for this job, an American, that Kipling travelled to Australia. 'The female of the species is more deadly than the male' is a phrase that Kipling later added to the English language. Trying to work out if this woman would be beneficial or 'deadly' to his happiness, Kipling needed space, and so put half the world between them as he tried to make up his mind. Flight was his preferred method of coping with emotional entanglements.

In 1889 he'd travelled to America with his friends Edmonia (known as 'Ted') and her husband Alex Hill. Kipling was half in love with Ted, a maternal figure and a mentor to him, his feelings for Ted had soon included an affection for her younger sister Caroline Taylor, to whom he became unofficially engaged within two weeks of their meeting. He appeared to be courting one sister to remain close to the other. Instead of staying to enjoy Caroline's society, he set off almost immediately to travel the United States. But as the months passed Kipling became more and more convinced of the pointlessness of the engagement. In 1890 Ted's husband Alex died suddenly, leaving the woman for whose company Kipling had ill-advisedly proposed to her sister, free to marry again. Kipling had no idea what to do, so he fled, rushing off on a sea voyage to Naples.

On his return to London after that voyage he became entangled with the woman who would send him to the other side of the world, and who would then draw him back again to become her husband. Her name was Caroline Balestier or Carrie, as she was known, through her brother. Wolcott Balestier, an American literary agent, had arrived in London late in 1888 and had soon latched on to Kipling, now a world-famous author. Wolcott was a charmer, with great force of character, and biographers have endlessly debated his precise role in Kipling's life. Kipling's feelings for Wolcott were certainly intense; he could hardly stay away from him, took his advice on literary matters, and the two men even

*Carrie Balestier,
the woman
who became
Kipling's wife
soon after
his visit to
Australia.*

*Wolcott
Balestier,
ca.1890,
Carrie's brother
and Kipling's
friend and
literary agent.*

co-wrote a novel (*The Naulakha*), something Kipling never stooped to with anyone else. Some biographers are convinced the two were lovers despite Kipling later speaking with loathing of homosexuality. However, there's no doubt that their friendship was a vital one for Kipling. No other man ever meant as much to him as Wolcott Balestier.

Carrie came to London to keep house for her brother in 1889. Few people who met her actually liked her. Biographer Adam Nicolson titled his life of Carrie *The Hated Wife* and she was indeed hated by Kipling's family, friends and relations. His father Lockwood once described her as 'a good man spoiled'. She was opinionated, imperious and possessive and even Carrie's own daughter would write of her mother's 'uncertain moods' and 'difficult temperament'. For Henry James she was 'a hard devoted capable little person' and 'poor concentrated Carrie'. With straight, dark eyebrows, a determined jaw and solid build, Carrie was no beauty and, at twenty-seven, already 'on the shelf'. 'That woman', said Kipling's mother on first meeting Carrie, 'is going to marry our Ruddy'. It was soon plain to everyone that Carrie was determined to be Mrs Kipling. And so Kipling slipped again into what had become a pattern—attaching himself to an older, more forceful woman and then retreating in alarm before anything definite could come of it. With Caroline Taylor and with Carrie Balestier there was a highly attractive sibling in the background who was the reason for the relationship with each woman in the first place.

Surrendering himself to Wolcott's charisma, Kipling began, under Carrie's efficient and energetic management, to court her. When he met a second

Balestier sister, Josephine, he tentatively flirted with her as well. By the summer of 1891 there appears to have been some sort of 'understanding' with Carrie. An early biographer, Hilton Brown, claims that Rudyard and Carrie were engaged in June of that year and that it was temporarily broken off. The whole courtship is shrouded in secrecy, but there are hints there was some sort of unofficial engagement by the early autumn. Victorian engagements were normally very public affairs with parental permission asked, marriage contracts drawn up and notices placed in *The Times*. It speaks worlds for Kipling's lack of enthusiasm that, if there was an actual engagement, it was all kept so secret and so vague.

Yet again, at this time of crisis, Kipling planned his escape. This time he would go as far as he possibly could—to the Antipodes. Emotional strain was taking its toll on his health. He'd been working on *The Light That Failed*, a novel that is far from positive about marriage as well as poems and stories, and he was physically and emotionally exhausted.

So Rudyard Kipling embarked on the SS *Mexican* on 22 August 1891, on what he called 'a small excursion to the other end of the world'. The ostensible reason he gave for the trip was that he was going to visit Robert Louis Stevenson in Samoa. What he desperately needed was to 'get clean away and re-sort myself'.

⚶

The SS *Mexican* took him first to South Africa, a land that would 'bind chains round his heart' in years to come. He reached Cape Town on September 10 and spent two weeks in that 'sleepy, unkempt little place'. He also managed an excursion to Matjiesfontein in the Karoo to

137

visit novelist Olive Schreiner (famous for her book *The Story of an African Farm*). Cape Town was a city he would one day come to love, but on this first visit he had a brief recurrence of malaria which persuaded him that 'of all vile lands, South Africa was the worst'. On September 25 he set off on the SS *Doric* for Tasmania, but the ship only called briefly at Port Hobart on October 13 before departing immediately for New Zealand.

Kipling enjoyed his time in New Zealand, describing it as 'the loveliest land in the world'. He visited Wellington, where he was impressed by how good looking the people were and where he took a moonlit cruise in a Maori war canoe on the harbour. 'A small grey mare, and a most taciturn driver' took him in a buggy through 'bush country after rain' in the thermal district, and north to Auckland. At one of the halts en route he was 'given for dinner a roast bird with a skin like pork crackling, but it had no wings, nor trace of any. It was a kiwi'. Auckland he found enchanting, 'soft and lovely in the sunshine', a 'magic town'. From there he travelled by boat to Lyttelton, Christchurch, Dunedin, Bluff and Invercargill. This New Zealand visit resulted in two of his short stories—*One Lady at Wairakei* which he wrote while there, and *Mrs Bathurst*, written ten years later but inspired by a woman who sold him beer at a hotel.

New Zealand was, he felt, 'a new land teeming with new stories' and he accurately predicted that women would play a determining role in New Zealand writing of the future. Little Katherine Mansfield turned three in Wellington a few days before Kipling arrived in the city, and although the two would never meet (and would probably not have liked each other if they had), they would both become masters of the short story form.

The SS *Talune* then took Kipling around New Zealand's coast and across the Pacific to Melbourne which they reached on November 6. Plans for travelling to Samoa had been abandoned in New Zealand when he found the captain of the boat that was to take him there was habitually drunk. Robert Louis Stevenson died in 1894 so Kipling lost this last chance to meet a writer he deeply admired.

Once again Kipling touched at Hobart before sailing on to Melbourne. Both Tasmanian visits were unfortunately too short to give him a chance of seeing anything beyond the harbour. The Melbourne *Age* commented that Mr Kipling 'caught something of the tone of that quiet retreat between the Derwent and the hills'. What Kipling was too tactful to mention was Tasmania's criminal past, but he knew that Port Arthur was an infamous blot on the island's history. His later poem 'Song of the Cities', a description of some of the cities he visited in Australasia, has one verse on Hobart in which Kipling includes the line 'man's hate made [Tasmania] Hell'.

It took only one day of Kipling's presence in the country before Melburnians were described as suffering from 'Kiplingitis', but even before 'the hero of the hour' arrived in the city his approach had excited attention. On November 7 *The Age* reprinted an interview with Kipling from New Zealand's *Otago Daily Times* that had been conducted in Wellington. The article told readers what he looked like: 'He is rather below middle height, youthful looking and slightly built, with a great air of briskness and activity, almost of restlessness, as if always on springs'. Kipling was quoted as saying that he had come to this part of the world to 'loaf' (the excuse about visiting Stevenson in Samoa having worn thin by this time). Kipling then went on to say: 'There were some Melbourne people on board . . . and I was amazed at the extent to which they did "blow" (to use Trollope's word) about Melbourne. They seemed convinced there was nothing like it in the whole world'. Such a remark might have been acceptable in a New Zealand paper, but it inevitably marked the beginning of the media controversy Kipling created in Australia.

The SS *Talune* delivered the author to Port Melbourne the morning of November 12 and he went straight to the Oriental Hotel in Collins Street. The hotel seemed to suit him for he returned there when revisiting Melbourne after his excursion to Sydney. Kipling was a private man and had arranged no lectures or publicity, but he wasn't allowed to remain private long. The very day of his arrival saw him being interviewed by reporters for both *The Argus* and *The Age*. He didn't seem to mind: 'He lolls at ease on a couch', reported *The Argus*, 'in a conversational mood'. He chatted happily about his experiences in India and America, warned in his most imperialistic fashion of the 'Yellow Peril'—'Why, the Chinese must come in and swamp you. It's only a matter of time'—and answered questions about his works.

The piece in *The Age*, published on November 13, was longer and gave details of Kipling's Anglo-Indian background, his personal appearance and his travel plans. Kipling began by emphasising that he'd only just arrived—'I can't say anything about the people, for I have not met any of them'. However, in spite of commenting 'I am not going straight away, after 24 hours stoppage here, to write criticisms', he did manage to make many observations about Australia, most of them far from complimentary. 'This country is American, but remember it is secondhand American, there is an American tone on top of things, but it is not real. Dare say, by and bye, you will get a tone of your own', he remarked. Although he later told the reporter that he liked America, his comment must have been seen as unflattering by Australian readers. Both New Zealand and Australia came under attack for Labor politics and for having too much government for the size of population. 'Why', he said of New Zealand, 'there is more machinery for running their little handful of people than we have for the whole of the 300 million people of India', while Australia, he felt, had 'too much politics for a young country'. Once again he issued warnings: 'there are the Chinese close against you waiting their time'. All this from a man who claimed he shrank 'from dogmatising on the strength of a flying visit'. There was praise for the Melbourne trams, criticism that 'half the population [is] crowded into the cities, while the lands lie an idle wilderness', strong disapproval of strikes and the unemployed, and the 'very pleasant interview' came to an end.

Not surprisingly, it ruffled feathers. Those of a Mr Charles James Potts, Chancery Lane, Melbourne, were particularly disturbed and *The Age* published his letter to the editor on November 14. 'Could impudence go any further?' began Mr Potts, who insisted that Kipling's critical remarks were 'pregnant with ignorance and offensiveness'. He ended his letter with a warning: 'henceforth trespassers will be prosecuted! Everyone who, in dealing with the people of these colonies, trespasses beyond the limits of good taste, common sense, sound reason, must expect to receive the retaliation which his own rashness or malice has provoked'. Mr Potts' fury provoked a flurry of letters in response, as readers hurried to defend Kipling. But Kipling wasn't in Melbourne to read either the attack or defence. He was on his way to Sydney.

In the year before he died Rudyard Kipling wrote an autobiography, *Something of Myself*, which was published posthumously. The book is notoriously selective and unreliable; Kipling mis-remembers the ships he travelled on, speaks of exploring New Zealand *after* visiting Australia, and reports that he was offered the honour of describing the Melbourne Cup (actually run before he arrived). He says little of what he saw and did in Australia, but one thing that clearly made an impression was the train travel. He writes of 'trains transferring me, at unholy hours, from one too exclusive State gauge to another [he would have changed trains at Albury]; of enormous skies and primitive refreshment-rooms, where I drank hot tea and ate mutton'. Looking out the window at this 'new land with new smells' Kipling decided it was a 'hard land . . . and made harder for themselves by the action of its inhabitants, who—it may have been the climate—always seemed a bit on edge'.

The train delivered him into Sydney at midday on November 14 and he settled into the Hotel Metropole in Bent Street. He claimed business was the reason for his visit, but whatever that business was, he spent little time transacting it, his stay lasting only from midday Saturday to midday on Monday. Years later his abiding impression of Sydney was of its residents

The Hotel Metropole in Bent Street, where Kipling stayed for his two nights in Sydney. Jack London, who stayed there twenty years later, thought it was 'managed by Barbarians'.

enjoying their Harbour on a sunny day: 'I went also to Sydney, which was populated by leisured multitudes all in their shirt-sleeves and all picnicking all the day'. He did not approve of picnics—the poet who insisted on cramming 'the unforgiving minute with sixty seconds worth of distance run' felt Sydney-siders were wasting precious time. However, his verse on Sydney in 'Song of the Cities' is more positive, although Australia's convict past is clearly still in his mind:

Sydney
Greeting. My birth stain have I turned to good;

Forcing strong wills perverse to steadfastness:
The first flush of the tropics in my blood,
And at my feet success.

Kipling's time in Sydney was so brief the media almost missed it. *The Sydney Morning Herald* noted his departure on the RMS *Valetta* on November 16, while the *Sydney Mail*, a few days later, published a long article about the young writer's 'world-wide reputation', comparing him to Bret Harte, the American writer whose tales of adventure were popular at the time. It stressed how well Kipling's books sold in local bookshops and how familiar his works were to Australians.

On his arrival back in Melbourne on Wednesday November 18, Kipling was informed of the Potts controversy that had taken place in his absence. Disinclined to add to the media fuss, he nevertheless bore Mr Potts in mind for the remainder of his Australian visit. From this time he was more careful to be complimentary—when he visited a cake fair at Melbourne's Town Hall on the 18th, his gushing praise was happily reported in the journal *Bohemia*: 'Mr Rudyard Kipling has given it as his opinion that Melbourne girls are the finest in the world'; while at a dinner on November 23 he had 'none but complimentary references to make to Australia'. A few days later, speaking as guest of honour at the Yorick Club, Kipling obliquely but humorously referred to Mr Potts' criticism by announcing 'that having been nearly a week in Melbourne he felt competent to draft a new constitution'. *The Sydney Bulletin* had the last published word on the Potts saga, reporting on November 21 that 'Rudyard Kipling landed in Australia at noon and delivered himself of a new Australian National Policy at 12.15'.

Melbourne seemed determined to make the most of him. His first night on Australian soil had been spent at The Austral Salon for the Advancement of Women in Music, Literature and the Fine Arts, where, sporting a new pair of boots, he sat quietly and listened to a lecture on The Geological Strata of Victoria. But he was recognised and members who had 'long been Mr Kipling's worshippers' asked him to sign their visitors' book and say a few words. Anxious to avoid any more fuss or attention, Kipling then escaped as quickly as he could. Several papers reported this visit, each adding elaboration in the retelling until it grew into a small urban legend. As the *Bohemia*, *The Argus*, *The Sun* and *The Melbourne Herald* each had their say about the visit to the Austral Salon, it became impossible to know what was fact and what was fiction.

Separating truth from legend is also difficult when it comes to chronicling Kipling's Melbourne outings. Rosalind Kennedy and Thomas Pinney in *Kipling Down Under* have examined the evidence, the newspaper reports and the stories and have come up with the likeliest programme for the six days:

> **Wednesday, 18 November**: return to Melbourne and visit to the Cake Fair, Town Hall;
> **Thursday, 19 November**: perhaps a call at the Melbourne Club and a visit to the Trades Union Congress, Trades Hall;
> **Friday, 20 November**: no particular engagements— . . . he *might* have dropped in on the Wheeler family, or he *might* have called at the Club, or have done all these things;

Saturday, 21 November: supper with the Yorick Club;

Sunday, 22 November: a day with the Wheeler family;

Monday, 23 November: lunch with Dr Adam, seeing off Rolf Boldrewood at Spencer Street Station, and a theatre party in the evening;

Tuesday, 24 November: a morning of farewells, and the departure for Adelaide by the Express in the afternoon.

Kennedy and Pinney dismiss rumours that Kipling also managed a jaunt to Lorne, at that time a day's travel from Melbourne. The tradition that he did go there is based on his poem 'The Flowers' which contains the lines:

Buy a frond of fern
Gathered where the Erskine leaps
Down the road to Lorne—
Buy my Christmas creeper
And I'll say where you were born!
West away from Melbourne dust holidays begin.

Kipling's imagination, stimulated perhaps by pictures, could just have imagined the road to Lorne and the leaping Erskine River. Another rumour has Kipling travelling by train to Ballarat with Alfred Deakin, firm Federationist and later Australia's second prime minister who, at a Working Men's Club in Brighton, had picked up on the Potts controversy and added his own view that 'Mr Rudyard Kipling's airy criticisms on Australia and Australians' had been taken too seriously. Yet another has him dining at the Athenaeum and doing memory tricks to impress his fellow diners. Both stories are almost certainly apocryphal.

We know, however, that Kipling lunched with physician Dr George Rothwell Adam at the Oriental Hotel. Nothing is known of their table talk during lunch, but Kipling's collection of medical books was presented by his widow, according to her husband's wishes, to the Royal Australasian College of Surgeons in Melbourne. Kipling had always had an interest in medicine, but whether this unusual posthumous gift was a result of his lunch with Dr Adam can only be speculation.

Then there was the Wheeler family with whom Kipling spent a relaxed Sunday. David Wheeler, a former journalist, was by 1891 a recorder of parliamentary proceedings for *Hansard*. Wheeler had the misfortune to be related to Mrs Holloway, the owner of Lorne Lodge, who had made young Ruddy's life such a misery; but he shared Kipling's dislike of the woman and so his guest was able to relax in 'a hammock under the plane trees' at his East Melbourne home (it's hard to work out why he felt lying in a hammock was any less time-wasting than enjoying a picnic). Kipling adored children and shared with the young Wheelers his delight in *Alice in Wonderland*.

Rolf Boldrewood was the most famous Australian that Kipling met in Melbourne. Rolf was actually Thomas Browne, whose novel *Robbery Under Arms* had been a success in 1888. Kipling met this fellow writer at Spencer Street Station on his last day in the city. According to the *Bohemia*, Boldrewood was a 'friend', but it's not known when or how this friendship came about.

There was dining and singing at the Yorick Club, there was a theatre party to see *The Gondoliers*, probably a visit to the Melbourne Club (Kipling was later able to describe the building), and possibly a visit to the Trades Hall where a prominent Labor leader, William Arthur Trenwith, was holding forth. But there were no more public occasions after the November 21 dinner at the Yorick Club. There was a report that Mr Kipling was 'resting and coquetting with an attack of influenza', but he was well enough to spend Sunday with the Wheeler family so the 'influenza' could well have been a polite excuse to avoid the sort of more formal engagement which might be reported in the press. For on that day 'Kiplingitis' had reached an extreme that had made this very private man very angry indeed—it had intruded, misleadingly, into his love life.

On November 21 *The Argus* stated, as part of a long article on 'our distinguished visitor', that he was contemplating a 'great leap in the dark'; in other words, that he was planning to get married. While admitting that the source of this information had come, vaguely, from 'a letter from a lady in England' and was unsupported by any further evidence, the paper then announced: 'Florrie Garrard is engaged to a Mr Rudyard Kipling, a fashionable young author'. Florence Garrard had been Kipling's first adolescent crush. He'd written her love poems, but enjoyed his relationship with her from a distance, hurrying away at any possibility of commitment from her. He had characterised her as 'Maisie' in *The Light That Failed*, but any 'romance' they had shared was over. Yet the newspaper gave Florrie's family history, mentioned her slight connection with Australia (a brother had worked briefly at a Melbourne bank), and delivered hearty congratulations.

It's easy to understand Kipling's horror at reading this announcement. His obsession with privacy grew stronger and stronger throughout his life, but incidents such as this must have intensified his increasing reserve towards the press. His relationship with Florrie, tentative at best, had been replaced by his confused feelings for Carrie Balestier. For a man fumbling through his feelings for one woman to open a newspaper and read that he was supposed to be engaged to another was far from pleasant. He had come to Australia to sort out himself and his emotions—the papers had apparently decided to do the job for him! He did not deign to make any reply to *The Argus*.

Nor was he keen to be interviewed when, on November 25, he arrived by train in Adelaide and found journalists waiting for him at the station. As the *South Australian Register* reported, he 'had only a few minutes to stay here' as he had to get to his ship. But a pushier reporter from the *Adelaide Advertiser* made Kipling 'submit' to a short interview, even while commenting that 'Mr Kipling does not like being interviewed and says so'. He was then allowed to board the SS *Valetta* which was en route for Colombo.

Kipling had not quite finished with Australia. Four nights later the ship called briefly at Albany to take on coal for the rest of the voyage. This was done in the early morning and the *Valetta*'s famous passenger was probably asleep in his cabin as the ship left Australian shores, but he later described the very slow sea journey to Ceylon in verse:

It was a ship of the P & O
Put forth to sail the sea

Her passengers were all aboard
Her hold was full and her larder stored
And her speed was ten point three (10.3)

Kipling usually loved sea travel. Was his frustration at
the slow pace a reflection of his desire to get away from
Australia? He had told a reporter that he'd 'had a most
delightful time'. How true was that statement? On their
honeymoon he made plans, which never eventuated,
to show his bride New Zealand, but Australia never
tempted him again. Had Australia brought about the
're-sorting' this young author desired? It seems unlikely.
It had helped resolve his citizenship issues for he never
regarded it as a place he might call 'home'. But he was
still rootless, still searching for a country to settle in. His
trip back to England took him via India, the only 'real
home' he felt he'd ever known. While this was in fact
his last visit there, his great Indian novel *Kim* was yet
to come. America was still a possible home. Perhaps
Australia's 'second-hand' Americanism made Kipling
feel he had to choose either Britain or America, but not
a mixture of the two. Probably it reinforced his belief
that the British Empire was the best thing that could
happen to a country on the other side of the world but
that Britain suited him better than her dominions.

Only one letter written by Wolcott Balestier to
Kipling has survived from this time. In it Wolcott
cautions his friend to 'return only when copper-
fastened, double-rivetted and warranted not to fade,
tear or unravel', but added 'I want you back most
hideously'. He also informs Kipling that Carrie
'counts the days' until his return, but neither Wolcott's
'wanting' nor Carrie's 'counting' shortened Kipling's

travel plans, indicating that his feelings for them both were as ambivalent as ever.

It took a death to make Kipling decisive. On December 6, two weeks after Kipling left Australia, Wolcott Balestier died of typhoid fever in Germany. Kipling, who was in Lahore, responded immediately to Carrie's cable, sailed to London and eight days after his arrival he became a married man in a depressing little ceremony with a special licence. In a letter to a favourite aunt he said that he would be 'married tomorrow to the sister of the man with whom I wrote the *Naulakha*'. Carrie was 'the sister of . . .' rather than a woman he adored for herself alone. Memories of Wolcott, from this time, were hidden deep within Kipling, never mentioned publicly and omitted from his autobiography (as were any details of his marriage, the mental disturbance of his sister and the deaths of two of his adored children). The Kipling marriage, which he would often describe as a 'committee' run by Carrie, has long fascinated and mystified biographers.

Kipling's 1891 visit to Australia left him unenthusiastic about Australians. He found they 'insisted a little too much that they also were new'. They were direct of speech, 'a bit on edge', and 'would do wonderful things some day', but in the meantime were too busy having picnics.

This negative view changed eight years later when he went to South Africa for the Boer War. There, amid Australian troops, Kipling felt he had discovered 'a new nation—Australia' which he'd never properly appreciated before. Never had he come across a 'cleaner, simpler, saner, more adequate gang of men' and he rejoiced that Australia was forging its own national identity as it competed with New Zealand to see which country could send the most men to fight the Boers. He delighted in the enthusiasm with which these troops were offered: 'You 'ad no special call to come, and so you doubled out'. In his poem 'The Parting of the Columns' the English 'Tommy' thanks these colonial soldiers for having 'learned us how to camp and cook an' steal a horse and scout'. Tommy also affectionately recalls the comradeship he enjoyed with men from all corners of the Empire:

> Think o' the stories round the fire, the tales
>   along the trek—
> O' Calgary an' Wellington, an' Sydney and
>   Quebec.

Kipling told his friend Cecil Rhodes that he'd recently been seeing a good deal of the Australians involved in the war. He met and liked Colonel James Mackay, Australian Chief of Staff Officer of Overseas Colonial Forces, and in his work as sub-editor of *The Friend* (a Boer War newspaper for the troops), Kipling was always delighted to receive contributions from AB ('Banjo') Paterson, soon to become known as 'the Australian Kipling'. It also pleased him that the six colonies of Australia (that 'parochial' system whose separate rail gauges had forced him to change trains) were joining to become a single independent dominion of the British Empire. For Kipling this was an imperial coming of age and he celebrated the event in a poem. 'The Young Queen' portrays Australia as a woman warrior, 'her hand . . . still on her sword-hilt, the spur . . . still on her heel', riding out from a Boer battlefield to be crowned by the 'Old Queen', the Empire. Australia's coming of age as a nation is often seen as taking place on the cliffs and beaches of Gallipoli, but for Rudyard Kipling it was amid the kopjies and dust of South Africa that Australia, 'Tempered, august, abiding, reluctant of prayers or vows / Eager in face of peril', became a true 'sister' of Britain and a nation with a well-earned, rightful place within the Empire.

His newfound respect for Australians also appears in a story that arose out of his Boer War experience. *A Sahib's War* is about a Sikh soldier in South Africa, there accompanying his English officer. This Sikh greatly approves of the Australians he meets. The 'Ustrelyahs' might speak 'through their noses', but are 'a new breed of Sahib'. They are also brave: 'They said on all occasions, "No fee-ah", which in our tongue means *Durro mut* ("Do not be afraid"), so we called them the *Durro Muts*. Dark, tall men, most excellent horsemen, hot and angry, waging war *as* war, and drinking tea as a sandhill drinks water'.

Kipling had always shown sympathy for the common soldier facing hardships away from home, whether in India or Africa. In a beautiful poem written during the Boer War, he describes an Australian soldier riding, with his New South Wales contingent, into Lichtenberg, a town in the Karoo. It is raining heavily and the scent of rain-soaked wattle brings memories of home flooding back. The tone is poignant and homesick. Kipling, who had seen some of what he described in the poem on only two train journeys and who had never seen the Hunter Valley where he places the soldier's 'homestead', still manages to evocatively capture

Australian smells and landscapes giving a good sense at the same time of the larrikin young man who is missing 'all Australia':

'Lichtenberg'
Smells are surer than sounds or sights
To make your heart-strings crack—
They start those awful voices o' nights
That whisper, 'Old man, come back!'
That must be why the big things pass
And the little things remain,
Like the smell of the wattle by Lichtenberg,
Riding in, in the rain.

There was some silly fire on the flank
And the small wet drizzling down—
There were the sold-out shops and the bank
And the wet, wide-open town;
And we were doing escort-duty
To somebody's baggage-train,
And I smelt wattle by Lichtenberg—
Riding in, in the rain.

It was all Australia to me—
All I had found, or missed:
Every face I was crazy to see,
And every woman I'd kissed:
All that I shouldn't ha' done, God knows!
(As He knows I'll do it again),
That smell of the wattle round Lichtenberg,
Riding in, in the rain.

And I saw Sydney the same as ever,
The picnics and brass-bands;
And my little homestead on Hunter River

All my new vines joining hands.
It all came over me in one act
Quick as a shot through the brain—
With the smell of the wattle round Lichtenberg,
Riding in, in the rain.

I have forgotten a hundred fights,
But one I shall not forget—
With the raindrops bunging up my sights
And my eyes bunged up with wet;
And through the crack and the stink of the
cordite,
(Ah Christ! My country again!)
The smell of the wattle by Lichtenberg,
Riding in, in the rain!

Kipling had finished with visiting Australia physically, but he was far from finished with it imaginatively. In June 1900 the *Ladies' Home Journal* published one of his *Just So Stories*—*The Sing Song of Old Man Kangaroo* with illustrations by the author. As with so many of these superb stories, this concerns a search for individual identity, a subject close to Kipling's heart. The kangaroo in Kipling's tale does not yet look like a kangaroo; he is 'a Different Animal with four short legs; he was grey and he was woolly, and his pride was inordinate'. He goes to see 'Little God Nqa' and asks to be made different from all other animals by five o'clock. This god sends him packing, as does the next god he visits from whom he requests the gift of 'wonderful' popularity. Finally he asks Big God Nqong to make him both popular and 'wonderfully run after', and this god calls up Yellow-Dog Dingo. Dingo proceeds to chase the kangaroo all across Australia: 'He ran through the desert; he ran through the mountains; he ran through the salt-pans; he ran through the reed-beds; he ran through the blue gums; he ran through the Spinifex; he ran till his front legs ached'. But there is no rest—Dingo continues to chase him and Kipling gives his reader a wonderful sense of the vastness of Australia as the animals race through its varied, scrubby vegetation: 'Still ran Kangaroo—Old Man Kangaroo. He ran through the ti-trees; he ran through the mulga; he ran through the long grass; he ran through the short grass . . . he ran till his hind legs ached'.

As he hops, the kangaroo tucks up his front legs, sticks out 'his tail for a balance-weight behind him', and finds his hind legs growing longer and stronger. By five o'clock his shape has permanently changed as a result of all this running. Big God Nqong tells Kangaroo to thank Dingo for fulfilling his wish—he has been 'wonderfully run after' and he certainly looks 'different from all other animals'.

The story has various sources. Kipling's own train journeys within Australia made him aware of the scale of the country. He'd always been interested in folk tales and fables and when *Australian Legendary Tales* was published in 1896, with an introduction by his friend Andrew Lang, Kipling read in it the story of a kangaroo which is transformed during a tribal dance. A few years later *The Native Tribes of Central Australia* was published and attracted considerable interest in England. Pursued by dingoes, this kangaroo is magically returned to life each time the dingoes catch him and his tail and bones become features of the natural landscape. The story uses the phrase 'Old Man Kangaroo'. Kipling would appear to have combined his own impressions, plus elements of these two books, to create his own myth of a proud and demanding marsupial who is tripped up by the ambiguity of his request to be a celebrity ('wonderfully run after').

In the process, Kipling created an intensely Australian story. He captured the flora and fauna—ti-tree, mulga and blue gum, and he clearly depicted the landscape—the 'Flinders', the deserts, 'the sand-banks' and land that is 'dusty in the sunshine'. Aboriginal place names must have intrigued Kipling, who had a highly attuned ear for the musicality of words, and in the story he had fun creating his own versions of them with 'Warragaborrigarooma' and the 'Wollgong' river. It is not known whether Kipling saw either a kangaroo or a dingo while in Australia, but he was able in the story to convey their essential characteristics. The hungry dingo is described as 'grinning like a rat-trap', while Old Man Kangaroo 'stuck out his tail like a milking stool behind him'. Even the narrative style of the story, written in a kind of free verse, as a 'sing song', with repetition and long irregular lines, designed to be intoned like a ballad or folk song, feels 'Australian'. The lines catch the dry drawl and humorous tone of 'ocker' speech, the characteristic 'let's not take ourselves too seriously' approach to life.

Kipling's two illustrations add further commentary to the tale, the first depicting the kangaroo before his transformation, 'dancing on an outcrop . . . in the middle of Australia'. His long caption to the picture adds that 'the Kangaroo hasn't any real name except the Boomer. He lost it because he was so proud'. The second illustration is a superb portrayal of motion. The kangaroo is bounding on his new strong hind legs, hotly pursued by dingo ('black, because I am not allowed to paint these pictures

Kipling's illustration of Old Man Kangaroo hopping about Australia from The Just So Stories.

with real colours out of the paint-box; and besides, Yellow-Dog Dingo got dreadfully dusty after running through the Flinders and the Cinders'). The Big God Nqong is bathing in a saltpan, with toes sticking out of the water, and the 'two little squatty things out in the desert' are the other two gods. In a reference to Australian federation, the kangaroo's pouch (which has buttons to do it up!) is labelled 'Patent Fed. Gov't. Aus.', making the point that Australia, like the kangaroo, had just evolved its own unique identity. Kipling, son of an artist, was an excellent draughtsman, and his two illustrations add important commentary to the wonderfully Australian story. The tale ends with a poem which retells the events in a more formal verse form, and once again stresses the immensity of Australia.

'The Lost Legion', a poem published in 1893, contains allusions to 'the wallaby track' (meaning any track one feels like taking), to 'seven-ounce nuggets' from the Australian gold rush, and to the Kanaka workers on Queensland sugar plantations. In the same year he wrote 'The Song of the Cities' with its individual stanzas on Sydney, Melbourne, Hobart and (interestingly, as Kipling never went there) on Brisbane as well. This poem ruffled the pride of Australians anxious to forget their convict ancestry and provoked an annoyed parody by Randolph Bedford in the *Bulletin*:

> I put on my specs in Port Phillip, and I spat on
>   Sydney Quay,
> For I'm the bloke that hits it in once: no serving
>   my time for me!
> And I cleaned my nails over Brisbane, and I
>   sneezed for an hour at Perth,
> And then I came home on the English mail and
>   I wrote of the Big Wide Earth.

When a conference of colonial ministers was held in London in the Queen's Jubilee Year of 1897, Kipling wrote a dramatic sketch for the *St James's Gazette* on 'Premiers at Play'. The Australian premiers, named Victoria, New South Wales, Westralia et cetera, together discuss their problems. Favourite Kipling issues emerge in the dialogue: the problem of separate rail gauges for each state, sand and heat and emptiness, and the fear of 'a lower civilization prowling round your fence'. A short story written in 1924, *A Friend of the Family*,

The Melbourne Shrine of Remembrance, for which Kipling wrote his Ode.

concerns a sheep-herder from Queensland getting his revenge on a family who cheated his dead friend. He is single-minded in his purpose. Kipling had become convinced that Australians were 'the most vindictive haters within the Empire on account of their heavy meat diet'. Coming from Kipling, this odd remark is a compliment. He admired good haters who would make determined fighters in a battle if they had, as the Sikh in *A Sahib's War* puts it, a 'just lust for war'.

In 1934 Kipling was asked to write an ode for the Melbourne Shrine of Remembrance. The invitation came from the Victorian Agent General in London. Although ill and greatly troubled by a duodenal ulcer, Kipling accepted the invitation because the cause was dear to him. John, his only son, had been killed in World War I. His body had not been found (being correctly located only after Kipling's death) so his grieving parents had no grave to visit. Kipling had worked tirelessly for War Graves Commissions from that time on and public memorials to the dead were personally important to him. With memories of John fresh in his mind, it's not surprising that this ode was hard for him to write. He worked on it for nine months, an unusually long time for a man who normally composed very rapidly.

The poem is not only a tribute to those whose lives had been cut short by war. It is also specifically appropriate to the Australian dead. Kipling writes, in words reminiscent of the national anthem, of 'great waters girdling' the land; of Gallipoli as 'a beach / Which shall outlive Troy's tale when Time is old'; and of the brave and heedless men who thronged to the 'Western War' and lost their lives there. The obsession with sport gets a passing mention ('as cities throng to watch a game') and Australians are seen by the poet as people of 'stubborn pride', living in a 'desired land'. It's the only poem called an 'ode' that Kipling ever published and the words, on a metal panel within the shrine, end with a moving image of the Australian sun lighting up the memorial in the pages of history:

> Having revealed their nation in earth's sight
> So long as sacrifice and honour stand,
> And their own sun at the hushed hour shall
>   light
> The shrine of these their dead!

Australia no longer suffers from 'Kiplingitis'. These days Kipling's works are rather out of fashion. Children are familiar with Mowgli, Sheer Khan and Balloo not from reading *The Jungle Books*, but from the Disney movie of those stories. Australian tennis players about to walk onto centre court to play at Wimbledon might pause to read the words of Kipling's poem 'If' that are inscribed there, but probably don't. Tourists stop to read the brass plaque at Sydney's Circular Quay, but most Sydneysiders walk past oblivious to this record of a famous literary visitor.

And yet Kipling's influence can still be felt. He is one of the world's most quoted writers and Australian newspapers and journals repeat his words almost subconsciously. There are Kipling treasures in Australian libraries—Monash University Library has an excellent Kipling collection and the original manuscript of *The Five Nations* is in the National Library of Australia. A film about Kipling's son John, made in 2008, is teaching a new generation of Australians about the horrors of World War I and reminding viewers of Kipling as a man and a father who suffered great loss.

Kipling spent only two weeks in Australia and saw very little of the country in that time. The visit may or may not have achieved his purpose of 're-sorting' himself. But it did leave a rich legacy—an ode, the beautiful poem 'Lichtenberg' and a delightful explanation of how Australia's most memorable animal, the kangaroo, came to look the way it does.

The plaque for Rudyard Kipling at Sydney's Circular Quay.

CHAPTER SIX

Mark Twain

The air in the Horsham Mechanics' Hall was heavy with expectation. It was a warm night, and those who had rushed inside when the doors opened at 7.30 pm were jammed in like the proverbial sardines. Around the walls were the people unlucky enough not to have booked seats—they would stand during the whole performance. There were even people sitting on the sides of the stage. Bodies shifted restlessly on chairs, fans swished to bring cool breezes to heated cheeks, legs crossed and uncrossed in anticipation.

And then, onto the stage with a strange, half-capsized sort of gait that left many wondering if he'd had a bit to drink, walked a man. He stopped and looked at his audience. He could see a mass of eager faces, and could certainly hear them, their roars of applause, the cheers and stamping of feet. And they, looking back at him, could see hair—lots of it. Mark Twain had a great thatch of grey hair, still showing hints of the auburn it had once been, all wild and untamed. Below it grew great shaggy eyebrows and a bushy moustache. The man's head was so riveting that the audience barely noticed he was wearing black evening dress and shiny black patent-leather shoes. When the cheers and clapping faded, the audience stilled, but the man on the platform hardly moved. And still the silence went on . . . and on. Their expectation was by now at fever pitch, their bodies perspiring from excitement and heat, and still the silence continued . . . And then, finally, Mark Twain began to speak. His voice was a slow quiet drawl, but the people of Horsham could hear every word, right to the back rows. Ambling through a chat with his audience, he narrated a story of a fishing excursion that netted a dead body instead of a fish, the audience began to laugh. In a languid monotone, he moved on to his silver-mining days in Nevada: 'I could remember everything, whether it happened or not', he told them, and the audience held their sides, in stitches. As if conversing with old friends in a smoking room, Twain continued, telling of his very own Huck Finn wrestling with his conscience over whether or not to turn the escaped slave Jim over to the authorities; the audience found their throats tightening with sadness. Then, with another quick change of mood, he regaled them with the saga of how he once stole a watermelon but then returned it to its owner, complaining it was green! Buttons popped off garments, straining beyond endurance with fits of laughter.

With each story, Twain would pause, sometimes for seemingly unendurable lengths of time. And then would come his 'snapper', as he called his punchlines, all delivered as if there were nothing funny about them at all, and Horsham's tension would dissolve in yet another storm of laughter.

Mark Twain in a photograph taken at the time of his visit to Australia. It looks as if his carbuncle was troubling him!

Finally, after nearly one and a half hours, it was time for a lesson in the peculiarities of the German language, a tongue which 'neutered' an unmarried girl, yet made a turnip feminine. A man sitting next to Twain's wife 'began to pound his sides' in mirth, much to her consternation. Feet and walking sticks thumped the floor. Mark Twain played his crowd like an experienced fisherman landing a big one, as he told the crowd just what those Germans did with words. There was one last pause . . . a long one that stretched to breaking point . . . one last dazzling 'snapper' . . . then the final eruption of applause and laughter. The audience hurled hats and hankies into the air, and lurched, drunk with laughing, out of the hall into the warm October night. The people of Horsham had just been treated to one of the best lectures Mark Twain had ever given. The Victorian township would never have another night like it.

⁂

If a theme song were needed as an accompaniment to Mark Twain's tour of Australia, it would have to be 'Money, Money, Money'. Financial problems prompted his visit to Australia in the first place, potential earnings precipitated every lecture he gave while on tour, and money motivated him to write a book about his travels. It's not surprising that an Australian reporter explained away Mark Twain's long pauses in his lectures as opportunities to listen to his tour agent counting the takings in the back room.

Financial worries had been part of his life from its beginning. He was born Samuel Langhorne Clemens in a two-bedroom rented shack in Florida, a small village in Missouri, in 1835 and his father, a merchant and lawyer, was hopeless with money. Full of ambitious plans, John Marshall Clemens invested in scheme after scheme, moved his family from place to place, and endured perpetual disappointment. When he died, unprosperous, in 1847, his wife, three sons and one daughter were left to fend for themselves. Sam and his elder brother inherited their father's eternal optimism about making money, and with it his total lack of business acumen. In the ensuing years Sam tried his hand at many careers— printer, river-boat pilot on the Mississippi, reporter, silverminer and, finally, lecturer and writer.

He gained fame with a short story, 'The Celebrated Jumping Frog of Calaveras County'. *An Innocent Abroad*, his first travel book, soon followed, and before long there were novels, plays, articles, essays and letters pouring from his pen. He worked hard (Twain's idea of a day off from writing books was to write sixty-four letters instead), and the money came in at quite a rate. The trouble was, it went out just as fast. He struggled with the copyright laws of the time, which meant he unfairly lost royalties unless his books were published simultaneously in the United States and Britain, but he struggled even more with making sensible decisions about how his money should be spent.

By the time of his tour to Australia, there were many financial drains on his pocket. He was keeping an expensive home in Hartford, Connecticut, and supporting a wife and three daughters. Jane Clemens, his mother, had received regular cheques from her 'Sammy' until her death in 1890. He enjoyed travel and the best cigars, luxurious hotel suites and whisky cocktails— none of which came cheaply. But what really did the damage was technology. All his life Sam Clemens had had a passion for the latest gadgets. He claimed to be the first person in New England to install a telephone in his home for private use. His *Life on the Mississippi* was almost certainly the first novel in history to be typed before being sent to the printer. He even invented things himself—a bed clamp to keep babies from kicking off their covers; a glass hand grenade filled with chemicals to extinguish fires; and a board game for children.

Marvellously inventive as a writer, he was also inventive as a designer. The problem was, no one wanted to finance his inventions. Undaunted, he began to finance those of others, and the one that dragged him into the bog of bankruptcy was the Paige Compositor, a typesetting machine developed by James W. Paige. The machine would, its inventor promised, do the work of six men and revolutionise the printing industry. Sam, who could remember hours spent as a printer's apprentice laboriously setting type, was enchanted with the machine—everything a human could do, he boasted, the machine could do better, except drink, swear and go on strike. Convinced he was about to become a multi-millionaire by supporting its design through its final stage, he poured money into the scheme. He signed an agreement to pay Paige an annual salary of $7000 (even when warned he was courting bankruptcy by doing so); he handed over more and more money to finance Paige's fine-tuning and adjustments; and he grew beside himself with excitement whenever he thought the machine was ready to be launched on a receptive world.

Of course, the machine was never ready. Something was always going wrong with at least one of its *eighteen thousand* movable parts, and Sam failed to see that this state of affairs was unlikely to be mended. Paige was all too plausible: 'he could persuade a fish to come out and take a walk with him', Sam confessed. 'When he is present I always believe him. When he is gone away all the belief evaporates. He is a most daring and majestic liar.' Too many cheques were signed *before* Paige went away, money was borrowed so that more could be thrown into the Paige quicksand, and the financial mess went from bad to worse.

There were other investments that failed as well. Convinced he was being cheated by publishers,

The Paige Compositor which brought Mark Twain to financial ruin and necessitated his lecturing tour of Australia.

Sam Clemens had created and become part-owner of his own publishing firm, and had put his nephew in charge of it. A bookkeeper embezzled $25,000; books he was convinced would be bestsellers flopped pathetically; creditors began to demand payment, and the situation grew more precarious by the day, as debts reached $200,000. The Clemens family moved to Europe—life there was cheaper then—but Sam had to make regular transatlantic crossings to negotiate new deals to stave off disaster. Pacing the floor and endlessly adding up the mounting totals did no good at all and in April 1894 his publishing company was declared bankrupt. And, finally, he accepted the truth that the Paige machine would never work. Exactly how much money was poured into the hopeless device will never be known, but estimates range from between $170,000 and $300,000.[1]

---

1   Mark Twain's biographer, Ron Powers, who made these estimates, states that their equivalent in modern money is US $3.5–4.9 million.

In the final weeks before bankruptcy, Sam Clemens found a fairy godfather. Henry Rogers, a hard-nosed capitalist nicknamed 'Hell Hound Rogers', was an ardent Mark Twain fan, and his shrewd advice was just what was needed. He untangled the mess, took over the Clemens' business affairs, and set about finding solutions. Declaring that bankruptcy was necessary, Rogers saved what he could for Sam from the wreckage, and worked out just what could be done to finance the Clemens' family future. Thanks to Rogers' arrangements, the whole amount of the debt did not, legally, have to be paid back.

But 'honour is a harder master than the law', and Sam felt the 'moral necessity' of paying what was owed. He could do it by writing, but he could also do it by talking. He'd been a lecturer on and off for thirty years and was adept at handling audiences and promoting talks. He knew the best way to earn money fast was a huge lecture tour, so plans were made to travel to America, Canada, Australia, New Zealand, Ceylon, India, Africa and England, in a trip lasting over a year. Sam Clemens didn't want to put on the Mark Twain hat again in this way. He was fifty-nine, in poor health, his wife was frail, and one daughter was suffering from epilepsy: 'Travel has no longer any charm to me. I have seen all the foreign countries I want to see except heaven and hell, and I have only a vague curiosity as concerns one of those'. But bankruptcy left little choice and, on 14 July 1895, he set off on what he would afterwards describe as 'our lecturing raid around the world. We lectured and robbed and raided for 13 months. I wrote a book and published it. I sent the book money and lecture money to Mr Rogers as fast as we captured it'.

At his side was Olivia 'Livy' Clemens, his devoted wife. Marrying her, Sam was convinced, was the best thing he'd ever done. It had taken 134 ardent love letters to persuade her into an engagement, but once persuaded Livy never stopped adoring her erratic, temperamental and demanding husband. In Australia she attended almost every lecture he gave, dealt with his correspondence,[2] tried to keep him tactful, and supported him with her love and care. He was the first to admit he could never have survived the tour without her. Fortunately, Livy kept better health on the trip than she'd enjoyed in years.

Clara, their middle daughter, came too. She was at a loose end (she was keen to have a career as a musician), so invited herself along on the journey. Jean, their youngest, suffering worsening epilepsy, remained in the States. One unwelcome guest did join the travelling party just before it departed—a carbuncle, which attached itself to Sam's left leg and refused to go away. 'I could have done without it', he told Rogers, 'for I do not care for jewelry'. This 'adornment' and its replacements (carbuncles, a bacterial infection, are very contagious, and he got three more of them during the trip) would become well known as 'personalities' in Australia. Reporters took a great interest in their current state of health, size, and whether or not they might prevent a lecture (which, on occasion, they did).

The tour that would cover 53,000 miles and would

---

2   One letter that Mark Twain did write himself while in Australia was to 22-year-old Ethel Turner, who was about to publish *The Family at Misrule*. He had greatly admired her *Seven Little Australians* and wrote to tell her so.

bring in about $25,000 in receipts, began in Elmira, New York state, when the family boarded a train for Cleveland. On the platform, waving goodbye, was Susy, their eldest, who had elected not to go. Sam adored Susy, the daughter most like him, and hated leaving her behind. Little did he know, as he kissed her farewell, that he would never hold his darling Susy again.

Mark Twain arrived in Australia aboard the RMS *Warrimoo*, having followed Robert Louis Stevenson's directions—cross America to San Francisco, sail west and it's the first turning on your left. He knew he had quite a reputation to sustain. His travel books were well known, the characters Tom Sawyer and Huck Finn were already much loved in Australia, and their creator was said to be 'the funniest man in America'. No wonder he was welcomed like visiting royalty, besieged by reporters in every town, and faced packed halls at his fifty talks around the country. But, with money-making so crucial, Twain's fame could not be left to do all the promoting unassisted. Robert Sparrow Smythe, his manager for the tour, was there to give that fame a helping hand, and to count those all-important takings. An experienced theatrical manager and impresario, Smythe and his son Carlyle ran a successful agency.[3] Between them they would ensure that lamp posts were plastered with pictures of Mark Twain, advertisements for his talks were inserted in all the leading papers, hotels and venues booked, and the whole show got on the road.

---

3 Carlyle Smythe would act as manager for Sir Arthur Conan Doyle's tour in 1920.

Olivia and Clara Clemens, Twain's beloved wife and daughter, in a photograph taken at Falk's Photographic Studio, Sydney.

The reporters were there from the very beginning. They even came out in a launch to greet the *Warrimoo* when it pulled into Watson's Bay, on 15 September 1895, calling out questions to its famous passenger. Interview conditions were far from favourable (a ship's pipe was gurgling and hissing in the background) but Twain was still able to give them good copy: 'I'm going to write a book about Australia', he announced. 'I think I ought to start now. You know so much more of a country when you haven't seen it than when you have. Besides, you don't get your mind strengthened by contact with the hard facts of things.'

Unlike Rudyard Kipling, who had arrived and immediately given opinions on Australian politics and people, Twain was more cautious.[4] Asked again and again throughout the tour for his views on the cities he visited and the people he met, he resisted giving answers. After all, he'd firmly believed there was a small ferry boat running as often as 20 times a day between Melbourne and New Zealand before he arrived, so how could he possibly make pronouncements when he was so ignorant? Still, it didn't take him long to get into trouble with reporters by being rude about the novelist Bret Harte ('he has no heart, except his name', said Twain, and 'his work is shoddy'). Harte's books were extremely popular in Australia at the time. Livy tried to hush her husband up on the subject, but Bret Harte had tried his patience for years and still owed him money, so he refused to be hushed, and Australians were offended by his frankness.

Once the *Warrimoo* had docked at Circular Quay (crashing into the wharf as it did so), the passengers disembarked in a light rain. Soon the Clemenses were settled in the Australia Hotel, their base for the next nine days. From there they explored the Domain; had tea on board the warship *Orlando*; visited the NSW Fresh Food and Ice Co. to inspect the 'huge establishment where they kill and clean and solidly freeze a thousand sheep a day, for shipment to England' (how pleased Trollope would have been that the refrigeration he'd predicted was now up and running); and watched a game of polo.

---

4   The issue of Federation was being much discussed at the time of his visit. There had been a Federation Conference in Melbourne in 1890 and another in Sydney in 1891 and Twain was often questioned about his views on the idea. Other topical issues included the 'Woman Question', and the new fashion for riding bikes which failed to excite him, though later in life he did buy a bicycle.

*Mark Twain
with his literary
agent and
tour manager,
Carlyle Smythe.*

They danced at a ball at Government House, with
Livy resplendent in white figured silk and Clara in
buttercup satin. It must have been quite a sight—Sam
had once described his dance style as 'a step peculiar to
myself—and the kangaroo'.

There was also a session at Falks' Photographic Studio where the family were photographed.
They enjoyed a private lunch with Sir Henry Parkes,
four times Premier of New South Wales between 1872
and 1891, who presented Sam with a volume of his
own terrible poems. Sam had been shown a photo of
Sir Henry at Falks' studio and was impressed and
envious: 'I reverence that man's hair . . . I'm sure,

had he lived his life in the States, he would have been President. That head of hair would have been irresistible'. Cartoonists had fun portraying these two hirsute men together, and found Mark Twain's hair a never-ending source of amusement. 'His head is like an amazed gum tree', recorded *The Bulletin*, his hair 'gives him the wild expression of a man who has just found a baby's shoe in the soup'. One reporter was completely carried away: 'I'd love to run my fingers reverently through Mark Twain's silky grey hair', he purred. Larrikins at his talks sang out 'Get your hair cut, Mark', which always raised a laugh.

Sydney's Athenaeum Club made him an honorary member. In the mild spring weather he enjoyed going out onto the Harbour with local dignitaries (the former Mississippi pilot loved travelling on water), and he noted with approval (unlike Kipling) the many picnic parties on the Harbour shores. The beauty of Sydney Harbour had its usual effect—he had to try to capture its wonders in words:

> It is shaped somewhat like an oak-leaf—a roomy sheet of lovely blue water with narrow off-shoots of water running up into the country on both sides between long fingers of land, high wooden ridges with sides sloped like graves. Handsome villas are perched here and there on those ridges, snuggling amongst the foliage, and one catches alluring glimpses of them as the ship swims towards the city. The city clothes a cluster of hills and a ruffle of neighbouring ridges with its undulating masses of masonry, and out of those masses spring towers and spires and other

Cartoon of Mark Twain and Sir Henry Parkes from The Bulletin, September 1895.

Mark Twain—"Alas! that I should envy you!" Parkes—"What do you envy? My politics, my poems, or my brains?" Mark T—"Alas! neither, 'Tis your hair consumes me with envy!" *The Bulletin*, September 1895.

architectural dignities and grandeurs that break the flowing lines and give picturesqueness to the general effect.

But he had not come to admire the scenery. He had come to make money, and on Thursday September 19 he began doing so. His 'At Home', as he called his performances, were held at the Protestant Hall in Castlereagh Street, and two thousand people were there to hear him. He was almost overcome by the ovation he received, and the papers next day went into an orgy of praise. *The Sydney Morning Herald* remarked that 'more spontaneous, heartier, or more prolonged roars of welcome' had rarely been heard. The audience 'trembling all the time between tears and laughter' adored him. They had paid a lot to be there (there were complaints in the press about how much Smythe was charging);[5] but they all went home happy—lawyers, politicians, clergymen, working

---

5   At most of his lectures seats cost five shillings, while two shillings got you standing room.

men, women and children. Even the Presbyterians laughed.[6]

During the tour Twain delivered three different lectures, though sometimes he was inspired to mix and match as he went. There were personal reminiscences (but in these he never let actual truth get in the way of a good story), there were versions of his own novels and travel stories, there were dry asides, and there were moral lessons. As he delivered each one, his drawl became more pronounced (by the end of the tour he was known as 'Mark Twang' speaking 'Murkan'), his face more deadpan, the pauses judged by 'the five-millionth of an inch'. Telling a funny story, he had always said, was a 'high and delicate art'. In Australia he perfected this art. Clara, who had sat through hundreds of his talks, commented of his stagecraft: 'Father knew the full value of a pause and had the courage to make a long one when required for a big effect. And his inimitable drawling speech, which he often lost in private life, greatly increased the humorous effect on the stage . . . Cries that resembled the cries of pain could often be heard.'

Australians loved his stock favourites: the 'Golden Arm' story about a man who robs his wife's grave to steal her prosthetic arm of solid gold (a dialect tale he'd been addicted to since boyhood); the story about a lost dime which left audiences rolling in the aisles; the stolen watermelon anecdote; the one about the diary

---

6   One of Twain's Sydney lectures was attended by
    Henry Lawson, who sat in the front row because he
    was hard of hearing and, in fits of laughter, kicked the
    stage so hard that it shook. Twain did not meet the
    other famous Australian poet of the day, AB 'Banjo'
    Paterson, whose poem 'The Man from Snowy River'
    was published that year.

Adam kept in Eden; the jumping frog tale; and episodes from the fictional lives of Huck, Jim and Tom. Passing easily from one story to the next and barely giving his audience breathing space as he did so, he was described by one reporter as 'mount[ing] a balloon' and throwing out 'anecdote, story, incident, scraps of dialogue, short readings from his books, and spontaneous . . . observation', before returning to earth.

It's not possible now to reproduce Mark Twain's humour—so much depended on his stagecraft and his silences—but some of his jokes about the language he'd spent twenty-eight years trying to learn have survived. German puzzled him: why, if 'neck', 'elbow' and 'body' were masculine, was a 'foot' neuter and a 'toe' feminine? 'In France a cat is a male; in German a cat is female. Why if I were a cat I would sooner die than live in such a condition of uncertainty.' A fish was a 'he', 'his' scales were 'she', but a 'fishwife' was neither. He hoped that 'a deceased fishwife would be rewarded for the uncertainty of gender during her life in Germany' by having in her eternal home 'only one good square sex and have it all to herself'. When it came to cases, Twain had a field day.

> A dog is *der* Hund *the* dog . . . now you put that dog in the Genitive case, and is he the same dog he was before? *No* sir; he is *des* Hundes; put him in the Dative case and what is he? Why, he is *dem* Hund. Now you snatch him into the Accusative case and how is it with him? Why he is *den* Hunden. But suppose he happens to be twins and you have to pluralize him—what then? Why sir they'll swap that twin dog around thro' the four cases till he'll think he's an entire International Dog-Show all on his own. I don't like dogs, but I wouldn't treat

a dog like that. I wouldn't even treat a borrowed
dog that way.

And as for verbs . . . well 'a verb has a hard time enough
of it in this world when it's all together. It's downright
inhuman to split it up. But that's just what those
Germans do'. He'd far rather 'decline two drinks than
one German verb'. He concluded with a joke about
German's famously long sentences: 'Whenever a literary
German dives into a sentence, that is the last you are
going to see of him till he emerges on the other side of
the Atlantic with his verb in his mouth'. His audiences,
from Sydney to Tasmania, lapped it up. Only once, in
Geelong, did his German jokes fall flat. Even when he
insisted that 'Wagner's music is better than it sounds',
he never failed to raise a smile. And when he learned
that Geelong had a suburb called Germantown because
of the many German immigrants who'd settled there,
he understood why.[7] Everywhere else this 'moral lesson'
and the many others he rambled his way through were
received as the lecture in Horsham had been received—
with applause, gales of laughter, and absolute delight.

After their luggage was weighed for the train trip
(much to their astonishment) the Clemenses, and
Sam's carbuncle (which 'reminds me of its company
occasionally. I have a greater respect for it than any
other possession'), all took the night train to Melbourne.
Nobody was happy to change trains at Albury at 5 am, just
as Kipling had been forced to do. Twain was convinced

7   The name of the suburb was changed to Grovedale
    in 1915, because of anti-German feeling roused by
    the war.

that standing on the cold platform gave his darling Livy 'an acute attack of rheumatism' and he was myst-ified by the system of different rail gauges for different states: 'Think of the paralysis of intellect that gave that idea birth', he mused. En route the train had passed through Wagga Wagga; he'd actually met the Tichborne claimant and loved the story of how the Wagga butcher had left behind his sausages and tripe to go off and claim an English inheritance.

Two hundred people were waiting to greet them at Spencer Street station. The carbuncle was giving him pain and he was glad, once yet another official welcome was over, to rest in bed at the Menzies Hotel, reading *For the Term of his Natural Life* and regaining strength for his first Melbourne lecture. All his Sydney talks had been well reported in *The Argus* and Melbourne's three other daily papers, so audiences had high expectations; but Twain, who'd just been to a fortune teller and was told 'the owner of these hands has no sense of humour', was wondering if he'd been deceiving his public all these years. He needn't have worried. His 'At Home' at the Bijou Theatre in front of former premiers and the cream of Melbourne society was so funny that even his wife and daughter, who'd heard it all many times before, were half paralysed with laughter. At all his Melbourne talks 'people were packed like sandwiches into boxes, the gallery was brimming over, there were two perspiring rows of spectators in the orchestra, and a side glance at the wings showed a background of eager faces'.

Twain had started to intrigue his audiences with a poem: 'If I am going to write a book about this trip round the world, why a book of such a character ought to have some poetry in it. I felt that . . . then I thought of the fauna of Australia . . . I made a list of them and began'. The trouble came with the rhymes, 'for if you get the sense right, why then there is no word that will rhyme with it. If your rhymes rhyme then there is no sense in it'. And he began . . .

> Land of the ornithorhynchus
> Land of the kangaroo,
> Old ties of heredity link us . . .

Of course, he was stuck. What on earth rhymed with kangaroo, he begged his audience. Suggestions to help him were sent to the papers and it became an ongoing tease that he would add improvements and further stanzas to create the great Australian epic. Much of Australia was drawn in to the writing of this poetic gem.

He delivered five lectures in Melbourne, dined at the Yorick Club and gave that club the best evening it had ever had, chatted in his hotel with Rolf Boldrewood (who seemed to make a habit of calling on visiting authors), and tried to rest as much as possible in between. When he made a side trip to Bendigo (leaving his ladies in Melbourne) his lecture there had to be cancelled: the carbuncle was reminding him too forcibly of its presence. A doctor was called to lance it, drain it, then bandage it in moist cloths. In spite of this, dress trousers were too tight for comfort; the people of Bendigo were disappointed. Sam Clemens was in bed, so Mark Twain would not appear.

On October 11, with Robert Smythe in tow, the party began the seventeen-hour train trip to Adelaide. This time Sam had the chance to see a bit more of the countryside. He was fascinated by the trees he saw: 'Your gum trees require long study. I think I should grow fond of them. I know I would try to very, very hard. They look so reproachful, and grave, and serious'. Of all the authors discussed in this book, only DH Lawrence would feel an instant rapport with the Australian eucalypt. Twain admired their 'assertive, aggressive green' and was convinced they must be intelligent because of their ability to find water in such harsh conditions. Later, he was enchanted by a pepper tree with its 'fountain-sprays of delicate feathery foliage', and admired the vistas of blue hills in the distance: 'they are of a blueness not to be paralleled in the world. They are of a blue that is a blue . . . It seems to have a light from behind, and is endowed with spirituality'.

Adelaide, determined not to be outshone, had assembled the city's best and finest to welcome the great American. But the Clemenses left the train twenty miles outside Adelaide and travelled through its hills to the South Australian Club Hotel. Twain joked he'd smuggled his carbuncle past Customs. Everywhere he looked he saw his own face, and his hair. Marshall's Department Store had a particularly large photo of him in their front window, but other shops displayed his image as well.

He gave three lectures in Adelaide. The crowds rocked with uncontrollable laughter at his story of a widow whose husband, having fallen into a carpet-making machine, was returned to her as fourteen yards of three-ply carpet, but who was reluctant to roll up his remains. He attended soirees, endured more toasts to the 'King of Humorists' and 'the funniest man on earth', more welcoming receptions and speeches, and more interviews.

Mark Twain had become one of the most interviewed figures of his century.

He had always been a disappointment to religion. He'd once wanted to mount the pulpit, but could not supply himself 'with the necessary stock in trade, i.e. religion'. Rich people might have a God looking after them, he decided, but the poor certainly didn't. It amazed him that Adelaide was such a religious city. With a population of 320,000, it managed to cater for 'about 64 roads to the other world'. Twain tabulated the varieties: Wesleyan (49,159), Congregationalist (3884), Primitive Methodist (11,654), Unitarian (688), Jews (840), Confucians etc (3884), and Other Religions (1719), which included Deists, Freethinkers, Maronites, Memnonists, Moravians, Pantheists, Shakers, Welsh Church, Zoroastrians, Zwinglians (Adelaide boasted one proud Zwinglian in its population) and, intriguingly, Infidels, of whom the city had nine. 'You see how healthy the religious atmosphere [of Adelaide] is. Anything can live in it', he claimed.

Smythe left them in Adelaide to return to Melbourne and make arrangements for the final performances there, but the ship he travelled on was quarantined when smallpox broke out on board, and it would be some time before they saw him again. However, he left them in the capable hands of his son, Carlyle. Carlyle was keen on billiards, which Twain also loved, so the two men played and smoked together for relaxation between lectures and money-counting. When playing billiards at home, Twain made up his own rules and if one of his beloved cats was asleep on the table, the game had to take place without disturbing it; but with Carlyle he stuck to conventional rules and their ongoing competition lasted the rest of the tour.[8] It's a wonder they could see the billiard balls for smoke. Twain had packed 3000 fine manila cheroots in his trunk before departure and smoked his way through them as he went round Australia. It was a habit he'd had since boyhood—he'd first smoked in public at the age of eleven. It wasn't that he'd not *tried* to give up smoking—he had, hundreds of times!

The shillings accumulated at quite a rate in the next two weeks as the 'raid' moved on to Victorian country towns. Horsham came first. Twain had been feeling particularly well for a few days which perhaps accounted for his triumph there. They reached Stawell on October 18 to be greeted by the mayor and be taken to the Commercial Hotel. His twenty-four hours in the town included a visit to the Great Western Vineyard where he admired the supply of 120,000 bottles of champagne (a drink he loved). His talk was given in the Stawell Town Hall. In Ballarat the big excitement was receiving their first letters from home since mid-August. It was a relief to know that Susy and Jean were managing without them. Ballarat appealed, with its mining history and rough and tumble past, and the story of the Eureka Stockade fascinated him; he included it in the book he wrote about his travels. The town had a 'Pioneers of California Society' which turned out to welcome him.

Another carbuncle had put in its intrusive appearance and, again, Twain was sent to bed. By the end of the tour he felt qualified to write a book on Australian wallpapers—he'd studied such a variety from his various hotel beds. Often in pain, he was frustrated

---

8 The billiards competition carried on to Ceylon as Carlyle accompanied the Clemenses there as well.

when journalists asked the same questions yet again: 'The interviewed has nothing to say, and the interviewer does not know how to make him say it'. In Bendigo, the next stop, he was driven mad by the station clock that woke him several times a night.[9] The ear that was so finely tuned to dialect and the nuances of speech was also acutely sensitive to other noises; his 'German Language Lesson' invariably contained jokes about cuckoo clocks, a particular *bête noire*.

But when he walked onto the stage, his pain and crossness were forgotten. In town halls, theatres and mechanics' institutes across the country, he was cheered and applauded. He was never introduced before speaking—he needed no introduction—but just ambled on stage and, instantaneously, connected with his audiences. He played with his pauses, as a child plays with a toy, and he played with his audiences too. As he moved along, he added new jokes: Mr Smythe's quarantine provoked howls of laughter before Twain had done with it, while 'Ballarat English' was another favourite lesson for a while ('Q' is the end of the phrase "I thank you", while 'Km' is "You're welcome"). He made comedy out of his attempts to get a kookaburra to laugh (no kookaburra ever found his jokes funny); he joked about Australian place names (Woolloomooloo was a favourite because it had eight o's, and was 'musical and gurgly'); and he kept the famous poem going—he'd added dingoes and dugongs to it by this time, but refused to add lyre birds (a lyre couldn't be a bird, he insisted, as he'd met so many without feathers). On one occasion he was challenged to

---

9 He was not the only person to hate that clock. Dame Nellie Melba insisted on its being disconnected when she visited Bendigo.

put the names Geelong and Prahran into a poem and, with barely a pause this time, came up with:

> Lo! There is Geelong
> Where the righteous belong;
> And there is Prahran,
> Where they don't give a _____.

The national risk of apoplexy induced by laughter increased considerably, the papers warned those going to hear Mark Twain *not* to wear tight clothing, and the shillings kept pouring in.

Maryborough came next, with what must have felt like the thousandth mayor on the platform to greet him, and then it was back to Melbourne. In fourteen days he'd lectured eleven times in six different towns, gone to five public 'welcomes', given three interviews, and spent far too much time on Victorian trains, which he hated, drinking railroad coffee which, in his view, would be vastly improved by the addition of sheep dip. He still had to get through one more Melbourne address, talks in Geelong, Prahran, and a dinner at the Cathedral Hotel in Swanston Street hosted by the Institute of Journalists. He also squeezed in an outing to the Melbourne wool sales ('feeling the market before visiting a barber', quipped one journalist, unable to resist one last 'hair' joke), and then, on October 31, he, Livy and Clara, but not the carbuncle, were off to Tasmania. He had hoped to visit Queensland so he could experience its heat—he'd been told the 'hens laid fried eggs' up there—but time did not permit.

In Tasmania Twain was desperate 'to get a glimpse of any convicts that might still remain on the island', given the country's 'picturesque history'. 'Indeed, it is so curious and strange that it is itself the chiefest novelty the country has to offer . . . It does not read like history, but like the most beautiful lies.' He only sailed past Port Arthur, but he did visit a Refuge for the Indigent which housed 223 convicts—some of the oldest people he'd ever seen. 'It was like being suddenly set down in a new world—a weird world where Youth has never been, a world sacred to Age, and bowed forms, and wrinkles.' He learned the average age of death in the refuge was seventy-six: 'Too healthy. 70 is old enough for me', was his comment on that. He was given a rusty convict's leg-iron as a souvenir, which delighted him. His travel book would contain several pages of notes about the transportation of convicts.

In Hobart—'the neatest town that the sun shines on'—he found time to visit the museum and admire the collection of stuffed marsupials. Kangaroos and Mark Twain had much in common, he stated—both had very deep pockets. However, he couldn't joke about the Aboriginal artefacts he also saw there: 'There are many humorous things in the world; among them the white man's notion that he is less savage than the other savages'. He never laid eyes on a single Aboriginal during his Australian travels, much to his disappointment. He loved hearing stories of their amazing tracking abilities and wished James Fenimore Cooper was still alive to write tales about them. He remained acutely conscious of racial issues—no man who'd lived through the Civil War could fail to be—and he was full of sympathy: 'The Whites always mean well when they take human fish out of the ocean and try to make them dry and warm and happy and comfortable in a chicken coop'.

Trans-Tasman rivalries were stirring as Sam left Hobart for New Zealand—'the England of the Far South', as he called it. He grew weary of being asked in both countries how New Zealand compared with Australia, but remained diplomatic. He loved New Zealand scenery, came close to shipwreck on an inter-island crossing, celebrated his sixtieth birthday in Napier (and got a fourth carbuncle as a present), envied the Maoris their 'flowing and graceful' tattoos which were so much better than his own adornment, made thousands of dollars from his lectures, and collapsed once more onto a ship that took him back to Sydney. During the voyage he read a Jane Austen novel, and wasn't impressed with it. Was it *Persuasion* with its reminder that 'a person who has contracted debts must pay them'? While he'd made good money so far, the debt back home in America was still very large, and he was getting tired of trying to pay it off.

From 17 December to 1 January 1896 Twain squeezed in more lectures for his adoring public in Sydney, Scone and Melbourne. And he managed a bit of festive relaxation before Christmas, with a trip to the zoo and an outing to the theatre to see *For the Term of his Natural Life* which his daughter found 'gruesome', but which he thought went far 'to enable one to realize that old convict life—invented in hell and carried out by Christian devils'. Sharks were a problem in Sydney Harbour at the time, with bounty offered for any captured (one pound paid for any shark over twelve feet long), and he was duly taken shark fishing. 'I caught one myself', he claimed, 'but he thought he caught me—and as he was doing most of the pulling I conceded the argument and let go', so no bounty payment was added to what he'd so far 'raided' in Australia. He did, however, raid a shark story—an amusing anecdote about how a young Cecil Rhodes made his first fortune in Australia through finding in the stomach of a shark a copy of *The Times* only ten days old, which had been swallowed in the Thames and which brought the news of a European war and its effect on wool prices faster than the news could have arrived by ship. 'Nothing beats inside information', quipped Twain, and he put this tall tale into his book about his travels.[10]

When it was time to depart, all the Clemenses felt sad to be leaving Australian hospitality behind them. They'd enjoyed the 'English friendliness with the English shyness and self-consciousness left out', and had found people 'good and kind to us everywhere'. Twain called Australia 'the cordial nation'. He was also, he said, impressed with the rapid development of cities and towns and with the Australian willingness to spend money on public works and buildings. He found the hospitals, asylums, botanic gardens and town halls all excellent, and his personal love of technology had been especially taken with the speedy lifts installed in the hotels he'd stayed in—they were so much faster than European lifts which carry 'two people and a half, and you arrive at old age on your trip to the 6th floor'.

The Australian vernacular also pleased him, with its differences from American speech ('In America if your uncle is a squatter, you keep it dark, in Australia you advertise it'), and with wonderful phrases all its own. 'No Man's Land', 'never-never country' and 'new chum' became favourites, and as for 'My word!'—well, he wasn't impressed when he saw it written down, but when he heard it spoken, 'it was positively thrilling'. His quick ear caught the accent and soon he was joking

---

10 It was a tall tale—Cecil Rhodes never visited Australia.

Mark Twain lecturing at Dunedin City Hall, in a sketch done by William Hodgkins from the audience.

about the Australian fondness for the letter 'y', as in the case of the hotel maid who announced: 'The tyble is set, and here is the piper; and if the lydy is ready I'll tell the wyter to bring up the breakfast'.

The 'funniest man in America' clearly enjoyed Aussie humour and Aussie larrikinism. One of the most amusing after-dinner speeches he ever heard was in Australia, and he liked the jokes and comments called out to him whenever he appeared in public. One that came close to going too far, but in the end succeeded, was the tale about the 'Mark Twain Club of Corrigan Castle'. Many years before, he had started to receive mail from Australia, all signed by a man who called himself the President of this Mark Twain fan club. He was sent the club's constitution and by-laws, a list of the names of its thirty-two members, programmes of their planned events and other information concerning the club activities. He was asked for a photograph, which he duly sent, along with a letter. But soon he was being bombarded by letters from the club, each requesting more photos, comments on those aspects of his novels which puzzled members of the club, and also his opinions on the club's speeches and reports:

> These reports came every month. They were written on foolscap, 600 words to the page, and usually about twenty-five pages in a report . . . a solid week's work . . . By and by I came to dread those things; and this dread grew and grew and grew, grew until I got to anticipating them with a cold horror. For I was an indolent man, and not fond of letter-writing, and whenever these things came I had to put everything by and sit down—for my own peace of mind—and dig and dig until I got something out of my head which would answer for a reply.

This went on for five years, then 'at last I rose in revolt. I could endure my oppressions no longer. I pulled my fortitude together and tore off my chains, and was a free man again, and happy. From that day I burned the secretary's fat envelopes the moment they arrived, and by and by they ceased to come'. It was one night in Bendigo that Twain finally learned the true history behind all those letters. The entire fan club had originated from one man—he had sent the letters, imagined the members, invented the speakers and their speeches, and had written every long report. He'd even invented the name of 'Corrigan Castle'. Twain was delighted, even though he'd been the victim of the joke: 'It was wonderful—the whole thing; and altogether the most ingenious and laborious and cheerful and painstaking joke I have ever heard of. And I liked it; liked to hear him tell about it; yet I have been a hater of practical jokes as long back as I can remember'.

'Good breeding consists in concealing how much we think of ourselves and how little we think of other persons', Twain once commented. As Mark Twain he was certainly polite: he praised the landscape and its animals, responded with cordiality to the thousands of people he met around the country. How much was he concealing? Were the opinions expressed by Mark Twain also those of Sam Clemens? It's hard to be certain— both men regarded too much truth as an impediment to good literature—but it's probable that the real views emerge in Sam's personal notebooks and diaries. There he records that, like Trollope, he was inclined to think Australians 'blew', and he was far from sure they had that much to blow about: 'The truth is that the native Australian', he wrote two months after his departure, 'was as vain of his unpretty country as if it were the final masterpiece of God, achieved by Him from designs by that Australian. He is as sensitive about her as men are of sacred things—can't bear to have critical things said'. Did he leave with any desire ever to return to its shores? 'My word no!'

The Clemenses sailed from Australia on a P&O liner, the *Oceana*. It called in at Largs Bay in South Australia, where Twain showed up at Glenelg for Commemoration Day festivities, lunched with the governor, and also stopped briefly at 'desolate-looking' Albany (here he shared Darwin's view of the place, not Trollope's), then the ship passed Cape Leeuwin and went onwards to Ceylon. Whether or not the carbuncle was still a passenger has not been recorded.

⚜

But the pain from his infected leg was nothing to the pain that awaited them all at the end of the tour. After lectures in Ceylon, India and South Africa, they set off for Southampton which they reached fourteen months after first leaving Elmira. Twenty-five thousand dollars of debt had been repaid, thanks to the gruelling itinerary; and the book on those travels which he was about to write could bring in another $50,000 or so. First though, there was family to see. Susy would soon join them in England, and money worries could be put aside for a while.

Then came a cable: Susy was unwell, her departure had been delayed. Then another one: Susy was no better, she couldn't think of travelling. Livy decided to go to her daughter, so she and Clara packed their bags and headed to Southampton. There, another telegram assured them that Susy's recovery would be 'long, but certain', but they boarded anyway. Sam waved his wife and daugther goodbye and returned to Guildford where they'd rented a house. And then one more telegram came. Livy and Clara, learning the news as their boat reached New York Harbour, cabled Sam: 'Susy was peacefully released today'. Susy Clemens had died on August 18 from spinal meningitis at the age of twenty-four.

GK Chesterton once remarked that Mark Twain was 'serious to the point of madness'. Twain himself said the secret source of his humour was not joy, but sorrow. For the rest of his life his humour would be fed only too well from that source. Now, in his devastation over his darling Susy, he turned to work and began the chronicle of his recent travels. Through a damp English winter and through his bitter grief, he wrote mechanically, pacing the floor whenever he waited for inspiration. Livy, looking twenty years older, edited the pages as he finished them, seeking in the task some fraction of sanity. Few books have been written during such months of misery.

And yet the book he created out of his despair was full of 'lying cheerfulness'. Incredibly, it is a funny book—Mark Twain reached beyond death to find his humour. He wrote fast, taking only six months and, unusually for Mark Twain, he wrote continuously, without putting it aside for other writing projects. It's as if he held grimly to his course until that last leg of the journey was done. By the time he'd completed it, even finding a title was beyond his mental energy. *Another Innocent Abroad* and *Imitating the Equator* were considered, but finally in November 1896, handsomely adorned with an African elephant on its cover, the unexcitingly titled *Following the Equator* was published in the USA. Simultaneously, it was released as *More Tramps Abroad* in England and elsewhere. It was the last travel book Mark Twain ever wrote.

The book is a mixture of anecdotes about his experiences, padding from other books about history and geography, and tall tales put in for some light relief. It is scathing about missionaries and colonists and reads like a relaxed chat with its author. It covers Hawaii, Australia, New Zealand, Ceylon, India and South Africa. Some reviewers were not excited by it (the work of 'an old man fallen on evil times, trying to joke'), while others found it an 'unalloyed pleasure' and 'stunning reading'. It contains inaccuracies and some 'beautiful lies' but also shrewd observations about Australians and their land. Recently reprinted, it is a book that has stood the test of time.[11]

Sorrow may have been the wellspring of Twain's humour, but as tragedy upon tragedy piled on Sam Clemens, the humour slowly silted up. In 1904 Livy died from heart disease: 'She was my life, and she is gone; she was my riches, and I am a pauper'. By this time his finances were back on track, but he was too full of sorrow to notice. His brother Orion died in 1897, his sister Pamela in 1904, and in 1908 his nephew. Jean suffered increasingly from her epilepsy, drowning in her bath during an epileptic fit on Christmas Eve, 1909. In the jumbled autobiography he wrote in his last years there is little mirth (nor is there much evidence of Australia—the book hardly mentions his Antipodean tour). In his final years he regarded the most precious of life's gifts as death. And it came to him gently on 21 April 1910. He was seventy-four.

According to Ernest Hemingway, American literature began with *The Adventures of Huckleberry Finn*. That novel

---

11 The Australian parts of it have recently been reissued
in *The Wayward Tourist: Mark Twain's Adventures in
Australia*, with an introduction by Don Watson.

remains an integral part of the syllabus for American students in schools and universities and Mark Twain is considered one of the greats of their nation's literature. Two of his homes are popular museums. In America Mark Twain is alive and well, but what about in Australia?

It is a generally known that Mark Twain once visited Australia, his comments are frequently quoted in the papers, there are questions in quiz shows about what he saw and did, his descriptions are reproduced in regional museums, and media references to his visit mean that, of all the writers in this book, his visit and that of DH Lawrence are the most familiar. Sydney's Circular Quay plaque, which quotes Twain's words about Australian history being composed of 'beautiful lies', reminds locals and tourists that the man described as the most famous American of his day once stepped ashore at that spot.

One-man stage shows *Mark Twain Down Under* and *The Mark Twain You Don't Know* have toured Australia in recent years—Sam would have been delighted that money is still being made on the stage in the name of Mark Twain. But when it comes to the Australian Mark Twain Society with its official website, its public lectures and its presentations for schools, he'd probably have said, in the words of Huck Finn, that 'it ain't shucks', to that old Mark Twain Club of Corrigan Castle.

The plaque for
Mark Twain
at Sydney's
Circular Quay.

CHAPTER SEVEN

Jack London

The fight was not due to start until 11 am, but by three in the morning the queues were forming up the hill from Rushcutters Bay into Paddington, and hordes of men and boys were making their way down to the bay from the city. Extra trams had been laid on—they'd been arriving since 6 am, packed tight, boys clinging to the outsides. Hansom cabs were at a premium and the old Sydney omnibuses had doubled their prices, but they too arrived bursting at the seams. The most eager had camped out on the grass near the stadium, a strange way to spend Christmas night, but it got them a better chance of a seat on one of the wooden planks inside. It had rained during the night, but everyone soon steamed dry. The day was overcast, but warm.

It got even warmer when twenty thousand bodies packed into the open-air stadium by 9 am. The structure was designed to hold sixteen thousand, but promoters were happy to take the money from those willing to squeeze in.[1] Tickets ranged from ten shillings to ten pounds—you could buy two new shirts from Gowings for ten shillings, so it was no mean investment; but who thought of the price when there was a chance to watch history being made? Those unfortunates who missed out on tickets didn't consider turning round to go home. Somehow they were going to be part of the occasion too, so they pressed up close against the wooden fences of the stadium, the younger ones climbing trees and telegraph poles, and all waited to be on the spot when their man won the fight. Another forty thousand or so men had gathered outside by the time the match started.[2] They couldn't see anything, but they were desperate to express solidarity by their very presence.

They were all there to support Tommy Burns, a white man, fight Jack Johnson in the boxing ring. Johnson was a black American—big and powerful, and arrogant enough to challenge a white boxer in the world's very first professional heavyweight world championship between fighters of different colours. Black boxers had been recognised for some time, but considered beneath the honour or right of fighting for the major prize. There had been enormous pre-match publicity. This had become far more than a fight between two men wearing leather gloves—this would be a battle of racial supremacy, as the press well knew: 'Citizens who have

1 The take for the day was twenty-six thousand pounds, then a world record for a boxing match.

2 Estimates on the numbers of those present outside the stadium vary considerably, from ten thousand to two hundred thousand, but forty thousand seems to be the most reliable figure.

*Jack London
in a 1909
photograph
taken in
Melbourne.*

never prayed before are supplicating providence to give the white man a strong right arm with which to belt the coon into oblivion'. The 'black bastard', that 'big buck nigger' needed to be shown who was boss and Tommy Burns was the man to do it. Journalists waited in the crowd to be among the first to cable the news of his victory around the world.

The fight was late starting and the crowd waited tensely. There was no sense of post-Christmas cheer; too much was at stake for any merriment to break out. But they waited patiently, all twenty thousand pairs of eyes on the small square 'ring' where the two men would slug it out. Of those pairs of eyes, 19,999 were male. Only men and boys were allowed to buy tickets and those women who had dressed as men in the hopes of sneaking in had been roughly turned away. Only one woman was allowed in and she was sitting ringside next to Attorney General Billy Hughes and a former prime minister, John C. Watson. She was there as the invited guest of the event's organiser Hugh McIntosh. She watched as eagerly as the rest for the contestants to appear, unfazed at being the only woman in that huge crowd of men. Her name was Charmian and she was no mean boxer herself. Her husband had taught her and she'd given him black eyes, though had also been knocked unconscious by him, in their sparring sessions. She knew what was at stake in the coming match and would type the articles her husband had been commissioned to write about it. But for now, that husband was there at her side, invited because he was one of the most famous writers in the world at that time. His name was Jack London.

Jack London had not planned to come to Australia to see the Burns–Johnson fight. He had intended to come a year or so later as part of his seven-year literary pilgrimage through the Pacific. Books and travel had always been Jack's preferred forms of escape. On the voyage of the *Snark* he combined the two, journeying in the footsteps of his favourite authors, in a boat that had over five hundred books on board, and which even bore a literary name (from Lewis Carroll's 'The Hunting of the Snark'). Even the seven-year length of the voyage made it seem like a task from a fairytale.[3]

Jack London had survived the harsh realities of his childhood because fiction gave hope and meaning to

3   The number seven has long had magical properties in fairytales and mythology, as in 'Snow White and the Seven Dwarves', 'The Wolf and the Seven Little Kids', the Seven Wonders of the World, the seven books of the 'Harry Potter' series, the Seven Deadly Sins, etc.

his life. Born John Griffith Chaney in San Francisco in 1876, he was the illegitimate child of an astrologer and a Spiritualist. When he was a baby his mother married John London, a failed entrepreneur who died young, so Jack went early to factory work, fishing, and whatever else he could find, to support his mother and young step-siblings. Only in Oakland Public Library did he find any joy in life. There, librarian and author Ina Coolbrith guided him into the wonders of fiction (she had been a good friend to Mark Twain) and opened up a whole new world for the lonely boy. He worshipped the memory of Miss Coolbrith for the rest of his life.

Herman Melville's and Joseph Conrad's tales of the sea inspired Jack to save to buy his own little boat and learn to sail her in the treacherous waters of San Francisco bay. Mark Twain's *Jumping Frog* story left him longing to find gold as a miner (he did strike 'gold' in the Klondike, but it was the fictional gold of *The Call of the Wild*, not the metallic sort), and Kipling's call to 'Take up the White Man's burden / Send forth the best ye breed' was one he longed to answer. Jack copied out story after story of Kipling's until he felt the master's style had seeped into his very pores, a lesson he always acknowledged: 'I would never have possibly written anywhere near the way I did had Kipling never been'.

In his teens he discovered Darwin, whose theory of 'survival of the fittest' he'd see tested between Burns and Johnson in Sydney. And as for Robert Louis Stevenson, he filled Jack's head with dreams of ships and pirates and the blue Pacific. Stevenson's *Treasure Island* remained Jack's favourite novel. He longed to see the places these writers had described. Stevenson himself had started from San Francisco when he sailed the *Casco* to the Pacific, so

Jack planned to trace that journey from its beginning to the grave where his literary idol slept on the top of a Samoan mountain. On his travels he could visit the Marquesas Islands, setting for Melville's *Typee*, and call at islands visited by the *Beagle*; he could see where Twain had convulsed audiences with laughter in Australia; he could anchor his *Snark* in the same ports where Conrad's *Otago* and *Torrens* had halted; and, with luck, he might even encounter Kipling's Old Man Kangaroo hopping across Australia. In true Jack London style, it would be the literary tour to beat all literary tours.

Unfortunately it had about as much practical planning behind it as any heroic journey in a novel. Jack London poured money into the construction of the forty-five foot *Snark* (some thirty thousand dollars in all), but things went wrong from the very beginning. The day the keel was to be laid, San Francisco was flattened by the 1906 earthquake—costs skyrocketed, supplies were shoddy, delays never-ending. When the boat finally set sail, she soon began to leak, taps broke off in the expensive bathroom, the gas tanks filled the boat with fumes, and the lifeboat was unsafe. Serious design faults in Jack's plans meant the boat refused to sail before the wind in a stiff sea.

The crew could equally have been the cast selected for a stage farce. Roscoe Eames, uncle of Jack's wife Charmian, was ship's navigator, but had no idea how to use a sextant and knew nothing about boats—he would abandon the *Snark* in Hawaii, but only after leaving it out, unvarnished, in harsh sunlight to warp and crack, which necessitated an almost total re-build. Then there was Herbert Stolz, a university student with no sailing experience. He was to be ship's engineer. Ship's cook was

Martin Johnson; he'd never even seen a ship under sail and he didn't know how to boil an egg.[4] And the cabin boy, a Japanese youth called Tochigi, spent most of his time being seasick. He too was replaced in Hawaii by Yoshiatsu Nakata, another Japanese whose one word of English was 'Yes' and who joined the ship in the mistaken belief it would take him straight home to his beloved Japan.

Charmian London, also on board, was Jack's second wifc. He'd married his first wife for domestic comfort rather than for love. She'd given him two daughters and, reluctantly, a divorce. Charmian was delighted to be setting off on the *Snark* pilgrimage. It meant she could get Jack away from alcohol and his drinking cronies, have him all to herself, and make love with him in their tiny cabin to her heart's content. They'd only been married a little over a year when they set off and she looked forward to a seven-year honeymoon.

Lastly there was Jack London himself. Charming, handsome, adventurous and prolific Jack, who'd been an oyster pirate, a goldminer, a seal hunter, a packer of pickles in a factory, a prisoner, an ardent socialist, atheist and Darwinian, and was now a bestselling author. *The Call of the Wild, White Fang* and the Klondike stories such as *The White Silence* and *An Odyssey of the North* had made him an international name. His literary career had not come easily. He'd kept working away, perfecting his style, as the rejection slips piled up; but now fame had arrived he intended to enjoy its proceeds. 'No writer of prominence in the days of his prominence has ever gone sailing around the world', he grandly announced,

---

4   Martin Johnson later had a famous career as a big-game
    hunter and motion picture director.

but he would do it. Stevenson had sailed only the Pacific and London had to out-do Stevenson. So his itinerary included the South Seas, Tasmania, New Zealand, Australia, New Guinea, the Philippines, Japan, China, India, the Red Sea, the Mediterranean, the Black Sea and the Baltic. The *Snark*'s journey was planned to end in Paris when a triumphant Jack would moor her in the Seine and enjoy a Latin Quarter dinner in celebration. How the boat would reach one destination after another to cover this extraordinary route was something none of the crew ever discussed. Jack ignored the dire predictions of friends, the scoffing of his ex-wife and fears of his daughters, and the mounting debts that threatened imminent arrest, and on 23 April 1907 (Shakespeare's birthday and therefore an auspiciously literary day), he sailed his leaky boat and inexperienced crew out of San Francisco harbour. Once out in the ocean he had to teach himself navigation, but often no one on board had any idea where they actually were. It didn't matter to Jack—he could read aloud to them all from *Treasure Island* and they'd all be happy. Jack London was a Peter Pan who didn't want to grow up, but his dreams of Never Never Land did not eventuate, and the *Snark* would force upon him adult lessons he'd never wanted to learn.

Somehow the *Snark* limped its way to Honolulu. There, while repairs were carried out, Jack joined local Hawaiian chieftains riding the enormous waves on big heavy boards and wrote about the experience, thus introducing the sport of surfing to American readers. Following Robert Louis Stevenson's trail took him to nearby Molokai to visit the lepers. Wanting to allay public terror of the disease, London wrote an article,

The Snark *in a photograph taken after she was sold.*

Jack London (seated) with Charmian and the crew on board the Snark.

'The Lepers of Molokai', and he and Charmian stayed with the 'noseless, lipless' lepers for five days. *The Sheriff of Kona* and *Koolau the Leper* were powerful stories resulting from the visit. Next came the Marquesas Islands, important to Melville who sent his sailors there in *Typee*; they were also visited by Stevenson. The Londons were able to rent the very cottage Stevenson had stayed in, and hire the cook who had prepared his meals. As she cooked, Jack read Melville's *Moby Dick* to his wife.

By the end of 1907 the *Snark* had reached Tahiti, in better shape than when she'd first set out. There Jack had to leave her for a lightning trip back to America on the SS *Mariposa* so he could sort out the tangle of his business affairs and raise more cash (the bank account was down to sixty-six dollars), but he spent only eight days in San Francisco before rushing back to Papeete to continue the pilgrimage. In Apia, Western Samoa, he and Charmian climbed Mount Vaea to see Stevenson's grave: 'I wouldn't have gone out of my way to visit the grave of any other man in the world', he told her. Fiji came next, and then 'the terrible Solomons', as he titled them in one of his stories. *Heart of Darkness* was another favourite novel—Jack's quest into the interior of wild places was an imitation of Conrad's white trader hero taking his boat into the heart of Africa. He found his 'Congo' in the violent, remote Solomon Islands, inhabited in some parts by ferocious headhunters and cannibals. Jack, penetrating too close, came near to being turned into a trophy by one tribe.

Throughout all these travels he had written books. One thousand words per day were churned out, regardless of the conditions, no matter how he felt. *Martin Eden* and *Adventure*, both novels, were completed, along with many short stories for *South Sea Tales* and the autobiographical *The Cruise of the Snark*. But finally, after extended discomfort, he couldn't hold his pen and the writing had to cease. A doctor needed to be found, and soon. There were bad sores on his ankles and feet. He'd self-doctored with burning corrosive sublimate (a mercury poison), but they refused to heal and had turned into 'yaws', painful, messy tropical ulcers. Large centipedes had infested the boat—at night they munched away at the fingernails of the sleeping crew. Everyone on board had severe headaches, the onset of malaria, and also 'scratch-scratch', a skin irritation, while Jack was crippled by what he called 'dropsy', his hands swollen enormously and the skin turning silver in colour and flaking off. Horny new skin grew in its place and if he cut his toenails at night, they'd doubled in size by the next night. Since almost dying from scurvy in the Klondike, Jack had also been troubled by his teeth—they ached and his gums bled. He'd been seriously sunburned several times, had enjoyed drinking binges in any port that supplied alcohol, had been burned in the *Snark*'s kitchen, and had pushed his body beyond endurance for eighteen months. Now it could take no more and he was forced to concede defeat. If he couldn't write, he couldn't earn the money they needed. He turned the *Snark* towards Guadalcanal and there the Londons, Nakata and Martin Johnson boarded the SS *Makambo* bound for Sydney. He had not yet admitted it, but the *Snark*'s literary journey was at an end.

※

Jack London's own literary travels, however, were not over. After arriving in Sydney on 14 November 1907, he

booked into the Hotel Metropole, the very hotel Kipling
had stayed in for his two nights in Sydney. The Bent Street
hotel was the Londons' base for a week while Jack consulted doctors, who then decided he must be hospitalised.
The St Malo was a private hospital in Ridge Street, North
Sydney, a Victorian house originally connected with the
St Ives Church of England Hospital nearby, but from
1903 run by Nurse Gertrude Walker.[5] Jack's surgeon,
Dr Clarence Read of Chatswood, operated to repair his
double fistula. He was dosed with quinine for his malaria,
and his yaws were treated with an arsenic compound
which left unsightly troughs on his skin, and which
permanently undermined his health, creating bladder
problems among other ailments. But his swollen, flaking
hands had the skin specialists flummoxed: 'The biggest
specialist in Australia in skin-diseases has examined me,
and his verdict is that not only in his own experience has
he never seen anything like it, but that no line is to be
found about it in any of the medical libraries'. Although
proud of being a medical rarity, Jack was frustrated at
being without the use of his hands, 'unable to cut a piece
of cold meat with a knife and fork', and incapable of
holding his pen. Charmian shared his hospital room as
her malaria was treated, while Martin Johnson went
off to have his yaws seen to at the Sydney Homeopathic
Hospital in Cleveland Street. They both got better, but
Jack's condition failed to improve: 'No case like it had
ever been reported. It extended from my hands to my feet
so that at times I was as helpless as a child. On occasion
my hands were twice their natural size, with seven dead
and dying skins peeling off at the same time. There were

5   The St Malo Hospital was demolished in 1956 when
    the Warringah Freeway was constructed.

times when my toe-nails, in twenty-four hours, grew as thick as they were long'.

Jack and the specialists thought it must be nerves. He'd been well in his 'own climate of California', so he thought he'd better return there. After five weeks he was dismissed from the St Malo, though he continued to visit as an outpatient for the next few weeks. It is now thought that Jack London was suffering from pellagra (a vitamin deficiency disease, caused by lack of niacin and protein) and also psoriasis (a skin and joint disorder, believed to be caused by stress and excessive alcohol consumption, which produces red or silvery scaly patches on the skin. It also causes excessive skin production and often affects fingernails and toenails). But whatever the causes, it was clear he could not go back to life on the *Snark*. Charmian cried for two days when he told her the beloved boat must be sold. She'd experienced the adventure of a lifetime—she'd steered the boat, shot, hunted and fished, ridden mountain trails, visited active volcanoes, seen headhunting cannibals, explored and, best of all, she'd had Jack constantly at her side throughout. Now the drink, editors, bank managers and publishers would all have a share of him as well. Martin Johnson was despatched to the Solomons to find a skeleton crew and sail the *Snark* to Sydney where she would be sold. In the end, Jack had copied his literary idol once too often—like Robert Louis Stevenson he too was sick in Sydney.

❧

And so it was that Jack London found himself sitting ringside at a stadium in Sydney instead of sailing the Pacific as he'd planned. Hugh McIntosh, match promoter, was delighted to hear that the legendary author was in town and rushed to invite him to the big event. Still feeling 'weak and wabbly' *(sic)*, and only days out of hospital, Jack nevertheless lined up payment from New York newspapers, the Melbourne *Argus* and *The Australian Star* for reporting on the event.

The Sydney Stadium was only a year old. Entrepreneur Hugh McIntosh had built it to make a killing from fights put on for the sailors of America's 'Great White Fleet', which had come to Sydney Harbour in August 1908. One and a half acres in Ruchcutters Bay, serviced by tram lines from the city, were ideal for his purpose and he'd rented them at four pounds per week on a two-year lease from the ironmonger who owned them.[6] No investor was prepared to finance a permanent structure, so McIntosh spent two thousand pounds erecting a wooden fence and seats, billing it as 'the greatest open-air stadium in the world'. The opening fight, Tommy Burns versus Bill Squires, was a huge success. Burns, the victor and heavyweight champion of the world, became a friend to McIntosh and stayed on in Sydney. McIntosh offered Burns six thousand pounds when he finally agreed to take on Jack Johnson.

Jack Johnson, his 'dusky Cyclops' antagonist, was a Texan streetfighter. At six foot one and 192 pounds, he towered over Burns, who might have been built like a firehydrant but was only five foot seven and much lighter. The racial discrimination of the American South had left Johnson with a hatred for the white man and he

6   McIntosh was a crafty businessman and, in order to get
    a cheap rent, had indicated to the owner that he just
    wanted to hold a few small entertainments for friends.
    The owner was horrified, but powerless, when he
    discovered how much money McIntosh was making on
    his land.

arrived bitter, cocky, and determined to win. From the moment of his arrival in Australia, the press was full of Jack Johnson—his stylish clothes, his gleaming gold tooth studded with a diamond, the way he sipped expensive wines through a straw and quoted Milton, his flashy footwork and his 'shadow-sparring' (something new in Australian boxing then). The man had once challenged Rasputin to a vodka-drinking contest (which Rasputin won). But what was considered worst of all was that this brazen 'nigger' dared to ogle white women, had brought with him his white 'wife' (she was not actually married to Johnson and was a prostitute), and before fights wrapped his penis in gauze bandages to exaggerate its size.

In promoting the 'Championship of the World' McIntosh played to the public's weaknesses. Australia was intensely xenophobic in the early twentieth century. The 'Great White Fleet' had come to Sydney as 'a symbol of a racial ideal to be upheld'. Australians wanted protection from the 'Yellow Peril' and from negroes (Martin Johnson thought Australians were 'worse negro-haters even than the Americans'). The fight, if it went the wrong way, could be a demonstration of White Australia's worst racial fears. Tommy Burns, of Canadian and Scottish heritage, who looked like Napoleon and was proud of it, just had to win. Pre-fight publicity emphasised the racial message. Artist and writer Norman Lindsay's advertising poster portrayed heroic white Tommy squaring up against an animalistic monster of a black man.

The fight was nasty from the start. Johnson, aware that his fee of fifteen hundred pounds was far less than the amount paid to Burns, refused to go on at the last minute. McIntosh's pistol held to his head soon changed

Photograph of Sydney Stadium on the day of the Burns–Johnson fight.

The Norman Lindsay poster advertising the Burns–Johnson fight.

his mind on that score. The crowd booed when he appeared, while Burns was cheered. There was an argument over whether Burns was allowed to have his arms bandaged, which Burns lost, so he then refused to shake his opponent's hand. On that sour note, the twenty rounds began.

In the first seconds Johnson felled Burns with a right uppercut, and the crowd roared with rage. Johnson didn't care. He taunted 'Tahmy' and promised to bed his wife, which made Burns yell at him to 'Fight like a white man!' Like 'a great black cat' with a helpless mouse, Johnson played with his opponent. By the eighth round Burns' face was battered and bloody and his manager fed him pep-up strychnine tablets between rounds (and neatly combed and parted his hair for him as well). Johnson, his black skin as polished and gleaming as the diamond in his smiling mouth, was hardly ruffled. He was in complete control. As Jack London described it for *The New York Herald*, 'A dew drop would have had more chance with a giant Texan. When Johnson smiled, a dazzling flash of gold teeth filled the wide aperture between his lips, and he smiled all the time. The fight? The word is a misnomer. There was no fight. No Armenian massacre would compare with this hopeless slaughter. Burns never landed a blow. The fight was like that between a colossus and a pygmy'.

The massacre went on for fourteen awful rounds. Within the stadium and outside it, there was a deepening silence. No straw boaters were hurled into the air, no cheers echoed the resounding blows. The audience sat, stunned and disbelieving, as their man was beaten to a pulp. Then Police Superintendent Mitchell stopped the fight and McIntosh, the referee, declared Jack Johnson the winner. Sporting history had been made and global race relations had been permanently changed; but no man there was happy to have witnessed it. The crowd left in an eerie silence, as if a bereavement had taken place. According to *The Bulletin* it was as if 'sunlight had found darkness and lost'.

Few were gracious in defeat. *The Sydney Mail* refused to publish pictures of the match and asked 'whether the spectre of this grinning, capering negro punching a white man was actually worthy of the city of Sydney', while the *Sportsman* insisted that 'Johnson has shown that he has only the instincts of a nigger—pure nigger'. Churchmen prayed that God would 'grant that the defeat . . . may not be the sullen and solemn prophecy that Australia is to be out-classed and finally vanquished by those dark-skinned people'. Burns was washed-up as a fighter; he became an evangelist and went off to fight the devil instead.

Jack London was no happier than anyone else about Johnson's victory, but was more gracious than most and did go and shake hands with him at the end of the fight. In his articles he made it quite clear that Johnson was the superior fighter: 'there was no fraction of a second in all the fourteen rounds that could be called Burns'—so far as damage is concerned Burns never landed a blow . . . He tried every moment throughout the fight, except when he was groggy. It was hopeless, preposterous, heroic'. Though the press was desperately implying otherwise, London admitted that Johnson was cleverer and quicker: 'All hail to Johnson! His victory was unqualified. It was his fight all through, in spite of published accounts to the contrary'. But he also made his own feelings plain. 'Personally I was with Burns all the

The memorial stone which marks the spot at Rushcutters Bay where the Sydney Stadium once stood. It was there that Jack and Charmian London, along with 20,000 other spectators, watched the Burns–Johnson fight.

way. He is a white man and so am I. Naturally I wanted to see the white man win. Put the case to Johnson. Ask him if he were [a] spectator to a fight between a white man and a black man which he would like to see win, and Johnson's black skin will dictate a desire parallel to the one dictated by my white skin.' His article ended with a clarion call to the white world. Somebody must dig the white boxer Jack Jeffries out of his retirement, so he could wipe the smile off Johnson's face.[7]

Cables rushed the news around the world and Jack's articles soon followed. His words provoked race riots in the American South, there were lynchings and black homes were burned. In Australia the 'White Australia Policy' grew ever more entrenched. Two years

7   Jeffries did fight Johnson in Reno in the USA in 1910 and was beaten. Jack London was there in Reno to report on that fight too. He bet four thousand dollars on Jeffries, and lost it all. Johnson remained World Champion until 1916. He then, like Burns, became a preacher.

later poet Henry Lawson was still pointing out the racial consequences of the Boxing Day match:

> You flock to your fairest city, for a thing that
>   you would not miss
> To see a sight that could never be seen in a
>   land but this.   ·
> You paid and you cheered and you hooted,
>   and this is your meed of disgrace
> It was not Burns that was beaten—for a
>   nigger smacked your face.
> Take heed—I am tired of writing . . . but O
>   my people, take heed,
> For the time may be near for the mating of
>   the Black and the White to breed.

The stadium went on to become a popular sporting and entertainment venue. Given a roof in 1912, it hosted boxing and wrestling matches, concerts and even The Beatles, before being demolished in 1973 to make way for an overhead railway. The historic site where Jack and Charmian London watched both a match and a racial battle being fought out, is now marked by a memorial stone and plaque.

After leaving the St Malo a few days before the fight, the Londons rented an apartment in Phillip Street in the city. There, his hands still badly swollen, Jack dictated his report of the fight to Charmian, was interviewed by reporters and mulled over his 'First Impressions' of Australia. These appeared as a front-page piece in *The Australian Star* on 7 January 1909. 'Whenever a traveller journeys to a far country the inhabitants of that country immediately set him up on a high place, and demand that he tell them what he thinks of them. And when he has told them they proceed to cast potsherds at him', his piece began. It was only twenty years before that his revered Kipling had arrived in the country and, within hours, had begun to generalise. Jack was not going to copy Kipling here: 'It is only the reckless and war-hardened foreigner who rushes into wide generalisations upon new things and places. Being neither reckless nor callous, I shall resolutely avoid wide generalisations. I shall make mine up so narrow, that though I be potsherded, I shall be content in the knowledge that my facts are irrefragable'.

Like Trollope, Jack was weary of the 'blowing' that went on about the glories of Sydney Harbour. He claimed the locals had nothing to blow about, as the Harbour was not manmade, but was an 'act of God' (in whom he didn't actually believe, but he didn't mention that fact in the article). After remarking that Australians were very like Americans (Kipling's view also), he moved on to the 'narrow' generalisations he'd promised—first a problem he'd encountered in the Hotel Metropole and secondly the garbage men of Phillip Street.

The hotel, he claimed, was 'managed by Barbarians'. Unable to sleep one night, Jack sat down to clutch a pen in his clumsy hand and write. The electric light bulb went out, so he lit the candle provided and went on writing. When the candle guttered, he rang for more and his request caused great consternation: 'three able-bodied nightporters' entered his room and 'held a conference', gazing at him as if he were 'Siamese twins'. Although it was a large hotel: 'I got no more candles. My conduct in asking for candles was unprecedented. They could furnish me with candles only by breaking the rules, and who was I that they should break the rules?' So he lay 'sleepless the rest of the night', his mind full of ideas he couldn't jot down.

In early January he was robbed of sleep again. This time the problem was metal garbage bins, put out in the evening and collected in the morning:

> Between midnight and 1 in the morning the first peace-destroyer arrives. And thereafter, at regular intervals, until 6 in the morning, Phillip-street is a combined boiler shop and lunatic asylum. I am a good sleeper, but morning after morning, by 4 or 5 o'clock, the last shreds of sleep are routed, and, with aching eyes and sanguinary soul, I gaze out of my window at the joyous garbage men juggling with the metal barrels, shouting at their horses, and bellowing interminable conversations back and forth until the street is a huge cavern of re-echoing sound.

He felt the garbos had awakened the 'essential depravity' of his nature: 'I know now the license of brutal thoughts, the lust for blood, the desire to kill. I devise cunning and diabolical schemes whereby I may murder and remain unscathed'.

One week later he was back in print. *The Australian Star* devoted two columns of its front page to his article 'The Future Belongs to Labor'. Like most other literary visitors, Jack found there were strikes on while he was in Australia. At Broken Hill strikers were 'blowing up water-mains and wrecking railroad tracks', but still he was impressed by the 'orderly' behaviour of the Australian striker, when compared with his American counterpart. Jack was a long-time and ardent Socialist. His factory work, his time in prison (he'd been arrested for vagrancy as an out-of-work teenager), and his reading of *The Communist Manifesto* which he'd found in Oakland Library, had left him convinced that 'the whole history of mankind has been the history of contests between the exploiting and the exploited'.

His views, however, were not socialist enough for the left-wing journalist Andrew M. Anderson, who attacked Jack in the magazine the *Socialist*. Anderson poured out his fury that the famous Jack London had done nothing to further the cause of socialism while in Australia, had turned into a snob, only interested in his own fame, and who, in his fiction, was 'too willing to honour the exalted' instead of the working man. Jack was furious and wrote to the editor to complain. He was not obliged, he pointed out, to accept another man's conception of what he should write about, socialist or not.

He also gave a long interview, speaking with 'well-phrased, clear-cut, aggressive eloquence' to a suspicious socialist interviewer. The article appeared in *The Lone Hand* on February 1. The interviewer was impressed in spite of himself, finding Jack London had 'nothing of the air of the great author about him', was funny and honest. Jack talked continually, leaving his interlocutor little to do. Six pages of the magazine, accompanied by photos of Jack, Charmian and the *Snark*, were given over to the piece in which Jack recounted his early travels, his eleven-hour days in a jute factory and job as a carpet-beater, and his struggles to get published as a writer. In no uncertain terms he defended his reputation as a socialist and had the last word on the subject in Australia.

A visit to the Theatre Royal to see *The Girl of the Golden West* provided light relief, as did a pleasant excursion to the Jenolan Caves. However, the humidity of a Sydney January was not what Jack needed. His hands were getting worse, not better. Charles Darwin had liked Tasmania, so the Londons decided to give the coolest state a try. They took the train to Melbourne, where Jack celebrated his thirty-third birthday on January 12 and had his photo taken. He left no record of what he thought of what was then Australia's largest city and the following day they sailed to Tasmania. The Mount Royal Hotel, Brown's River, Kingston Beach, was their quiet base for the next three weeks. Jack had been drinking in Sydney and Melbourne—wine, cocktails, Scotch highballs and whatever else came his way—but in Tasmania he found himself 'in a place where there was nothing to drink'. Instead he 'soaked in the cool air, rode horseback' and wrote his thousand words each day. As Jack dried out, his hands began to sweat again and the swelling subsided. Charmian built up their strength by providing lots of tomato soup. They ate and slept well and left on February 9 feeling renewed and invigorated.

The rest of February and all of March were spent back in Sydney, with the Australia Hotel in Castlereagh Street their base. This was Sydney's premier hotel at the time—it had been opened by actress Sarah Bernhardt in 1889—and its granite entrance, Carrara marble foyer and Moorish-style lounge were opulent and impressive.[8] Jack had no reason to complain of a lack of candles or anything else. Soon he was back to his old habits, drinking in the bars and pubs of the city, and also taking excursions out to Bondi Beach where a 'bucks' camp'—a carnival of barbecues, convivial songs, yarns and laughter—had

8   The hotel was demolished in 1969 to make way for the MLC Centre.

Brown's River,
Tasmania,
(ca.1900)
where Jack
and Charmian
London stayed
for three weeks
recuperating
in the cooler
weather.

been established on the northern headland. Men could escape their wives and drink in peace, with no closing time to stop them. Jack joined the fun and more than made up for the time spent drying out in Tasmania.

But the drink and the warmer weather again impaired his health and confirmed his decision to sell the *Snark* and end the voyage. In early March Martin Johnson sailed the boat into Sydney. With Tahei, a young Polynesian he'd taken on as crew, they all enjoyed a fancy dinner at the hotel and then a vaudeville show at the Tivoli Theatre. Nakata, the Japanese cabin boy, was still with the Londons as a servant; he remained in their employment for another six years and eventually settled in Honolulu and became a dentist. According to a remark London made in *The Lone Hand* article, the author also gave a talk which was well attended, but details of the venue and the exact date in March have not survived.

The *Snark* was moored at Pyrmont. Daily trips had to be taken by ferry to remove the books and other belongings—though many had disappeared when the boat was left in the Solomons—and to supervise the packing of items to be sent back to California. The *Snark* was then placed in the hands of the Londons' local business agent, Justus Scharff, an ironmonger with premises in York Street. He was to sell it as soon as a buyer could be found. In the event, this only happened in September, months after the Londons had left Australia, and the price paid was low—three thousand dollars, a tiny fraction of her original cost. She was sold to an English trading syndicate. The *Snark* ended her days, ingloriously, as a blackbirder—sailing the South Seas to trap unwary natives into lives of virtual slavery on tropical plantations. Robert Louis Stevenson had criticised the practice—what would he have said to Jack London about the final use of his beloved boat?

Financially and physically the voyage of the *Snark* had been disastrous; but the literary consequences of the journey were another matter altogether. The pilgrimage had been fulfilling—homage had been paid at Stevenson's grave, Melville's *Typee* had been explored, and the footsteps (or sailing paths) of Darwin, Kipling, Conrad and Twain had been reverently followed. The one thousand words a day had produced novels, an entertaining travelogue, and many short stories. But did any of those works have Australian settings? Had Australia triggered Jack London's creativity as it had triggered Kipling's and Twain's, or did Jack more resemble Conrad and Stevenson in remaining imaginatively unstirred by the Australian landscape and its people?

Jack and Charmian London left Australia on 8 April 1909, on board the SS *Tymeric*. In no hurry to get home, Jack reached San Francisco in July. Tired and depressed, he felt more like the 'Ancient Mariner' than any other literary hero. On board the *Tymeric* he'd done some boxing with the ship's officers. He managed to give the first mate 'a couple of beautiful black eyes', the second 'a gum-boil that raised his face four inches', and the third a badly swollen nose. He was anxious about the cramps that plagued him while he boxed, and depressed by his own physical deterioration. So he sat down to write a story about a fight, and with Boxing Day and the most memorable fight he'd ever seen still fresh in his mind, he set his story in Sydney. Called *A Piece of Steak*, it's a powerful, evocative tale, one of the finest short stories he ever wrote.

Tom King, an ageing, impoverished boxer, returns to the ring to fight Sandel, a young New Zealander. He needs to feed his family and the prize money, if he can win it, will keep them all going some time. The tale opens poignantly:

> With the last morsel of bread Tom King wiped his plate clean of the last particle of flour gravy and chewed the resulting mouthful in a slow and meditative way. When he arose from the table, he was oppressed by the feeling that he was distinctly hungry. Yet he alone had eaten. The two children in the other room had been sent early to bed in order that in sleep they might forget they had gone supper-less. His wife had touched nothing, and had sat silently and watched him with solicitous eyes. She was a thin, worn woman of the working class, though signs of an earlier prettiness were not wanting in her face. The flour for the gravy she had borrowed from the neighbour across the

hall. The last two ha'pennies had gone to buy the bread.

Jack London had always associated red meat with success and prosperity. Nobody could ever have too many steaks. In his view, meat barely needed cooking and dinner guests, for he was a hospitable man, had to turn their eyes from the still bloody meat he loved to feast on.[9] What he called a 'Cannibal Sandwich' was a particular favourite: it consisted of raw beef and onions, finely chopped. In his tale, the 'piece of steak' of the title comes to symbolise strength. Tom King feels the need of just such a meal before the fight: ' "Blimey, but couldn't I go a piece of steak!", he muttered aloud'. His wife has tried the butchers, who refused credit.

> Tom King grunted but did not reply. He was busy thinking of the bull terrier he had kept in his younger days to which he had fed steaks without end. Burke would have given him credit for a thousand steaks—then. But times had changed. Tom King was getting old; and old men, fighting before second-rate clubs, couldn't expect to run bills of any size with the tradesmen.

Mindful of that Sydney journalist who'd accused him of being no true socialist, Jack depicts all too realistically the plight of the city's poor: 'It was a drought year in Australia, times were hard, and even the most irregular work was difficult to find'. Tom has to walk two miles to the Gayety Theatre, hardly the ideal preparation for his fight. He remembers how, when he was 'heavyweight

---

9 He was very fond of duck that had been cooked less than ten minutes and was still dripping blood. He also ate a lot of raw fish during his life.

champion of New South Wales', there'd have been cabs to take him, just as 'Tommy Burns and that Yankee Jack Johnson' had gone in cabs. Plodding wearily into the city, he remembers past fights at 'Rush-Cutters Bay'; thrashing old Stowsher Bill twenty years before and how 'Stowsher Bill had cried afterward in the dressing room'.[10]

Now Tom King is the old fighter, the 'grizzled old chopping block' who has to take on a younger, stronger opponent. His experience will be pitted against the other's brute strength: 'Always were these youngsters rising up in the boxing game, springing through the ropes and shouting their defiance; and always were the old uns going down before them. They climbed to success over the bodies of the old uns'.

For many rounds Tom King holds his own. He ducks, he feints, his 'policy of economy' forces his opponent to exhaust himself, while he conserves energy. By the seventh round the young Kiwi is tiring, but both men fight on grimly. King never makes 'a superfluous movement' and the match drags on into its tenth round. There's a tense moment when the referee could end the agony and 'the purse' would be King's, but the younger man protests that he can keep going and the eleventh round begins.

King knows he is almost finished:

He had not had sufficient strength in him to begin with. His legs were heavy under him and beginning to cramp. He should not have walked those two miles to the fight. And there

---

10 Boxer Bill Squires was known as 'Boshter Bill'. Jack London is using a variation of the name of the man who was beaten by Tommy Burns in Sydney.

was the steak which he had got up longing for that morning. A great and terrible hatred rose up in him for the butchers who had refused him credit. It was hard for an old man to go into a fight without enough to eat. And a piece of steak was such a little thing, a few pennies at best; yet it meant thirty quid to him.

The eleventh round begins with a rush from Sandel, but King inflicts more punishment than he gets, smashing with all his remaining strength while the crowd goes wild. And then he gains a chance to end the match; one great effort is all it needs, 'one stiff punch would do it' and the prize would be his. 'And Tom King, in a flash of bitterness, remembered the piece of steak and wished that he had it behind that necessary punch he must deliver.' He hits out, but not hard enough. Reeling backwards from the impact of his blow, Tom King falls from weakness and the match is soon over. The roars of the crowd sound 'like the surf at Bondi Beach'. He'd tottered 'on the hairline balance of defeat. Ah, that piece of steak would have done it. He had lacked just that for the decisive blow, and he had lost. It was all because of the piece of steak'. Dully he wanders out into Sydney's Domain. Weak and sore, his knuckles smashed, his stomach empty, Tom King sits down on a bench. Once, in his glory days, he'd beaten Stowsher Bill and Bill had sobbed in his dressing room. Now it is Tom King's turn. 'Unnerved by the thought of the missus sitting up for him', a bruised failure, Tom King's eyes fill with 'an unwonted moisture' and, alone in the Domain, he too cries.

Jack London had watched in Sydney when, for him and for the crowd, the wrong man won. Like Tom

King, he too was troubled by his own physical weakness and deterioration. Like Tom's, his finances were a mess and he had dependents (his mother, step-siblings, wife, ex-wife and daughters) who all needed their share. At thirty-three he too felt that his time in the 'ring' was drawing to a close. *A Piece of Steak* was written directly from the heart. Devoid of sentimentality, spare and vivid, the story packs an emotional punch the reader does not soon forget.

⚶

A Piece of Steak appeared in *The Saturday Evening Post* in November 1909 and earned Jack five hundred dollars. Two years later he published *The Cruise of the Snark* and *South Sea Tales*, then began writing *John Barleycorn*, a memoir about his drinking binges. It's a courageous and groundbreaking book which added greatly to the impetus of Prohibition in America. Once again, it shows Jack London's honesty as a writer: 'I was carrying a beautiful alcoholic conflagration around with me. The thing fed on its own heat and flamed the fiercer. There was no time in all my waking time, that I didn't want a drink'. From that moment, when he still churned out a thousand words per day, his writing began to deteriorate. He kept writing to earn money, but the money went out faster than it came in. Generous to the end, Jack paid a fifty dollar per month annuity to an Australian woman who had lost both her sons. He and Charmian had their own loss to cope with—their baby girl died two days after her birth. Jack established Beauty Ranch, a magnificent property in California's Sonoma Valley, where he pioneered agricultural methods and planted sixty-five thousand eucalypts which flourish there to this day. But the ranch was beset by disasters, cost a fortune to run, and the dream home 'Wolf House' which Jack designed burned down just before construction was complete.

Physically, like his character Tom King, he was washed up. The body once compared to a Greek God's was flabby and tired. It was also scarred; the Australian medicines had left deep troughs in his skin. His kidneys were packing up, poisons began to accumulate in his body, he was tormented by headaches and bad dreams. Charmian nursed him with devotion, but in the days before renal dialysis there was little she could do. In spite of it all, his literary pilgrimage continued; he devoured books and discussed them with all who came near. Only months before he died he wrote to Joseph Conrad to thank him for the sleepless night he'd just spent reading *Victory*. Conrad replied, 'immensely touched', and sent 'a grateful and cordial handgrasp' across the oceans they had both sailed.[11]

In November 1916, reading *Around Cape Horn*, a travel book about a sea voyage, and while taking notes for a new book on a socialist theme, Jack London died. He was only forty years of age, but almost fifty books had been written during that short, dramatic life.

The plaque at Sydney's Circular Quay which commemorates Jack London's visit to Australia states his personal credo for life: 'I would rather be ashes than dust, a spark burnt out in a brilliant blaze, than be stifled in dry rot . . . For man's chief purpose is to live, not to exist: I shall not waste my days trying to prolong them; I shall use my time'. There's now little other evidence

11 Jack wrote to Joseph Conrad from Hawaii, where he spent some of his last months.

that Jack London's path once blazed briefly across Australia. Yet, in subtle ways, Australians still feel the impact of his visit. He helped to popularise surfing around the world and was one of the first writers to turn sport into exciting fiction. Farming techniques that he pioneered in California, such as the development of the first liquid manure and the first cultivation of alfalfa, are currently used in Australia. His journalism after the Burns–Johnson fight further entrenched the 'White Australia' policy which had long-lasting effects, still felt and debated today.

Jack London was a social and industrial reformer, an adventurous traveller, a pioneer farmer and an acutely observant journalist. He was also a formidable storyteller. *The Call of the Wild* has been translated into over eighty different languages and remains, deservedly, an American classic. Australians can feel proud that one of his best stories has an Australian setting. Grapes from the vines he planted at Beauty Ranch today produce the Kenwood 'Jack London' range of wines which are now available in Australia. So, with a glass of his Merlot or his Cabernet Sauvignon in hand, all Australians who appreciate good literature can, in a most appropriate way, raise a toast to the memory of a writer who visited and left his mark.

The plaque for
Jack London
at Sydney's
Circular Quay.

CHAPTER EIGHT

Sir Arthur Conan Doyle

As Sir Arthur Conan Doyle set sail on the RMS *Naldera* from England to Fremantle, the Presbyterians of Australia sent up fervent prayers to heaven that he'd be shipwrecked and drowned. And yet Conan Doyle[1] was a famous author, loved around the world for his creation of Sherlock Holmes. Australians should have been welcoming him with warmth, eager to hear about the great fictional

---

1   Mary and Charles Doyle named their son Arthur Ignatius Conan Doyle. Conan was a family name, but was not part of his surname, which was simply Doyle. However, he published his works under his full name and custom has dictated that he is referred to not as 'Doyle', but as 'Conan Doyle' or as 'Sir Arthur Conan Doyle', which are the names used in this book. He was knighted in 1902 and then became Sir Arthur Conan Doyle.

Sir Arthur Conan Doyle on board the RMS Naldera *on his way to Australia.*

detective and the mysteries he'd solved. Why were some of them hoping he would never reach these shores?

The problem was that Conan Doyle had made it all too clear that he was *not* coming to Australia to talk about Sherlock Holmes; there would be no talk of the rational, logical detective and his scientific friend and colleague, Dr Watson. Instead, Conan Doyle would be talking of the irrational, the unproven and the illogical, although of course he didn't see it that way himself. Séances and fairies were to be his subject matter. He would tell of the dead returning to chat to the living at table-rapping sessions and through spirit mediums. He would display objects which he was convinced had been brought by spirits from the afterlife. He would check out local psychic mediums and assess the current state of spiritual health in Australia. In fact, his aim was nothing less than to convert as many Australians as possible to Spiritualism. But as the praying Presbyterians well knew, most Australians had no desire to be converted.

There was nothing daunting for Sir Arthur Conan Doyle in the idea of travelling as far as Australia—his sixty-one years had included a lot of travel. Born in Edinburgh in 1859, the son of an artist, he'd left Scotland for Lancashire to attend a Catholic school, then gone to Austria for a year at a Jesuit institution and back to Edinburgh to study medicine at its prestigious university. He'd been lucky to survive two dangerous sea voyages as a young man, the first whaling in the Arctic and the second as ship's doctor on an expedition to West Africa. In his work as a doctor he'd settled in Southsea and then moved to London. He had lived in various homes in the south of England, and had enjoyed holidays in France, Ireland, Egypt, the Sudan, Germany, Switzerland, Canada and America. Some of these trips were made as part of a search to find a climate suited to his consumptive first wife, Louise. As a doctor, he'd taken part in the Boer War in South Africa, and he had visited the Western front in World War I. Travel had been a regular part of his life by the time he set off for Australia in 1920.

Conan Doyle trained as a doctor, but it was not medicine that had made him famous. In fact, so few patients came to consult him in his Southsea practice that he found himself with time on his hands and a growing family to support. He'd always had a love of literature and so he picked up his pen, hoping to earn a few pounds by publishing a story, and turned his mind back to a remarkable man he'd met at Edinburgh University. Dr Joseph Bell, one of his lecturers, was an inscrutable observer, a man able to deduce a great deal about a person's career, background and illness from the condition of his hands and clothing. This ability to make instant diagnoses from minimal evidence seemed like a party trick, but always had a rational explanation. Doyle put aspects of his teacher into the character he now began to create, a man initially called Sherrinford Holmes. This character acquired a friend and housemate at 221B Baker Street, Dr Ormond Sacker, and gradually the two fictional men took on the traits and the names of Sherlock Holmes and Dr John Watson. It was in 1887, with the publication of *A Study in Scarlet*, that the reading public first met these characters, who earned for their creator a welcome twenty-five pounds. The story was not an instant hit, but Holmes and Watson soon caught the public's imagination and editors asked for more stories. Just five years after Holmes' first appearance in print *The Strand Magazine* was paying Doyle one thousand pounds for six stories. Medicine gave way so Conan Doyle could write full time.

Sherlock Holmes brought him fame, but was always regarded by his creator as a distraction—useful for bringing in money, but not befitting his true vocation as a writer. In between Holmes stories Conan Doyle worked hard at historical novels, all painstakingly researched and sometimes very dull. *Micah Clarke*, *The White Company* and *Sir Nigel* were the books Sir Arthur Conan Doyle wished to be remembered for. Much better are his racy *Brigadier Gerard* stories set in the Napoleonic era, and *The Lost World* about dinosaurs and pterodactyls discovered in the jungles of South America; but those books have not really endured in the public taste either, whereas Sherlock Holmes took on a life of his own and is familiar to everyone from books, films, TV, cartoons and advertising.[2]

It is not surprising, therefore, that when his creator decided on his own bit of literary murder and sent Sherlock Holmes plunging down the Reichenbach Falls, locked in the fatal grip of his arch enemy Moriarty, the reading public went into mourning. *The Strand Magazine* was bombarded with letters of outrage and grief and editors offered vast sums of money for Holmes to be brought back to life. For a while he resisted, but the temptation to do so finally became too great and Conan Doyle succumbed. For the inducement of five thousand pounds for six new stories he resuscitated Holmes in 1903 and some of the best stories and novels in the canon appeared after that date. Conan Doyle never again attempted to kill off his hero, but instead sent him into retirement as a beekeeper on the Sussex Downs, to be hauled back into literary life if the mood took him or if financial problems ever made it necessary.

Sir Arthur Conan Doyle could easily have been an Australian. His father, Charles Altamont Doyle, was an artistic drunkard who failed to support his family on his meagre earnings from art. Just before the birth of his son he seriously considered trying a little gold-prospecting in Australia and talked of emigrating. In the end, he never went, but young Arthur could have seen the light of his first day on an Australian goldfield. It is no surprise that

---

2 More film versions have been made of *The Hound of the Baskervilles* than of any other novel.

he went on to put Australian references into his works and was pleased to have the opportunity to eventually visit.

He first began to connect Australia with crime when he was a schoolboy and read about a sensational case of fraud when an Australian butcher claimed to be Roger Tichborne, heir to an English fortune. The ensuing trial was a Jarndyce and Jarndyce of a case that kept the courts occupied from April 1873 to February 1874. Arthur was fascinated by every detail, wrote to his parents asking them to keep newspaper accounts, and questioned those staff members at Stonyhurst, his school, who had actually attended the trial.

It was inevitable, then, that when his mind turned to crime, or crimes, that could be solved by Sherlock Holmes, he should scatter Australian references through the stories, many of them concerning those goldfields that might have been his infant playground had his father gone ahead with emigration. In *The Boscombe Valley Mystery*, John Turner (or 'Black Jack of Ballarat') and Charles McCarthy are miners who have turned to bushranging. In *The Adventure of the 'Gloria Scott'*, Armitage is shipped out as a convict on the ship *Gloria Scott*, but escapes and eventually makes a fortune on the Australian goldfields. In *The Sign of Four* the grounds of Pondicherry Lodge have been so dug over in the search for a missing treasure that Dr Watson is reminded of the diggings at Ballarat, thus making it clear that he at least has been to Australia even if his creator has not. Goldfields were violent places and Conan Doyle reflects this in his stories too. In *The Disappearance of Lady Frances Carfax* the villain Henry 'Holy' Peters is 'one of the most unscrupulous rascals that Australia has ever evolved—and for a young country it has turned out some very finished types'. A 'saloon-fight in Adelaide' has left Peters with a jagged ear, by which he can be identified by Holmes. A murder victim in *The Adventure of the Empty House* is the son of a 'governor of one of the Australian colonies', while Mary Fraser and her maid Theresa in *The Adventure of the Abbey Grange* are South Australians.

Violence and gold-diggers make good fodder for detective fiction, but Conan Doyle did not focus only on that side of Australian life, aware that there were more positive aspects. A keen sportsman, he had long admired the Aussie cricketers (and on the sea voyage out was given the honour of captaining England against Australia in a deck-cricket match). He came also to greatly admire the Australian soldiers he encountered first in the Boer War (where, like Rudyard Kipling, he was asked to write for *The Friend*, a newspaper for the troops), and then again in World War I. He visited Amiens where Australian troops were bravely holding the town and also Mont St Quentin, 'the taking of which by the Australians was one of the feats of the war'. 'The reckless dare-devilry, combined with a spice of cunning' gave the Australian soldiers, he felt, 'a place of their own in the Imperial ranks'. The Diggers returned the compliment and were impressed by his courage under heavy artillery fire. At the front he lunched with Sir John Monash, Officer in Charge of the Australian forces, approving the splendid job he was doing. He also noted 'the perfect equality of the Australian system, which would have the best man at the top, be he who he might'—so different from the English system where promotion was still heavily based on birth and social class. He formed these judgements over the four days in September 1918 that he spent at Peronne with twelve hundred sodden but cheerful Diggers.

He knew about the goldfields and the sportsmen, he was aware of the Australian effort in the war, but none of his encounters with Aussies had given him any idea of how they responded to Spiritualist doctrines. When invited by Australian Spiritualists to come and lecture to the converted and unconverted, Conan Doyle couldn't resist the opportunity, hoping he might find Australians who were wavering on the edge of conversion to Spiritualism. There might be others just like himself. After all, he'd been mildly interested in Spiritualism for many years before his own conversion—his father had drawn spirit figures and chosen occult subjects to paint. Most Scots were aware of people with 'second-sight', and knew that Edinburgh was considered a particularly 'haunted' city. As a young doctor in Southsea, Conan Doyle had attended lectures on hypnotism and phrenology, on witchcraft and séances. But, like Sherlock Holmes, he had wanted proof, some sort of scientific evidence of what was going on. For years he remained unconvinced, but still attracted. After all, he was busy with other things—a large extended family depended on him financially, he wrote prolifically, was a keen sportsman who played regular cricket and golf and went on skiing holidays, and he was involved in the political and legal issues of the day. But amidst all that activity, something was lacking. He had early rejected the Catholic faith he'd been born into and was in need of something to replace it. The sense that some other dimension was missing from life was a feeling shared by many others at that time. For many, this lack was filled by Spiritualism.

By the end of World War I Spiritualism had become a flourishing concern. The loss of loved sons, fathers and husbands left many yearning for communication with those who had died. In the view of many, traditional religion had failed to answer questions about the evil unleashed by a world war, and the church had proved unable to provide comfort for all those who grieved. Soon there were fraudulent mediums aplenty ready to trade off this misery and need. Whether because of, or in spite of, the charlatans, many ordinary people were converted and the movement enjoyed unprecedented popularity. Conan Doyle was one of those who grieved—his eldest son Kingsley, his younger brother Innes, two brothers-in-law and a nephew had all died in the war. The séance table offered the one hope of reconnecting with them and Conan Doyle, like so many others, rushed to try. There he met with success and was able, through a medium, to talk to his loved ones on 'the other side'. At one spirit session he finally found the proof he needed to make his conversion complete. The spirits told him something known only to himself and his dead brother-in-law, Malcolm Leckie, and from that moment, as he revealed to a Sydney audience while on tour, his conviction in its truth had never wavered. Conan Doyle was not a man to do anything half-heartedly: he plunged into a hectic schedule of public lectures, donated large sums of money to Spiritualist movements and rushed into print on the topic.

Jeering from the press did not deter him: 'I seemed suddenly to see that this subject with which I had so long dallied was not merely a study of a force outside the rules of science, but that it was really something tremendous, a breaking down of the walls between two worlds'. Conversations with his dead son left him determined that others must share such joyful experiences. As he wrote in a poem to his son:

> When I heard thy well-known voice,
> Son of mine,
> Should I silently rejoice,
> Or incline
> To strike harder as a fighter,
> That the heavy might be lighter,
> And the gloomy might be brighter
> At a sign.

By the time he embarked on his voyage to Australia Conan Doyle was an experienced Spiritualist. He'd spoken six times with his dead son, twice with his brother and once with Oscar, his nephew. Many of these 'chats' were on private matters. Soon, he hoped, any Australians feeling 'gloomy' over the loss of loved ones would 'be brighter' for the comfort he was bringing them. This was his life's work: 'All other work which I had ever done, or could ever do, was as nothing compared to this'. He saw Australians as particularly worthy recipients of his message:

> I had spent some never-to-be-forgotten days with
> Australian troops at the very crisis of the war.
> My heart was much with them. If my message
> could bring consolation to bruised hearts and to
> bewildered minds ... then to whom should I carry
> it rather than to those who had fought so splendidly
> and lost so heavily in the common cause?

Even when he heard that some Aussies were praying for his death by drowning as he travelled towards them, he was not deterred. Like an ardent missionary, he was determined to bring them spiritual comfort, whether they wanted it or not.

Conan Doyle's second wife Jean, (his first, Louise, having died of tuberculosis in 1906), their children Denis, Adrian and Jean, who were aged eleven, nine and seven, the children's nanny Jakeman, and Major Wood, a friend and secretary, all set forth together. Jean had most conveniently discovered within herself a talent for automatic writing during séances. This was writing that appeared to be out of the control of the person holding the pen, guided totally by a spirit with a message to convey. In Australia Jean would assist her husband at private séances, something that can't have thrilled the dead Kingsley when he was called up by the spirit medium—the child of Conan Doyle's first marriage, Kingsley had had no love for his stepmother. Throughout the trip Jean would sit at her husband's right hand during every lecture and aid in fanning 'that smouldering glow of truth which already existed in Australia, into a more lively flame'. Tickets for the group's passage to Australia on the RMS *Naldera* cost sixteen hundred pounds, but profits from lectures would go to the cause, after all expenses had been deducted. Even if they failed to carry the message of truth to all Australians, at least they would all have a long family holiday.

As it turned out, the Presbyterians' prayers were *not* answered and the Doyles arrived safely in Western

Australia. The sea voyage had been refreshing and relaxing—deck-cricket, silent movies, time ashore in Gibraltar, Marseilles and Crete, and some whale watching—and Conan Doyle had kept in training by giving talks on Spiritualism to fellow passengers. He knew he'd need all his energy for the months ahead, for 'the lectures would be numerous, controversies severe, the weather at its hottest', but it was still exciting when on 17 September 1920 'a low coast appeared upon the port bow—Australia at last'.

A friendly letter from Prime Minister Billy Hughes was there for him on arrival, and a deputation of West Australian Spiritualists came on board with bunches of wild flowers for Jean. Time did not permit Conan Doyle to lecture in Perth but, unwilling to disappoint the faithful who turned up to greet him, he made plans to return there at the end of his visit to Australia. There was time for only a glimpse of Perth. They were taken for a drive along the Swan River and through King's Park, then into town for a lunch which impressed them all as being 'good and abundant'. Denis and Adrian, both overweight, found the Australian food much to their liking.

Not so impressive was the sight of local Aboriginals: 'Those poor black fellows! Their fate is a dark stain upon Australia', Conan Doyle noted. Yet he also wondered what on earth the settlers were supposed to do when Aboriginals speared their cattle. He felt it was too much to expect white farmers not to retaliate. Like so many before and since, Conan Doyle had no solution to the problem and he could only see it as a 'piteous tragedy'. In New Zealand two months later, he would compare the Aboriginals unfavourably with the Maori people:

'But the noble Maori is a man with whom one could treat on equal terms and he belonged to a solid race. The Aboriginals of Australia were broken wandering tribes, each at war with its neighbours'.

The Doyles reached South Australia after a calm journey across the Bight and arrived to find Adelaide rejoicing that a two-year drought had just broken. One countrywoman told Conan Doyle that her child of five had never seen rain—an astonishing concept for a Scotsman! He noted with sympathy the escalating prices of animals and crops as a result of the drought: a sheep which would normally have sold for fifteen shillings was retailing at three pounds. With a drunkard for a father, Conan Doyle was abstemious, but still enjoyed a visit to a South Australian vineyard. So impressed was he by the hard work that went into viticulture, he resolved that in future he'd pay his wine bills with better grace. His prediction that one day the world would know Australian wines was an accurate one, and Adelaide itself he thought 'so pretty, so orderly and so self-sufficing'.

But he had come to work, not to play. Even before leaving the ship, he conducted three press interviews, answered challenges for debates with Materialists and the Christian Evidence Society, and met his lecture tour agent Carlyle Smythe. He also set out from the Grand Central Hotel to visit local mediums to catch up on the news with his dead son.

Conan Doyle's first Australian lecture took place on 25 September 1920 in the Adelaide City Hall. Clearly the praying Presbyterians were in the minority in Adelaide for every seat was full, with two thousand in attendance. As the *Register* reported, 'Many of the intellectual leaders of the city were present . . . It cannot be doubted, of

Sir Arthur Conan Doyle (seated) with his Australian lecture tour agent Carlyle Smythe.

course, that the brilliant literary fame of the lecturer was an attraction'. The audience listened with rapt attention. Throughout his tour Conan Doyle presented a number of different talks—'Death and the Hereafter', 'The Vital Message' and 'Recent Psychic Evidence' were some of the choices on offer. He arrived with notes, but frequently disregarded them once he warmed to his subject. At six feet tall, and a decidedly heavy man, Conan Doyle was an impressive figure on the platform. All who heard him during the tour agreed that he spoke well, his light

Scottish accent sounding sincere and reasoned, rather than hectoring. Many applauded his message, gave him flowers or wrote to thank him for his efforts: 'I feel sure that many mothers who have lost their sons in the war, will, wherever you go, bless you, as I do, for the help you have given', wrote one bereaved woman. Not everyone, however, was won over. 'May you be struck dead before you leave this Commonwealth' was the curse of one man. The abusive cries and the hate mail which arrived daily did not dishearten Conan Doyle, but instead convinced him that his work was badly needed in Australia. He gave five talks in Adelaide, one attended by the Governor of South Australia, Sir Archibald Weigall, and his wife.

He also presented two exhibitions of psychic photographs. Conan Doyle was proud of the 'choice samples' in this weird and wonderful collection, especially of those demonstrating the psychic phenomenon of 'ectoplasm'. 'Ectoplasm' was a viscous, jelly-like substance used by spirits to build up temporary forms and show material evidence of their presence. Photos of spirit mediums with this revolting, gooey mess issuing from their mouths were a prized part of his collection. Other photos depicted vague spirit faces floating in the background, shining brightly. Most extraordinary of all were the photographs of fairies, showing tiny winged female forms fluttering past a young girl in a garden. These, known as the 'Cottingley Fairy' photos were supposedly taken on a Midg camera by sixteen-year-old Elsie Wright and her ten-year-old cousin Frances Griffiths, and then developed by Elsie's father, a photographer who lived in Cottingley, Yorkshire. Conan Doyle had been given the pictures just before his departure. It seems astonishing that the creator of the super-logical, rational Sherlock Holmes could have

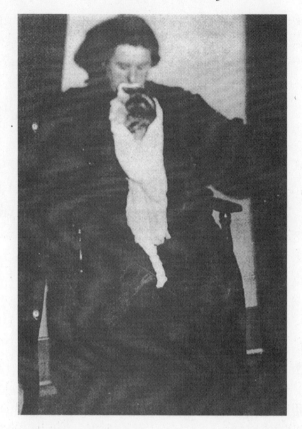

Spirit medium Eva Cox with ectoplasm issuing from her mouth. The manifestation is supposedly of a dead girl. This is one of the photographs Sir Arthur Conan Doyle brought to Australia as part of his 'choice' collection.

believed in the authenticity of these pictures and expected Australians to be excited by them, but to Conan Doyle they were simply marvellous proof. The girls in the photos were, he was positive, far too young to lie about what they saw. Besides, his two sons had seen sprites with their own eyes and would never dream of lying to him!

In 1922 in the face of public ridicule he published *The Coming of the Fairies*. Of course, it would later be established that his precious photos were frauds. The images had been cut out of *Princess Mary's Gift Book* and cleverly included in the photos, but in Australia Conan Doyle was filled with excitement at this genuine proof that spirits took on fairy forms and fluttered around the

This photo of the Cottingley fairies was first brought to Australia by Conan Doyle who, convinced it was genuine, showed it as part of his photographic collection. The picture and other similar photos were later exposed as fakes.

earth.[3] Australians just didn't know what to make of this startling photographic exhibition. Some photographers challenged their authenticity but failed to prove them fakes. The Aussie crowds came, looked and went away nonplussed.

Having written of bushrangers, Conan Doyle was keen to see the Australian bush and before leaving Adelaide, made time for such a trip with Denis and Adrian. There he admired the brilliant yellow wattle, a 'hideous lizard with open mouth', laughing jackasses and possums, and chatted with a strange old English eccentric who lived in the bush caring for local wildlife. If there *were* fairies in Australia, this man insisted, then they would be black ones, but Conan Doyle was uncertain what to say about the racial categorisation of fairies. Then it was off to Melbourne on the overnight train. It was light enough when they passed through Ballarat for him to experience a strange sense of déja-vu at the pitted landscape of the diggings which his own Dr Watson had seen in *The Sign of Four*, but which he'd never seen himself.

3 Elsie Wright admitted fifty years later that the photos had been an elaborate hoax.

Melbourne, spiritually speaking, was 'stony soil' and the five weeks he spent in the city were weeks of argument and abuse. The Presbyterians outnumbered the faithful and Conan Doyle had to deal with more scepticism and disapproval than he'd encountered so far. *The Argus* attacked him viciously, railing against the 'black evil', 'witchcraft' and 'shamanism' he'd brought to Melbourne. An editor described him as 'a force which we believe to be purely evil', while another headline read: 'The Five Fruits of Spiritualism: Fraud, Insanity, Depravity, Anti-Christianity and Futility'.

Had he been his own villainous creation Moriarty, he could hardly have drawn more opprobrium upon himself. For the first time in Australian history various religious sects and the agnostics united—they all agreed to vilify Sir Arthur Conan Doyle. 'Never in any British town have I found such reactionary intolerance', he concluded. He was cross that the press ignored his psychic photographs entirely, he had trouble getting large enough venues and had to speak at The Playhouse which seated only twelve hundred, and even the Spiritualists of Melbourne, who welcomed him warmly, had 'a tendency to divide and to run into vulgarities'.

Sightseeing came as a much-needed break from the media storm that surrounded him. Conan Doyle enjoyed a VFL game which he found 'extraordinarily fast' and thought an excellent spectator sport. Rugby had been his game at school, so he was used to violence on the field, but he'd never before witnessed a game where, on the blowing of the final whistle, 'a troop of mounted police cantered over the ground and escorted

*Sir Arthur
Conan Doyle at
his Melbourne
Town Hall
lecture on
12 November
1920.*

the referees to the safety of the pavilion'. He was
made an honorary member of the Melbourne Cricket
Club, which delighted him, but he chose not to watch
one of Australia's most famous sporting events, the
Melbourne Cup. Horseracing was, to him, 'the curse
of the country' and the famous Cup was an especially
'virulent bout' of racing fever. He regarded the event
as unsettling to decent people and a danger to honesty.
In his view, the Catholic Church should be ashamed
for allowing it to take place each year uncriticised and
he wondered how any sane nation could allow such
yearly madness to continue. He and Jean took their
children for a quiet day at a deserted St Kilda beach
instead. Such behaviour would not have endeared
him to Melburnians. As well as the sporting events, he
watched the procession of the new Governor General,
Lord Forster, make its ceremonial entrance into the city
(he knew Lord Forster from working on the Olympic
Games committee with him in London). He and Jean

attended lunches and dined with the Prime Minster, Billy Hughes, who was very deaf and talked too much. Sir Joseph Cook (former Prime Minister of Australia) proposed a toast to him.

There was one man in Melbourne who Conan Doyle was desperate to meet. Charles Bailey, a former bootmaker, was an 'apport medium', that is, a Spiritualist who specialised in bringing objects from a distance or from back in time. Conan Doyle had read candid accounts of Bailey being tested.[4] The man, after being thoroughly searched, was tied up in a large empty bag. He then began his 'apportising' and in these test conditions, managed to bring into the room 138 different articles—coins, newspapers, a leopard skin, precious stones, a de-fanged rock python, and even a sizeable shark entangled in seaweed! After reading this extraordinary account, Conan Doyle felt this was a man he just had to meet. The French had denounced Bailey as a fraud in 1910, so Conan Doyle approached him with some caution—he knew there were unscrupulous tricksters out there, eager to prey on ardent Spiritualists. But the man, he felt, must be given a fair chance and he was furious when he heard that before one session Bailey had been rectally searched. He met with Bailey twice while in Melbourne. At the first sitting, ten guests were invited, but it was a baffling session, producing only a slight attempt at the materialisation of a head, and a message written in bad Italian. Spirit hands were glimpsed in the darkness, but when Conan Doyle tried to grasp them, he was sharply reprimanded. The second sitting was more successful. Bailey was searched, lights turned off and Bailey went into a trance, chatting

4   A report by Dr CW McCarthy gave details of the test
    conditions Bailey underwent.

fluently to a Babylonian King. Suddenly he called out 'Ah! Here it is' and asked for the bag enclosing him to be opened. A tiny bird's nest was produced, complete with egg. The bird's nest was proof enough for Conan Doyle. Although he knew that ancient Egyptian amulets 'retrieved' by Bailey on previous occasions had been proven fakes by the British Museum, he was convinced that Bailey was a genuine medium who could bring objects across the divide between the living and the dead, and who could communicate with spirits.

Further proof of the spiritual hopelessness of Melburnians came with a story he heard while in the city. Mr Junor Browne, a local worthy, had lost two sons tragically in a boating accident. Frank Browne, one of those sons, made a ghostly appearance at a séance to reveal that his arm had been ripped off by a huge fish unlike any shark he had ever seen. Frank's body had not yet been found, but some weeks later fishermen caught a very rare deep-sea species of shark and Frank's watch was found inside it. Surely, Conan Doyle felt, incidents such as this were testament enough. Why would the people of Melbourne not listen and be converted?

A Melbourne voice medium, Susanna Harris, gave him four sittings. She'd been tested with her mouth full of coloured water, yet still produced a range of twenty different voices speaking from the spirit world. Conan Doyle felt he achieved true psychic results with her. Another medium, Mr Love, was controlled by a Chinaman called Quong, but Conan Doyle heard that Quong spoke in tongues when Ghurkhas and Chinese sages spoke through him from the world of the dead. No matter how busy his lecturing schedule, and there were talks in Bendigo and Geelong to fit in as well as those in Melbourne, he always made time for what he regarded as more important than anything else—his 'spiritual' health.

The Botanic Gardens were a favourite spot for the whole family to relax—'the most beautiful place I have ever seen'; he was impressed by the statue of explorers Burke and Wills, but so concerned that there was no plaque stating who the figures were, that he wrote to the papers suggesting this omission be rectified (and it was). Another spot the Doyles loved was 'Nerrin-Nerrin' station, a property in Western Victoria belonging to the Hon. Agar Wynne. The children were left in Melbourne under Jakeman's reliable care while their parents set off on a slow 140-kilometre journey. Looking back on the visit, Conan Doyle felt the station holiday, after all the stress of negative publicity and criticism, had been a haven of rest and peace:

> We shall always, however, be able in our dreams to revisit that broad verandah, the low hospitable façade, the lovely lawn with its profusion of scented shrubs, the grove of towering gum trees, where the opossums lurked, and above all the great marsh where with dark clouds drifting across the moon we had stolen out at night to hear the crying of innumerable birds. That to us will always be the real Australia.

'Nerrin-Nerrin' had a huge lagoon, alive with fish, eels and waterbirds, and merino sheep, which were being shorn by a very new device, an electric shearing machine (which, he noted, left the poor animals badly cut).

There was no sadness in leaving Melbourne when the Doyles boarded a train for Sydney on November 13. He had done his best for them, but the Melburnians had not, on the whole, wanted to listen to his message. At first it looked as if there might be more of the same reaction in Sydney, with the press there at the station to greet him (and, in the first print article about his visit, getting his name wrong by calling him Sir Conan). But the reception at the station was warm, with resounding cries of 'Thank God you have come' from local Spiritualists, no doubt welcome after the hostile Melbourne reception. But were the crowds greeting the Spiritualist or the author? One old Digger was heard to ask who he was. 'The bloke that wrote Sherlock Holmes', an urchin replied. The press of *The Sydney Morning Herald* wanted to know if Holmes was dead as far as any more stories were concerned. But to all who asked Conan Doyle gave polite, but vague answers. As *The Sun* reported, 'He seemed surprised when questioned about Sherlock Holmes. The impression he gave was that he had more serious and important things nowadays to think about'.

Conan Doyle was impressed with Sydney—he'd had 'no idea it was so great a place'. However, like so many of the other literary visitors, he worried that Australians crowded into cities round the edges of their country, leaving a vast empty space in the middle. 'It seems a weak point of the Australian system that 41 per cent of the whole population dwell in six capital cities. The local civic amenities pleased him, the zoo was 'among the very best in the world', and the Harbour, naturally, enchanted him.

To his relief, he found Sydney in a better spiritual state of health than Melbourne. Attendance at his lectures was all he had hoped for, even when an 'England versus Australia' cricket match offered a rival attraction. About 3500 turned up at the Town Hall, and he received a standing ovation after speaking for two hours. But there was no escaping controversy entirely. The press caricatured him, irate Christians screamed at him that his certainty of physical existence after death was blasphemous, the Plymouth Brethren branded him a devil, and anti-witchcraft agitators heckled him. Outside the Town Hall picketers denounced him as an Anti-Christ and even accused him of being Jack the Ripper. His beloved photographic display was mocked and its authenticity challenged, and the huge postbag that was delivered every day contained a good proportion of hate mail.

Conan Doyle tried to shrug it off: 'Wherever I go there are two great types of critics. One is the materialistic gentleman who insists on his right to eternal nothingness. The other is the gentleman with such a deep respect for the Bible that he has never looked into it'. He reasoned that 'if Spiritualism had been a popular cult in Australia, there would have been no object in my visit'. The attacks only made him feel that his work and his preaching were desperately needed and he consoled himself with the thought that 'any publicity is good publicity'. As there were over 500 articles in the press about him and his mission during his time in Australia, he certainly got the publicity he desired.

In between Sydney lectures there was the joy of the beach. The Doyles had gone first to Petty's Hotel in York Street, but soon moved to Manly's Pacific Hotel so the children could enjoy the sand and surf. Conan Doyle loved swimming in the waves—'a real romp with Nature'—and looked with interest at surfboards, which he had never seen. Although 'told that there were men competent to ride them', to his disappointment he saw no surfers in action. He picked up a jellyfish whose blue colour he admired, and was stung for his efforts; got seasick on a Harbour cruise and watched the England XI play New South Wales at cricket. (NSW won, but the barrackers were badly behaved.) The Pacific Hotel turned out to have a good psychic aura. Restless and unable to sleep one night, Conan Doyle was suddenly aware of a strong smell of ether and felt himself being wafted away into an intensely sound sleep, in what he felt was a deep spiritual experience.

Manly was a good place to leave Jean and the children while he set off for New Zealand on the *Maheno*.[5] His agent had arranged a whistlestop tour of Auckland, Wellington, Christchurch and Dunedin (a city whose intense Scottishness appealed to him). Feeling he was in 'enough hot water without seeking out a geyser', he avoided Rotorua. New Zealand provided the weirdest Spiritualist encounter of his whole trip—a session with a clairvoyant fox terrier, which barked answers to questions and could foretell the future. Darkie attempted to tell him how many coins he had in his pockets by the number of its barks, but was unfortunately having an off day when Conan Doyle called. In spite of the dog's obvious failure, he remained convinced that the animal 'clearly had these powers, though age and excitement have now impaired them'. Conan Doyle loved New Zealand: 'Every man looks on his own country as God's own country if it be a free land, but the New Zealander

---

5　Jean and the children did not stay in Manly all the
　　time Conan Doyle was away, but travelled to the Blue
　　Mountains to escape the city heat.

has more reasons than most'. New Zealand, he felt, stood 'supreme', above Canada, Australia and South Africa.

The joy he felt in being reunited with his family in Sydney was tempered by sadness at the news that awaited him there. 'The Ma'am', his adored mother, had died. Aged eighty-three and nearly blind, she had led a hard life caring for her depressed, alcoholic husband, and coping with the deaths of several children. She had refused to follow her son down the Spiritualist path, which had lessened the closeness of their relationship, but he hoped he'd soon be chatting to her over the séance table, even as he grieved 'that we should never see the kind face and gracious presence again in its old material form'.

Next stop was Brisbane. The original tour had included Tasmania, but strikes made it too hard to get there and necessitated a change of plan. Conan Doyle disapproved of striking workers: 'It is a terrible thing to see this young country frittering itself away in these absurd conflicts'. He suggested that fines and harsh penalties might sort out the problem, but was not optimistic anything would change as he saw the Labor Party as being too full of bullies.

The train trip to Brisbane on the old Darling Downs route took a boring, hot twenty-eight hours there. Exacerbating things was heat of more than one sort to encounter when he arrived: the clergy of Brisbane. This 'Abomination of the Lord', they demanded, must define his exact views in writing. During his tour, it was clear that many Australians were confused about his Spiritualist message, mistaking him for a fortune-teller, and filled his postbag every day with requests for advice about prospective marriage partners, future job promotions, and the best horse to back in the next race. Brisbane's heat was exhausting to a Scotsman, the mosquitoes—both of the real and the journalistic variety—plagued him, but the crowds still turned out to hear him speak. He was getting very tired, but the tour had to go on.

As Sir Arthur Conan Doyle had sent Sherlock Holmes into retirement on a bee farm, it was assumed that he was an expert on apiarism and so on 14 January 1921, he and Jean were taken to the largest bee farm in the country, Redbank Plains Apiary. Its owner, a Mr Jones, was horrified to find that Conan Doyle had no idea why the Queen Bee needed to be segregated. In fact, he'd never even seen a bee farm before thoughtlessly condemning Holmes to one in eternal retirement.

Another visit included the laying of a foundation stone for a Spiritualist church. Funds to complete the building had not yet been raised, but all present trusted to those 'who work with us on the other side to see the enterprise through'. Perhaps Bailey, the 'apport medium' would be able to whisk through enough money from the afterlife to enable those in this life to pay for the construction. A photograph taken at one public function showed Conan Doyle enveloped in a strange mist. No technical cause could be discovered and the photo became another exhibit in his psychic collection.

The return journey to Sydney was by ship on the *Orsova* and the family fled the January humidity for the fresher air of the Blue Mountains—'a little earthly paradise', with its kangaroos, wallabies, parrots and lizards. They loved the Medlow Bath Hotel, a restful place to summon energy for the farewell ceremonies and

*Sir Arthur
Conan Doyle
and his wife
Jean(centre)
visiting the
largest bee farm
in Australia,
near Brisbane.
Having sent
Sherlock
Holmes into
retirement as an
apiarist, Doyle
was supposed
to know a lot
about bees,
but didn't.*

lectures of the last days in Australia. Conan Doyle paid one final visit to Charles Bailey, the apport medium, and delighted in the Turkish coins and baby tortoises that were apported into the room. He had a session in Castlereagh Street with Mrs Foster Turner, reputed to have 'the highest general level of any sensitive in Australia' and was deeply impressed by what she told him. Then it was time for the goodbyes. A Spiritualist service was held at Stanmore Road, Enmore, to thank him for his mission and Jean for her loyal support. Finally the Doyles collapsed with relief onto the same ship that had delivered them to Australia, HMS *Naldera*. It took them back to Melbourne, on to Adelaide where thieves came on board, and then to Perth where he gave one last talk to a full house. On Friday 11 February 1921 the ship drew away from Australian shores. Whether the Presbyterians were still praying for it to sink has not been recorded.

Life magazine reported, 'The one thing clear is that Sir Conan Doyle's mission [they were still getting his name wrong in the press] to Australia was a mournful and complete failure'. His agent Carlyle Smythe declared it a total success. Conan Doyle had certainly done his best to deliver his message, with twenty-five talks, averaging 2000 people at each. The profits had enriched the coffers of the Spiritualist movement and many people had been touched and enlightened by his words. 'Long after you leave us your message will linger', read one farewell note. But he remained unconvinced about the tour's success: 'It is the unliveliness and spiritual deadness of this place which gets on my nerves'.

On top of that, there had been other irritations—the poor postal service, trains and ferries that were never on time, an inefficient telegraph service. To him such problems were all a sign of 'the failure of State control' and of a nation 'less disciplined' than it ought to be. He hated the big empty spaces of the country, regarding them as a danger—'that little fringe of people on the edge of that huge island can never adequately handle it'. 'History abhors a vacuum and finds someone to fill it up', he warned. Australia was to him 'like an enormous machine with a six horse-power engine to drive it'. The strikes, or threatened strikes, they encountered almost everywhere were anathema to a man who had climbed out of a poverty-stricken childhood by sheer hard work and ambition. He worried about the large numbers of disaffected Irish, the lack of a well-trained standing army, and the ignorance and bias of the press. The drunkenness he saw everywhere appalled him.

And yet, in spite of it all, he liked the Australians: 'A fine handsome body of people they are when you see them en masse, strong, solid and capable'. He thought they ate well and played well.

> We like the people here very much more than we had expected to, for one hears in England exaggerated stories of their democratic bearing. When democracy takes the form of equality one can get along with it, but when it becomes rude and aggressive one would avoid it. Here one finds a very pleasing good fellowship which no one would object to. Again and again we have met with little acts of kindness from people in shops or in the street, which were not personal to ourselves, but part of their normal good manners. If you ask the way or any other information, strangers will take trouble to put you right. They are kindly, domestic and straight in speech and dealings.

Unlike Rudyard Kipling, who had visited thirty years before, and found the Australians 'second hand American', Conan Doyle felt that it was the English who had been Americanised, while the Aussies were 'more English than the English'. Nevertheless, he always returned to what he saw as Australia's greatest problem—that 'materialism and want of vision', and that 'moral cowardice' when it came to embracing Spiritualism. Most had not wanted the message he had brought. He had failed to convert the masses and could only conclude: 'They are dear folk, these Australians; but, Lord, they want spirituality and dynamiting out of their groves'.

❈

When Sir Arthur Conan Doyle left Australia he continued apace with Spiritualist activity. He established a psychic-themed bookshop and museum in London. He continued to lecture in Paris, America, Belgium, South Africa, Rhodesia, Kenya, Holland, Scandinavia and around Britain—five thousand people came to hear him speak at the Royal Albert Hall. He fought a campaign to have archaic witchcraft laws abolished as mediums were sometimes prosecuted under these laws, and he became President of the International Spiritualist Association.

When the famous mystery writer Agatha Christie disappeared in 1926, he took one of her gloves to a noted spiritualist medium, who reported that it belonged to a woman called Agatha, who was alive, and who would be heard from the following Wednesday. On that very day news broke that the missing writer had been located in a hotel in Harrogate, where she had registered under the name of her husband's mistress. Conan Doyle began advocating that the police should have a psychic on call at every station. He published books—*The Case for Spirit Photography* in 1922, *The History of Spiritualism* in 1926 (his assistant for this book was Leslie Curnow, a former journalist from *The Sydney Morning Herald*), *Pheneas Speaks* (Pheneas was his wife's personal spirit guide) and *The Edge of the Unknown*. As his old friends and relatives died off, he had an ever-growing number of people to contact through mediums. He, Jean and their children, who had grown up with séances a regular part of nursery life, had regular conversations with those who had passed over.

After returning from Australia, he wrote *The Wanderings of a Spiritualist* which was published in 1922. Dedicated 'To my Wife, This memorial of a journey which her help and presence changed from a duty to a pleasure', the book is a strange mix of travelogue and spiritualist propaganda. He even felt it necessary to preface the book with a warning about its controversial spiritualist content: 'Should the reader have no interest in psychic things . . . if indeed any human being can be so foolish as to not be interested in his own nature and fate—then this is the place to put the book down'. While the travel anecdotes are entertaining and of some interest to Australian historians, the book is heavily weighted towards Spiritualism and, unsurprisingly, has long been out of print.

Sir Arthur Conan Doyle died in 1930. The movement he had espoused reached its peak in the 1920s, and has never regained that degree of popularity. The 1930s ushered in the Depression, and then a world war, advances in technology and more complete exposure of fraudulent mediums. Today some Australians continue to dabble; there is an Australian Spiritualist Association, an Australian Ghost Hunters Society and an Association of Progressive Spiritualists. An Easter 2008 message from Dr Peter Jensen, Anglican Archbishop of Sydney, warned against attempts to communicate with the dead, or dangerous 'meddling in the occult', so perhaps the church senses a growing threat. If Sir Arthur Conan Doyle were to return now, he would find little evidence of any Spiritualist activity and might well have to agree with the press reporter who claimed that his 'mission' to Australia had been a total failure.

In all the Spiritualist activity of his last decade, Conan Doyle churned out stories, plays and novels with great regularity. Mistakenly, he converted the irascible Professor Challenger of *The Lost World* to Spiritualism in *The Land of Mist*, a dull, didactic story, crammed with pedantic footnotes. Fortunately Sherlock Holmes was spared the fate of being born again as a Spiritualist and in 1927 *The Casebook of Sherlock Holmes* was published, but it contains some of the poorest stories in the canon.

Sherlock Holmes has been a curious phenomenon. There's almost certainly no other fictional character whose image is so instantly recognisable around the world. Holmes has been absorbed into our culture, has become an archetypal figure; his deerstalker hat, pipe and magnifying glass are universally recognised as the symbols of intellectual rigour, visionary insight and extraordinary detective skills. 'Sherlockian' words and idioms have entered the dictionary of English and of other languages. 'Elementary, my dear Watson' is a very familiar quote.[6] Holmes' beaky profile adorns puzzles and board games, Toby Jugs, tins of tobacco and even the walls of the Baker Street tube station in London. His statue stands in many cities around the world. A recent poll in the UK revealed that the majority of school children believe that Sherlock Holmes really existed, and his 'Life' has been reconstructed from the books and

6 The phrase was in fact never spoken by Holmes in any of the stories, but was first used by PG Wodehouse in *Psmith Journalist* in 1915. However, it captured the essence of Holmes's character and speech and has been regularly used in Sherlock Holmes films and pastiches ever since.

written up in numerous biographies. Post addressed to Mr S. Holmes is still delivered in large quantities to 221B Baker Street. Sherlock Holmes has attained a life quite separate from that of his creator—he has outstripped Sir Arthur Conan Doyle and left him far behind. Sherlock Holmes societies are numerous and active around the world (the largest currently in Japan), but there is only one small Conan Doyle society. Sherlock Holmes is celebrated universally as the world's greatest detective— film, theatre, cartoons, radio, sequels, prequels, pastiches, adaptations, imitations, Sherlockiana of all descriptions, and the canon itself, ensure that he is alive and well in the world today. Sir Arthur Conan Doyle, on the other hand, is dimly remembered as a Victorian writer. His fame has been eclipsed by that of the intellectual superman he created and reluctantly continued to write about.

Sherlockian societies flourish in many major cities in Australia. These groups publish journals, hold conferences, give themselves names drawn from the Sherlock Holmes stories, and endlessly discuss Holmes' cases. Australian Sherlockians can delight in the knowledge that the detective's career began as the result of a journey to Australia. In *The Adventure of the 'Gloria Scott'*, published in *The Strand Magazine* in 1893, Holmes takes on his first case. A sailor from the *Gloria Scott* ship appears at an English country house and causes Mr Trevor, the father of one of Sherlock Holmes' friends, to suffer a fatal stroke. Victor Trevor begs his friend to look into the cause of his father's death, and Holmes then uncovers the sailor's murky past, his role in a mutiny and what actually happened on that voyage to Sydney. According to Sydney Sherlockians 'The Sydney Passengers' (named after those on that fateful journey), the Orient Hotel in George Street in The Rocks is the spot where the sailor would have landed. If he had *not* arrived safely in Sydney, able to one day return to England and threaten Mr Trevor with telling his tale of the mutiny, then Sherlock Holmes would never have become a detective. As Dr Watson records:

> I had often endeavoured to elicit from my companion what had first turned his mind in the direction of criminal research, but I had never caught him before in a communicative humour. Now he sat forward in his arm-chair, and spread out the documents upon his knees. Then he lit his pipe and sat for some time smoking and turning them over.

To honour the commencement of such a great career, 'The Sydney Passengers' unveiled a plaque on the Orient Hotel in 1993. But crime is clearly as alive and well in Australia as it was in Victorian London, for the plaque was stolen. *That* is one mystery that Australians are still waiting for Sherlock Holmes to come and solve.

ARTHUR CONAN DOYLE
1859–1930

We all devoted ourselves to
surf-bathing, spending a good deal of our day in
the water as is the custom of the place. It is a real
romp with Nature, for the great Pacific rollers come
sweeping in and break over you, rolling you over
on the sand if they can catch you unawares.
It was a golden patch in our restless lives.
THE WANDERINGS OF A SPIRITUALIST (1921)
SIR ARTHUR CONAN DOYLE, THE CREATOR OF
SHERLOCK HOLMES, VISITED AUSTRALIA
IN 1920–1921 DURING A SERIES OF
LECTURE TOURS ON SPIRITUALISM.

NSW MINISTRY FOR THE ARTS
WRITERS WALK

*The plaque
for Sir Arthur
Conan Doyle
at Sydney's
Circular Quay.*

CHAPTER NINE

Agatha Christie

There were hundreds of corpses in Agatha Christie's life—corpses bloated with poison, gory with blood, bodies pushed under passing cars, riddled with bullets, or shoved off cliffs, corpses injected with overdoses, strangled and smothered. How they met their gruesome ends and who killed them would reach Australia via the pages of her eighty-three detective novels, and would be as popular with Australians as they were with everyone else around the world. Indeed, those corpses would make Agatha Christie the best-loved novelist the world has ever known.

She was only at the beginning of her career as a writer when she travelled to Australia. *The Mysterious Affair at Styles* had been published two years before, introducing a dapper Belgian detective named Hercule Poirot to the world. The book sold two thousand copies and was widely serialised. She had also completed

*Agatha Christie
as she looked at
the time of her
visit to Australia
in 1922.*

The Secret Adversary, featuring Tommy and Tuppence Beresford, and had sent the manuscript to her publishers who brought it out as a book while she was away. Several Poirot stories, commissioned and written, but not yet in print, would appear as *Poirot Investigates* in 1924. And she was close to finishing *Murder on the Links*, which was published the year after her Australian travels. The bestselling novels, the world's longest-running play, the translations that made her the most translated writer of all time, the TV versions, movies, radio adaptations, comics and video games—all those aspects of the Agatha Christie phenomenon were still a few years ahead. In Australia she was just Mrs Christie, author of one book, who was travelling with her husband who had a job to do.

And that job was a most unusual one. Her husband, Archie Christie, was part of a Mission whose purpose was to promote a forthcoming 'Empire Exhibition' to be held in London in 1924 as a showcase for the products of the British Empire. The Great Exhibition of 1851, held in Crystal Palace, had been a wild success, with a third of the population of Great Britain turning out to see it. It had displayed to the world the extent, power and diversity of the British Empire. This new exhibition was designed to do the same and to find 'in the development and utilization of the raw materials of the Empire, new sources of Imperial wealth. To foster inter-Imperial trade and open fresh world markets . . . To make the different races of the British Empire better known to each other, and to demonstrate to the people of Britain the almost illimitable possibilities of the Dominions, Colonies, and Dependencies overseas'. In other words, this exhibition was intended to herald a great imperial revival and a justified sense of British pride after World War I. It was Archie Christie's job to make sure that the colonies knew what was planned, to drum up interest among businessmen and politicians, and to encourage manufacturers to send their raw materials and finished products to the exhibition.

The Mission was the brainchild of a man who had taught Archie at school, Major EA Belcher. A colourful character, self-important and eccentric, he would not have been out of place in an Agatha Christie novel himself—in fact, he would soon appear, thinly disguised, as Sir Eustace Pedler in *The Man in the Brown Suit*. Belcher's talent lay in persuading others into believing that he had talent, and in sponsoring his wild schemes and placing him in charge of them. During the war, for example, he had invented and then filled the position of 'Controller of Supplies of Potatoes'. Agatha recalled that in the Torquay hospital where she did war work, there was never a potato to be had: 'Whether the shortage was entirely due to Belcher's control of them I don't know, but I should not be surprised to hear it'. The man was inefficient and knew nothing at all about potatoes, admitting: 'I didn't know a thing. But I wasn't going to let on. I mean, you can do anything—you've only got to get a second-in-command who knows a bit about it, and there you are!' It's not surprising that the Empire Mission, dreamed up because Belcher fancied the idea of exotic travel, came to look more like a touring comedy company than a serious trade mission.

The members of the delegation included Belcher's secretary, Mr Francis Bates, an anxious, credulous young man, thought by Agatha to have 'the appearance of a villain in a melodrama' with a decidedly 'sinister aspect'. Then there was Mr Hiam, a man who did know something about root vegetables. He came from East Anglia, where he grew them, and his role within the Mission was that of Agricultural Adviser. Alongside him were his wife, a stout, vigorous woman of the type Agatha would later depict running an English village single-handedly, and their slight, nervous daughter Sylvia.

Then there was Archie, handsome, debonair Archie, who at their first meeting had whisked Agatha away from the partner to whom she had been promised, and who had turned her life into a whirlwind with his aeroplanes, his motorbikes and his charm. He proposed to her soon after they met, undeterred by his own small income and uncertain career. Agatha's mother was against the match, but the young couple were besotted. War intervened and Archie left for France; soon proving his daring and bravery in the Royal Flying Corps. While he was flying into danger and appearing in despatches, Agatha was nursing and working in hospitals and dispensaries in Torquay, gaining invaluable knowledge about which poisons could dispatch wealthy relatives most efficiently, leaving the fewest clues. When Archie came home on leave in late 1914, they could resist no longer and were married on Christmas Eve. After the war, he found work in the city and they settled in London. Baby Rosalind was born in 1919, but Archie was restless. After the dangers and challenges of the war, a life of stockbroking seemed dull and routine. He was unsettled and more than ready for a change when Major Belcher asked him to be financial manager of the Mission, even though it was a risk as there was no guarantee of a city job when he returned. He'd be paid one thousand pounds, with all his expenses covered, but he would be away from England for nearly a year.

Agatha adored travel and remembered the excitement of seeing Egypt which she'd visited in 1910. A tour round the world was more than she could resist, and Archie's pay would just cover her costs. Two-year-old Rosalind was left with Madge, Agatha's older sister, who disapproved of the tour. Rosalind would end up getting used to being left while her mother travelled, and relations and boarding schools often cared for her as she grew up. Occasionally, on this world tour, Agatha worried that the toddler might forget her mother and instructed her in a letter (this to a two-year-old who couldn't read!) that, if asked who she loved best, she must always answer 'Mummy'. And so, without baby, but with a little Corona typewriter, Agatha and Archie boarded the RMS *Kildonan Castle* on 20 January 1920, along with the ill-assorted party of the Mission, and set off to see the world.

Agatha and Archie Christie (Archie to the left of Agatha) setting off on board the RMS Kildonan Castle *with the other members of the Empire Exhibition Mission party. The temperamental Major Belcher is the one with the cane.*

Agatha hadn't been on the ship very long before she was desperate to get off it again. Seasickness prostrated her. Instead of promenading the deck with her adored Archie, she was stuck in her cabin, 'sick without ceasing', only wanting to die. She resolved to abandon ship in Madeira, their first port of call, and even had wild thoughts of finding work as a parlour-maid while Archie travelled on without her. But the ship's doctor dosed her with medicines, Archie dragged her up on deck in Madeira and fed her beef essence, and she gradually recovered. For the rest of the journey she participated in deck games, watched flying fish and porpoises, and enjoyed meals at the Chief Engineer's table, which grandly included some pheasants from the royal estates which the King himself had presented to Belcher for the Mission to enjoy. With seasickness behind her, she found the journey to Cape Town enormous fun.

The *Kildonan Castle* reached South Africa on February 6 and left again on April 9. Agatha made the most of her time there, relishing the summer heat, the elegant Mount Nelson Hotel (also a base for Kipling and Conan Doyle on their visits) and the beaches. 'Bathing with planks', as she called surfing, was tried for the first time and Agatha became addicted—she was still surfing, or at least trying to, well into her sixties. Mission business kept her busy with official luncheons and garden parties and there were unexpected excitements; a journey to Johannesburg found the party caught up in the Rand Rebellion. Although bombs could be heard going off in the distance and Martial Law was proclaimed while they were there, they escaped safely to Rhodesia. Agatha delighted in the Victoria Falls—'very wonderful'—and in the carved wooden animals which the locals offered for sale wherever they travelled. She purchased so many of these that they had to be shipped back to England in three crates. Later, she put just such hippos, zebras and elands into a novel and used a wooden giraffe as a handy place for hiding diamonds. Back in Cape Town they boarded a different ship, the SS *Aeneas* of the Blue Funnel Line. It was typical of Major Belcher that the Mission's route was made up as they went along, with nothing booked in advance or properly planned. India and Ceylon had been on the original itinerary, but when sailings proved complicated, this plan was changed. Belcher left before the Christies and headed for Australia. He told them to meet him in Adelaide, but when they reached South Australia they were met

Agatha Christie around the time of her visit to Australia, with a wooden hippo purchased in South Africa.

with more of his confused messages—he'd gone to Melbourne so they were to join him there and then they would all immediately set off for Tasmania to officially start Mission business there.

In *An Autobiography,* Agatha Christie writes 'From Australia we went to Tasmania', as if she'd crossed the ocean to another country. As with other literary travellers, she adored Tasmania, falling in love with Launceston whose Tamar River reminded her of her beloved Dart River back home, and with Hobart, 'incredibly beautiful Hobart, with its deep blue sea and harbour and its flowers, trees and shrubs'. She found the climate cold, but invigorating. Interested in local history, she went to the museum to look at 'death casts of several of the Aborigines'. The museum also had old prints, 'sketches and water colour drawings of the Tasmania of a 100 years ago—some of them perfectly lovely'.

But what she loved most about Tasmania were its trees: 'Trees are always the first things I seem to notice about places, or else the shape of hills. In England one becomes used to having dark trunks and light leafy branches. The reverse in Australia was quite astonishing. Silvery-white barks everywhere, and the darker leaves, made it like seeing the negative of a photograph. It reversed the whole look of the landscape'. In Tasmania she was constantly fascinated by the 'silvery-blue gums' and other colours of the bush:

> All Australian scenery that I have seen has a faintly austere quality, the distances all a soft blue green—sometimes almost grey—and the white trunks of the blue gums give a totally different effect, and here and there great clumps of trees have been ringbarked and have died, and then they are ghost trees, all white, with white waving branches. It's all so—virginal—if there were nymphs in the woods, they would never be caught.

Nymphs in the bush were all very well, but Major Belcher was there to remind her that they were on a mission. There was a power station 3000 feet up, and freezingly cold, to visit, the Mayor of Launceston to meet, speeches to give at the Town Hall (Belcher usually made the speeches and he did it well. By the time the tour was over, Agatha knew all his speeches off by heart), official receptions to attend, a jam factory to explore and local produce to inspect. Agatha coped well with the pace—she attributed her remarkable stamina to the fact that she'd spent her youth doing nothing—but other members of the Mission found it hard going. Mr Bates had had a septic foot and was still limping. His boss kept the poor man in a constant state of nerves which meant Agatha spent much of her time cheering and reassuring him. Archie too needed wifely reassurance. As financial manager of the expedition, he was frustrated that Belcher kept a tight grip on the funds. Belcher even tried economising by making every member of the Mission pay for their own drinks. He had recently given up alcohol. 'We are resisting to the last ditch!' Agatha informed her mother. She was a teetotaller (she disliked the taste of liquor), but it was the principle she was fighting for.

Major Belcher proved to be a difficult leader—unpredictable, full of bluff, self-important (he threw a temper tantrum at the Launceston Town Hall when kept waiting by the Mayor) and vain ('He really does think he is a King', was Agatha's view). He was also struggling physically with a bad leg, which she kindly offered to bandage for him, but was growled at for her pains. The Christies worried that the friendly Australians they were meeting would be offended by Major Belcher's rudeness and vanity: 'Australians will *not* stand "side"—they are extraordinarily nice and kind, and awfully hospitable, but "swank" does not go down well'. But between the various members of the Mission, they managed to smooth over offences, calm the Major down, and keep the show on the road. Agatha left Tasmania with regret. One day, she decided, she would like to return there to live.

Three weeks in Victoria came next. Very little of that time was spent in Melbourne as it was in the country towns they found the canneries and freezing works they needed to visit. The Mission members took a two-day excursion by train to Shepparton, in the heart of the Goulburn Valley. The Shepparton Fruit Preserving Company (still in existence today as SPC) had begun five years before and was already processing huge quantities of peaches, pears and apricots. As she observed and sampled, Agatha became quite the expert. 'If you are buying canned peaches', she advised her mother, 'Shepparton Packing Co. Green Label "Fancy" are good'. The Ardmona Cannery was even newer (it had opened the previous year) and there she saw the tins of peaches, plums and other fruit being packed and despatched around the world with great efficiency. No fruit would ever replace apples as her favourite. They were what she liked to munch as she wrote her novels, a peculiarity she gave her detective heroine Mrs Ariadne Oliver. It is that character's apple obsession that helps Poirot solve a crime in *Halloween Party*.

Fruit was a major component of the Mission tour. Later on, in Queensland, Agatha was startled to discover that pineapples did *not* grow on trees. She had imagined them hanging gracefully from high branches: 'I was so astonished to find that an enormous field I had taken to be full of cabbages was in fact of pineapples. It was in a way rather a disappointment. It seemed such a prosaic way of growing such a luscious fruit'. Less disappointing were New South Wales' oranges. At one orchard, while Major Belcher and Archie were 'busy putting forth the claims of the British Empire, migration within the Empire, the importance of trade within the Empire, and so on and so forth', Agatha reclined on a deck chair and ate twenty-three oranges, straight from the trees around

The Shepparton Fruit Preserving Company building in Victoria which Agatha visited and where she learned about tinned fruit.

her, in one sitting. 'The most delicious things you can imagine', was her verdict.

They also visited Dookie College, an agricultural college opened in 1886, which had recently become part of the University of Melbourne. It was a place where students doing a Bachelor of Agriculture degree had to spend a year, but it also offered training for returned soldiers and short courses in domestic economy for countrywomen. There Agatha Christie saw cereal crops being grown and tested for quality, and young students learning the various aspects of dairying.

The farms and the orchards, the country towns and their factories, were reached sometimes by train, occasionally by horse-drawn carts, but more often by car. Coming from a county as densely populated, green and lush as Devon, Agatha found it fascinating to look out the windows at a seemingly vast and empty land: 'It always seems to me odd that countries are never described to you in terms which you recognise when you get there. My own sketchy ideas of Australia comprised kangaroos in large quantities, and a great deal of desert'. Instead she found 'the extraordinary aspect of the trees', the gums she regarded as both artistic and strange, and the birds—'macaws', she called them, but they must have been rosellas and lorikeets—'blue and red and green, flying through the air in great clustering swarms. Their colouring was wonderful: like flying jewels'. She didn't see the 'waste desert' she'd expected, but instead 'a green grassy desert' and 'enormous stretches of flat pasture land, with nothing to break the horizon except periodic windmills'. Like so many English literary visitors, she found such emptiness rather frightening.

Agatha Christie loved her food and was keen to sample local produce wherever she went, but Australian meals were generally a disappointment: 'We seemed always to be eating incredibly tough beef or turkey'. There was little imagination shown in Australian cookery at that time and the group soon wearied of overcooked, chewy meals placed in front of them every night. These invariably consisted of 'a plate with a slice of beef, a slice of turkey, a slice of ham, some parsnips, some carrots, two kinds of potatoes always, bread sauce, horseradish and stuffing and a portion of Yorkshire pudding, and a good strong cup of black tea. Then apple pie and enormous jugs of cream'. It could well have been a meal served in England. Even the cream was not as Agatha liked it—she preferred to drink cream from a glass, not have it diluted by apple pie!

In between the visits to brickfields, slaughterhouses and 'dried milk places', the speeches and tea parties, Agatha was pinned down by a Melbourne journalist from the *Herald*. After 1926, the year of her mysterious disappearance, she would avoid journalists like the plague. So this Australian interview is one of the few she ever gave that show her relaxed and happy, willing to chat about her childhood and her one published novel. The interview reminded her that there was more than just Mission work to be done—short stories needed to be added to *Poirot Investigates*, so were duly tapped out on her portable typewriter. The interview also taught her to treat all journalists warily. When the article was published, she was astonished to read that as a girl she had planned to enter a convent (Agatha wasn't even a Catholic). Getting Agatha Christie to sit for interviews or publicity photos five years later would prove an almost impossible task—the Melbourne journalist was lucky.

At the end of May the Mission set off for Sydney, a city that failed to live up to her expectations: 'having heard of Sydney and Rio de Janeiro as having the two most beautiful harbours in the world, I found it disappointing. I had expected too much of it, I suppose'.[1] New Zealand's Wellington Harbour which she saw a month later was more to her liking; she told her mother she had never seen anything so beautiful in her life. Sydney's hotels also disappointed. Her room reeked 'of stale commercial traveller'. Still, she photographed Sydney Harbour and sent pictures back to family in England.

By early June the Mission team had been together nearly six months and were all getting heartily sick of each other. Major Belcher continued to irritate. Even the fact that he was falling in love with an Australian girl didn't make him easier to work with. Agatha's position was a difficult one; she was not a fully fledged member of the team and had no official role, and yet she played a vitally important part in soothing tempers, nursing minor ailments, and keeping the mood as upbeat as possible in trying conditions. Her own batteries were

---

1   Agatha Christie never went to Rio de Janeiro, so
    was able to keep her imaginary picture of the place
    unchanged by the reality.

sorely in need of recharging. So she was delighted to receive an invitation to escape. In Sydney she and Archie met Major Charles Bell, a war hero from Queensland, who held long discussions with Archie about cattle and how best to promote the varieties and quality of Aussie beef at the London exhibition. Agatha avoided these agricultural discussions by chatting instead with the Major's sister, pretty Una Bell. The Bells came from Boonah in Queensland and a visit to their station property was planned for the Queensland part of the tour. But Una took a liking to Mrs Christie and suggested she travel there early, leaving the Mission team in Brisbane to carry out more of their dull engagements. This was an opportunity for a holiday, for a change of company and a break from the temperamental men she was travelling with. Agatha was delighted to accept the invitation.

'Coochin Coochin', the Bells' historic home, was part of a pastoral run established in 1842. It had been one of the earliest stations of the Moreton Bay district, and was a social centre as well as a thriving agricultural concern. The homestead that Agatha entered on June 6, feeling dazed and tired from a 'deadly journey of about six hours' on the train, was an elegant red-cedar structure, with deep verandahs and attractive gardens. Agatha was not the first distinguished guest to enjoy its 'homey' atmosphere and welcoming hosts. Two years before, Lord Louis Mountbatten and the Prince of Wales both visited 'Coochin Coochin' to see a fine example of an Australian station. Conrad Martens had admired and painted some of the lovely local views, and Frank Hurley had come to photograph it.

Agatha Christie had 'a glorious week' there and found the Bells perfect hosts. When she first arrived it

'Coochin Coochin' homestead in Queensland, where Agatha spent a relaxed and happy week and where the tree she planted still flourishes.

seemed that 'the Bell family numbered about twenty-six. The next day I cut it down to four daughters and the equivalent number of sons'.[2] Those sons included Charles, whom she had already met, another war hero Victor who was 'a wonderful flirt', Bert 'who rode splendidly' and Frick, who shared Agatha's love of music and whose son Guilford would later join Agatha and her second husband Max on archeological expeditions and, as their architect, help restore their own home to its original Georgian elegance. The matriarch Mrs Bell was a widow. She resembled Queen Victoria and 'was always treated as though she was royalty'. The Bells generally spent part of each year in Europe—they were cultured, sophisticated and gregarious. To Agatha they appeared to be 'really like the royal family with a little country of their own'.

Agatha's upbringing had been decidedly Victorian—restricted, proper, with rules and regulations governing every aspect of female behaviour. Aussie girls were

---

2   In her autobiography, Agatha Christie misremembered the number of daughters in the Bell family. There were three, not four girls and they were Una, Enid and Aileen.

fascinatingly different and proved to Agatha that women could lead energetic, exciting lives, while remaining ladylike and attractive. Una Bell and her two sisters donned breeches and rode for hours across a harsh landscape, then came home to dance half the night. They turned cheerfully to any task, they cooked her scrambled eggs and cocoa while talking nineteen to the dozen. They looked, she thought, 'like energetic young fillies'. Such bright, independent women were an example Agatha would imitate when, four years later, Archie left her for another woman and she set off, quite alone, for the Middle East. The Bell girls would also inspire some of the feisty young women of her novels, women like Lynn Marchmont in *Taken at the Flood* who does overseas service with the Wrens, Cinderella in *The Murder on the Links* who performs as an acrobat, and the only Australian heroine Agatha ever created, named Una after her new friend, in *An Unbreakable Alibi*.

'Coochin Coochin' provided Agatha Christie with a week of novel entertainments. She watched cattle being rounded up, attended a luncheon of Labor MPs who all got drunk, and played with the pet kangaroos and wallabies. Mrs Bell's diary, still in the family, records how Mrs Christie performed at a local concert (she was an excellent pianist and also sang well), danced with the local men, went off on drives round the station and enjoyed afternoon teas. Agatha also met Aboriginals for the first time:

> Among the various servants, station hands, general helpers, etc, most of whom were half-caste, there were one or two pure-bred Aboriginals. Aileen Bell, the youngest of the Bell sisters, said to me

almost the first morning: 'You've got to see Susan.'
I asked who Susan was. 'Oh, one of the Blacks.'
They were always called 'the Blacks'. 'One of the
Blacks, but she's a real one, absolutely pure-bred,
and she does the most wonderful imitations.' So
a bent, aged Aboriginal came along. She was as
much a Queen in her own right as Mrs Bell in
hers. She did imitations of all the girls for me,
and of various of the brothers, children and
horses: she was a natural mimic, and she enjoyed
very much doing her show.

By the time Archie and Major Belcher arrived, Agatha
felt at home at 'Coochin Coochin'. The visit had taught
her a great deal. The woman who had gone straight
from living with her mother to living with her husband
had discovered she could hold her own without either
of them. She had admired the energy, frankness and
independence of Australian women, and would soon
emulate them herself. She had enjoyed a much-needed
break from wearisome Mission business. She had
also experienced a gracious and restful little piece of
Queensland, while the Mission rushed here and there
talking cattle, crops and canned fruit. Before she
departed, she was (like other distinguished visitors to the
property) asked to plant a tree, an appropriate gesture
from a woman who loved them so. A Leopard Tree[3]
flourishes there today, along with those planted by Sir
Lawrence Olivier, Vivien Leigh and the Queen Mother,
who followed her there as notable guests.

---

3 The Leopard Tree, also known as the Brazilian
   Ironwood, gets its name from its shedding of large
   flakes of bark, which leave the trunk mottled and shiny,
   like the coat of a leopard.

Sydney was the last stop on the tour. She managed a brief glimpse of the Blue Mountains and once again was fascinated by the colours: 'I was entranced by landscape coloured as I have never seen landscape coloured before. In the distance the hills really *were* blue—a cobalt blue, not the kind of grey blue that I associated with hills. They looked as if they had just been put on a piece of drawing-paper, straight from one's paint box'. Agatha Christie always saw Australian landscapes in terms of art.

Agatha had appreciated Australian hospitality and frankness, but there had been customs and attitudes to which she'd had to force herself to adjust. It seemed Australian friendliness at times had no limits and, at others, had too many, and the diplomatic capacity in which she was travelling forced her to quickly learn the unwritten rules of local etiquette. As far as she was concerned, going to the toilet was far *too* social: 'the sanitary arrangements . . . were slightly embarrassing to one of Victorian upbringing. The ladies of the party were politely ushered into a room where two chamber pots sat in isolation in the middle of the floor, ready for use as desired . . .' but Agatha preferred to pee in private, rather than in the company of several chatting women. She also found it hard working out where to sit at formal dinners. Thinking she and Archie should separate and spread themselves around to talk Mission business, Agatha began the tour by placing herself next to some local worthy to make polite dinner conversation. She was told very firmly that she must sit by *her* husband; Australian women clearly thought she was intruding on their rightful territory if she attempted to sit by *theirs*.

These small social awkwardnesses aside, Agatha adapted well. In New Zealand she even gave a speech, one of the few times in her life she agreed to do so. Later in life, she would claim she was desperately shy but her Australian travels do not bear this out. She mingled and chatted, she drank tea and ate luncheons, she travelled to 'Coochin Coochin' on her own and formed new friendships there, and she promoted the Empire Exhibition wherever she went. After her disappearance in 1926, she became rather reclusive and her travels tended to be to remote archeological digs. Australia was lucky to see her at her most sociable and outgoing.

✼

On June 29 the Christies and the rest of their party sailed for New Zealand on the SS *Manuka*. There they visited Rotorua, Wellington, Nelson, the Buller Gorge and Kawerau Gorge and Agatha saw trees very different from the Australian gums, but just as wonderful. She loved it all: 'I still think New Zealand the most beautiful country I have ever seen. Its scenery is extraordinary', she wrote near the end of her life. From there she and Archie managed a holiday in Hawaii where too much time on the beach gave them both agonising sunburn and where Agatha's green woollen bathing dress was ripped in half by the power of the waves. Nevertheless, it was a holiday they both needed. Archie was fed up, sick with colds, blistered by sunburn, Agatha had neuritis, and their money was running out. On the last weeks of the Mission in Canada, she had to survive on dried meat extract turned into a thin soup, as they couldn't afford to pay for her meals. It was a relief when, on December 1, the RMS *Majestic* delivered them safely at Southampton

Docks, ten months and 40,000 miles after embarking from there. On the last night at sea they all signed the menu. Archie stated simply 'Finis Itinerum' (end of the journey); poor, frazzled Mr Bates wrote 'R.I.P'; Belcher showed off with a quote from The Aeneid about it perhaps one day being a pleasure to remember the tour. Agatha Christie, however, stayed cheery to the last, and used new-learned Aussie slang to express her view of their trip around the world. She wrote on a menu: '1st class! Good oh! Right here'.

The Empire Exhibition was opened by King George V on St George's Day in 1924. It cost £12 million and was the largest exhibition ever staged anywhere in the world. An astonishing 27 million visitors passed through its pavilions, the British Post Office issued a commemorative stamp for the first time, and Sir Edward Elgar composed an 'Empire March' and other songs for the occasion. One of the buildings that housed the event would afterwards be converted into Wembley Stadium, home of English football. The British Empire at that time contained fifty-eight countries (only Gambia and Gibraltar did not take part) and, thanks to the Mission, Australia had one of the largest pavilions. This comprised nearly six acres of exhibition space, in the middle of which was a sixteen-foot ball of scoured wool, reminding visitors that much Australian wealth came from the sheep's back. Among those who paid their shilling and sixpence to enter were the Christies, there to admire stuffed koalas and kangaroos in replicas of their natural habitats, a giant model of Sydney Harbour complete with working boats, impressive displays of canned fruit, a model station showing sheep being shorn, and a table elegantly set with Australian china for a formal dinner party. Each product brought back many memories for them both.

The Australian pavilion at the 1924 Empire Exhibition held in London. Agatha and her husband Archie visited to see the products sent for display as a result of their 'Mission'. The pavilion covered nearly six acres.

Many of those memories included the irrepressible Major Belcher. In the last weeks in his company Archie and Agatha vowed they would never speak to the irritating man again. It was a vow they failed to keep: 'To our enormous surprise we found that we actually *liked* Belcher'. So he came to dine with them in London and they met Gladys, his eighteen-year-old Australian wife (Belcher was fifty).[4] Agatha Christie had been tempted to turn him into a corpse many times on the tour, but once released from his daily presence she could think of him with some affection and put him into her next book, *The Man in the Brown Suit*. Sir Eustace Pedler, the character he inspired, turns out to be a villain, but a rather likeable one and his creator ultimately allows him to escape justice. In her eyes Major Belcher's worst crime

---

4   Major Belcher and Gladys were divorced eight years later. Agatha was not surprised when she heard the news.

was that, two years after the tour ended, he still owed her two pounds, eighteen shillings and five pence for a pair of socks. He never paid her.

While Agatha was travelling, her second book, *The Secret Adversary*, was published to good reviews. With the publication of three more novels and one volume of short stories her popularity began to grow. But in 1926 Agatha Christie became a household name when she disappeared for eleven days. Extensive searches were undertaken, the papers were full of the mystery. Agatha's mother Clara had just died and Archie wanted a divorce so he could marry his mistress. What had happened to her in this distressed condition? She was finally found in a Harrogate hotel, suffering from what could have been amnesia, or a nervous breakdown. Others were convinced it was a publicity stunt, though much of the ensuing publicity was negative. However, when it came to book sales, she found all publicity to be good publicity. Her next novel, the fiendishly clever *The Murder of Roger Ackroyd* took off like a rocket. After that, Agatha Christie never looked back.

She wrote about what she knew, sticking to the milieu of the English village, or taking her characters to places she herself had visited. She kills them off on the Nile and on the Orient Express, in Baghdad and in Jordan, in South Africa and in Torquay, as well as in Miss Marple's beloved St Mary Mead, and Poirot's London. But she does not kill anyone in Australia. No character meets a sticky end in Sydney or Tasmania, there are no corpses floating down the Yarra or pushed off cliffs in the Blue Mountains. Yet Australia does feature in her writing.

Readers do not pick up an Agatha Christie novel for an in-depth analysis of human nature. Her books are read for their plotting, their puzzles, the build-up to the exciting moment when Poirot points a finger and explains how the murder was committed. Apart from the memorable Hercule Poirot, Miss Jane Marple, and a few others such as Tommy, Tuppence and Mrs Oliver, there are few characters whose names are remembered for more than a day or two after the book is put away. They contribute to a picture of English life in the first half of the twentieth century, but they do not make a lasting impression as individuals. We feel no particular grief when one of them is bumped off, but we do want to know who did the bumping. Agatha Christie created stock characters—the crusty squire, the flighty parlour-maid, the young man-about-town, the absent-minded vicar and the embittered spinster, and variations on these stereotypes appear again and again in her writing. As an author she provided her readers with characters they recognised and expected, and then showed those characters having to cope with the unexpected in the form of murder. The exciting mix of the familiar and unfamiliar is a large part of the appeal.

It comes as no surprise that she decided Australians should be stereotyped along with the rest. She had liked the Aussie friendliness and openness and enjoyed a perfectly safe journey with no threat to life or possessions, but her readers did not, in general, know the Australia she had seen. Most had never been there. It suited her purpose to give them not what she had experienced, but what they expected; so her portrayal of Australians in her novels is a snapshot of how they were generally viewed in England at that time.

Botany Bay was still casting a long shadow when Agatha Christie began to write in the 1920s, and in the minds of many, Australia was the land of criminals. Anthony Trollope and Robert Louis Stevenson had portrayed it in their novels as a place where 'black sheep' were sent to be out of the way. Many English continued to regard it as a destination for undesirables. George, Poirot's manservant, certainly sees it this way. When Poirot asks him in *The Mystery of the Blue Train* if 'criminals are invariably drawn from the lower orders?' George replies:

> Not always, sir. There was great trouble with one of the Duke of Devize's younger sons. He left Eton under a cloud, and after that he caused great anxiety on several occasions. The police would not accept the view that it was kleptomania. A clever young gentleman, sir, but vicious through and through, if you take my meaning. His Grace shipped him to Australia, and I hear he was convicted out there under another name.

In *Mrs McGinty's Dead* a woman who has technically been cleared of killing her lover's wife, but who was almost certainly guilty of the crime, moves to Australia and there changes her name, while in *The Apple of Hesperides*, a short story in *The Labours of Hercules*, a thief called 'Red Kate' relocates to Australia to continue her illicit activities in a new arena. In *The Clocks* a woman abandons her illegitimate baby to begin a new life in Australia. The Willetts in *The Sittaford Mystery* pretend to be South Africans, but they are really the Australian wife and daughter of a man locked up in Dartmoor prison who have come to England to aid his escape. They give away their real nationality by calling 'Coo-ee' to each other across the garden. Ronnie Garfield in the same novel sums it up when he says: 'Fellows that go off to the Colonies are usually bad hats. Their relations don't like them and push them out there for that reason'. Transportation might have ended long before Agatha Christie began to publish, but in the minds of her English readers, a criminal record was still a requirement for travelling to Australia.

Another necessity among her fictional Australians is 'heartiness'. Genuine Australians and 'fake' Australians all put on a show of slightly overbearing cheerfulness and mateship. The women are all rather too 'jolly-hockey-sticks', and the men just a shade too hearty and matey. Australians are seen by other characters as being 'a bit too sociable', 'a bit too hospitable for English ideas' and 'over friendly . . . like Colonials are', rather too loud, and just a touch vulgar. In *Peril at End House* a middle-aged couple, forgers and thieves, masquerade as Australians. Captain Hastings, Poirot's sidekick, is taken in by their bluff talk, offers of 'a cuppa' and their delight in meeting such a 'bonza detective' as Hercule Poirot. But Poirot is suspicious: 'they were, perhaps, just a shade too "typical" . . . that cry of Cooee—that insistence on showing snapshots [of Melbourne]—was it not playing a part just a little too thoroughly?' And of course he is proved right. Mrs Croft is exposed as Milly Merton, well-known forger, who has never set foot in Australia. Australia is portrayed as a suitable destination for such hearty types as games mistresses (*Cat Among the Pigeons*), marine biologists (*The Clocks*) and those who strangely desire to go as 'jackaroos to an Australian station' (*Sparkling Cyanide*).

There is the implication in Agatha Christie's novels that cultured, sophisticated men and women wouldn't really want to go anywhere near Australia. In *They Came to Baghdad*, the heroine Victoria Jones has no job and no money. The employment agency offers her the chance of a job with 'a lady . . . with two little girls who was offering a passage to Australia'. Victoria is not *that* desperate—she 'waved away Australia'. When George Rowland of *The Girl in the Train* thinks briefly of emigration to the colonies, he asks the butler, Rogers, for his opinion of such a move:

> 'Which colony were you thinking of, Sir?'
> 'I'm not particular. Any will do. Let's say
> Australia. What do you think of the idea,
> Rogers?'
> 'Well, Sir, I've heard it said that there's room out
> there for anyone who really wants to work.'
> George looked at him with interest and
> admiration.
> 'Very neatly put, Rogers. I shan't go to
> Australia—not today at any rate.'

Tommy Beresford spends ten months searching for jobs, without success. But even that doesn't make him consider Australia: 'I shouldn't like the colonies', he tells Tuppence, 'and I'm perfectly certain they wouldn't like me'. Mr Badger Beadon in *Why Didn't They Ask Evans?* is described as being of the type 'who go to Australia and come back again'—there is clearly little hope for him if he can't succeed even in Australia! For an upper-class Englishman, with no criminal motivation, Australia is just not an attractive option in Agatha Christie's world.

The Aussie accent is also treated patronisingly. Agatha had been relieved to leave the 'Australian voice' behind when she left, but she gets her revenge on it in her writing. 'Cooee', 'bonza' and 'Good-oh' are scattered liberally through the speech of any Australian character. Whether real (as with the Willetts) or assumed (as with the Crofts, or the villain of *The Case of the Clapham Cook*), Aussie accents and slang never fail to indicate social inferiority. As soon as an Australian opens his mouth, he makes some Englishman despise him. In *Parker Pyne Investigates*, a lawyer masquerading as a crook even pretends to have an Australian accent, believing that this will make him more convincing as a shyster.

But the picture is not *all* bad, and very occasionally, Australia is shown in a more positive light. In *Third Girl*, Dr Stillingfleet, a charming red-headed psychiatrist, plans to marry Norma, the 'third girl' of the title, and emigrate with her to Australia at the end of the story. In *The Unbreakable Alibi* can be found Christie's one and only Australian heroine. Una Drake has travelled to England where a rather dim-witted Englishman, Mr Montgomery Jones, falls in love with her. Fun-loving Una sets him a challenge—she produces an alibi she's convinced no one can shake and gives Mr Jones receipts to prove she was in both London and Torquay on the same night. He is frightfully keen on her as she is 'simply one of the most sporting girls I have ever met', and is 'game for anything'. Even Mr Jones himself admits that he's 'not terribly clever' so he calls in Tommy and Tuppence to help. They know that Australians, with those vast distances to cover, can 'drive very recklessly', but even Una could not have covered the miles between London and Torquay in the time frame shown by the receipts. Tuppence checks out the hotel in Torquay where Una claims to have stayed and there the chambermaid remembers her as a 'very nice young lady, very merry and talkative. Had told her a lot about Australia and the kangaroos'. When Tuppence cables to Australia to do a background search on Una, she discovers she's an identical twin. Vera, the twin, is of course in England, so one twin was in London and the other in Torquay and the mystery is solved. Una is from a 'gambling family' so a hint of dubiousness is given to her background. Readers are expected to feel that the handicap of being born an Australian is balanced in the couple's marriage by his handicap of lack of brains.

Australia is also useful to Agatha Christie because of its distance from England. When she needed to place a witness or a suspect as far from the scene of the crime as possible, Australia came in handy. In *The Thirteen Problems* the writer of a dubious reference has conveniently left for Australia so the reference can't be checked, and in *Ordeal by Innocence* the alibi of a man who is hanged for murder is en route for Australia and then Antarctica while the trial is being conducted, so fails to hear that he is needed. In these days of emails, daily flights and text messaging, crime writers can't use Australia as a remote place to send suspects, but in Agatha Christie's fictional world it was only one step away from the icy wastes of Antarctica.

There is one Australian-inspired title among her works. *Why Didn't They Ask Evans?* was published in England in 1934, but when published in America it was given a different title, *The Boomerang Clue*. Its investigators, Bobby Jones and Lady Frankie Derwent, try to solve a murder that occurs in their tiny Welsh village of Marchmolt. The search for 'Evans' takes them all over the south of England, but eventually leads them to Bobby's home, the vicarage of Marchmolt— Evans, it turns out, is his father's housekeeper. Like a boomerang, the clues return them to the murder's point of origin.

The works of Agatha Christie are probably more familiar to the average Australian than the writings of any other author discussed in this book. Her mysteries have always sold well in Australia. The film and TV adaptations of her books have been extremely popular, whether starring the badly miscast Margaret Rutherford, the superb Joan Hickson (Agatha Christie's own preference for the role of Miss Marple), Peter Ustinov or David Suchet (whose aim is to film every Poirot story in the canon).

Agatha Christie has had many competitors for the title 'Queen of Crime', but she still retains it, and Australians have been among her greatest admirers. So it is ironic that her visit has *not* been commemorated by a plaque at Sydney's Circular Quay[5]. Most Australians remain unaware that she has ever visited. It's a crime that no brass memorial pays tribute to the visit of a woman whose tales of fictional corpses have given Australians so many hours of reading pleasure.

---

5   The Writer's Walk was originally planned to extend
    further than it does. Perhaps a plaque to Agatha
    Christie would have been placed there had the original
    scheme not been curtailed.

CHAPTER TEN

DH Lawrence

DH Lawrence came to Australia searching. He didn't know what he was actually looking for or where he would find it. But he had to get away from England, from Europe, and Australia was far enough away for him to search for 'something that brings me peace'.

And it proved to be the answer to his problems. The 'wrestling with the void' that he achieved in his three months in Australia brought him the peace he needed. As he struggled to get at the 'un-get-at-able' fascination of Australia, he also came to grips with part of his own self that had been 'un-get-at-able' for too long. Australia both soothed him and made him erupt, it enfolded him and then ejected him—Australia was DH Lawrence's desperately needed therapy.

He arrived in 1922 when he was thirty-six years old. He had already come a long way from his native

*DH Lawrence
in a passport
photo taken in
Sydney.*

Nottinghamshire, county of his birth and the root of his
creative stirrings. David Herbert Lawrence (known as
Bert to family and friends) was one of five children of
a coalminer and a schoolteacher. His family home, rent
by his parents' fighting and crippled by poverty, was
immortalised in *Sons and Lovers*, as was his complex
relationship with his dominating and ambitious mother.
Determined to keep her son from going 'down t'pit', she
scrimped and saved to have him educated, nursed him
through the many illnesses his weak chest brought on,
and rejoiced when Nottingham High School offered
him a scholarship. His three years there were followed
by a clerkship, and an intense literary friendship with
Jessie Chambers, who lived on a nearby farm. Jessie
encouraged and promoted his writing, her family

provided warmth and fun that were sadly lacking in his
own home, and the time spent at the farm showed him
that he could strike out on his own creative path in life.
Jessie's support was both punished and immortalised
in his writing—he turned her into Miriam in *Sons
and Lovers* and she never forgave him. Lawrence took
up teaching, endured some disillusioned years in the
classroom, then more disillusionment at Nottingham
University College. But his horizons were widening as
he began to write, and saw his first poems in print.

When he arrived in Australia there was a Mrs
Lawrence at his side. In 1912, while at Nottingham
University, he had called on a professor he knew, Ernest
Weekley, to ask advice about teaching jobs in Germany.
Professor Weekley was out, but his German wife Frieda[1]
invited him in. The next thirty minutes would change both
their lives. They fell in love, in a dramatic beginning to a
stormy, passionate, unfaithful partnership. Two months
later she left her husband and children (there were three
of them, the youngest only eight years old at the time)
and eloped with Lawrence to Germany. They married in
1914, as soon as her divorce came through, and together
they roamed the continent and now wed, they felt they
could return to England to face family and friends.

Sons and Lovers, published in 1913, brought Lawrence
critical acclaim and also connections in the literary world.
New Zealander Katherine Mansfield and her husband
John Middleton Murry became close friends and sources of
literary inspiration to him. Lady Ottoline Morrell invited
them to Garsington Manor, her home of patronage to
writers and artists, where Lawrence met Bertrand Russell,
EM Forster and Edward Marsh. Frieda had affairs (she

[1]   Born Baroness Frieda von Richthofen.

had enjoyed several affairs while married to Professor Weekley, and wasn't going to stop), but she proved to be just what Lawrence had needed in a partner and the marriage stimulated him creatively.

But just as everything seemed to be going well for him it all began to go wrong. War was declared, the conflict Lawrence described as the 'terrible, terrible war, made so fearful because in every country practically every man lost his head, and lost his own centrality, his own manly isolation in his own integrity'. DH Lawrence loathed its soulless mechanisation, its mindless patriotism, its mass slaughter and its 'obsolete, hideous stupidity'. He and Frieda tried to leave for America, but were refused passports, and in wartime a return to Italy was out of the question. 'The war is just hell for me . . . I can't get away from it for a minute: [I] live in a sort of coma, like one of those nightmares when you can't move', he wrote. Later he would declare, 'War finished me: it was the spear through the side of all sorrows and hopes'. His belief in English civilisation and his trust in humanity were ripped apart during these ghastly years.

British censorship added to his horrors. *The Rainbow*, published in September 1915, was prosecuted for obscenity by the Public Morality Council. Its analysis of human sexuality and its anti-war message were out of step with wartime Britain. The book was denounced as a 'menace to our public health' and was banned. Financially this was devastating, but it was also a blow creatively. He lost the right to publish what he liked; he felt he'd lost his freedom as a novelist. He could 'curse [the authorities] body and soul, root, branch and leaf, to eternal damnation', but no one knew better than Lawrence how impotent his curses were. When, in

1916, he tried to publish *Women in Love*, no one wanted to touch it. The war had prevented Lawrence from reaching his readers.

If he was not allowed to escape England, he could at least flee to the very edge of it. In 1915 he and Frieda went to Cornwall: 'the spirit of the war—the spirit of collapse and of human ignominy, had not travelled so far yet'. In the tiny, remote village of Zennor they dug themselves in to wait out the 'awful years', writing, growing vegetables, and smashing plates over each other's heads in their volcanic rows. But even a Cornish escape was not permitted them. Wartime paranoia and hysteria finally reached the seaside town and the locals became suspicious. Frieda was German, cousin to the famous air-ace, Baron von Richthofen, and the couple and their pacifist friends courted trouble by singing German songs and speaking openly of their feelings about the war. Zennor was on the coast, a good place for a loyal Hausfrau to send signals by flapping a brightly coloured scarf, or leaving a light on at night. 'The tales began to go round full-tilt . . . A chimney of his house was tarred to keep out the damp: that was a signal to the Germans. He and his wife carried food to supply German submarines. They had secret stores of petrol in the cliff. They were watched and listened to, spied on, by men lying behind the low stone fences.' There was some justification for local concern—English submarines and ships had been sunk by Germans just off the Cornish coast—but a depressed Lawrence could not endure it. It was all horror upon horror, 'poisonous', paralysing and obscene.

The invasion of Lawrence's privacy went further than the searching of his cottage. His body was searched too, anally, by jesting doctors, when he presented himself, on order, for military medical examinations. He underwent three such ordeals, twice in Bodmin and once in Derby. His bouts of pneumonia and weak chest left him unfit for service, but his naked humiliation under those inspections bit deep, killing something inside him. 'He had come to the end of his own tether' and lost that 'centrality' that was so fundamental to his sense of self and to his creativity.

Police surveillance continued even after the couple was evicted from Cornwall. They drifted from house to house, staying with friends, desperately poor. Lawrence prepared old poems for publications, worked on a play and essays on American literature and wrote a history book for schoolchildren. Worry and poverty dragged him down, his marriage was troubled, and when the influenza epidemic hit Britain after the war, it nearly put an end to his writing. Both he and Frieda were desperate to escape England. When he had sufficiently recovered, and they'd been granted visas, they set off for Italy. As they sailed away from English shores, Lawrence felt he was leaving the corpse of his country behind him. He raged against England, even as he went on writing about it, even as he felt it had left him 'broken apart'.

Lawrence did not find what he needed in Italy even though it was a productive period—two novels, a book of stories, a travel book, books on psychoanalysis, and some of his finest poems were written during this time. But problems with censorship continued and comments about his 'obscenities' appeared in the English press, leaving him absolutely disgusted with the civilised world, and unable to breathe from the misery of it all.

The old world could not give him what he needed, 'I've got to come unstuck from the old life and Europe', he told a friend, and so his thoughts turned to the new. His novels sold better in America than anywhere else and an admirer, Mabel Sterne, had invited them to Taos in New Mexico. Lawrence decided to go, though the place only 'half-cajoled' him. First, though, he would head east. Other friends, the Brewsters, had asked him to visit them in Ceylon. There, he hoped, he would cease to feel 'that tension and pressure' from which he was suffering. There he could perhaps break 'out of it all' and resolve his mental and physical needs. If Ceylon proved to be what he needed, they would stay on there.

But it wasn't, and they remained only six weeks. The heat was 'like a prison', Buddha irritated him ('Oh I wish he would *stand up!*'), it was all 'too boneless and negative'. The jungle seemed to close in rather than give him the breathing space he craved. It was as if there was 'a lid down over everything', and even moving up into the hills brought no relief. 'I thought we should get through the lid . . . no, it presses tighter here'. They moved on once more. On the voyage to Ceylon the Lawrences had enjoyed meeting Anna Jenkins, a musician and patron of the arts from Perth in Western Australia. She'd invited them to stay. 'One may as well move on, once one has started', Lawrence decided, so Perth became their next destination. Sixty-six pounds for each ticket was a shock, but he had hopes of a country he believed to be full of life and energy, so he paid up. Perhaps in this remote land he could achieve his ambition to recreate himself anew.

Mrs Jenkins was on the wharf to meet Lawrence and Frieda when they arrived at Fremantle on 4 May 1922. She quickly set about showing off this prize author who had fallen unexpectedly into her clutches.[2] She introduced him to the local literati who hung out at the Booklovers shop[3] where Lawrence was delighted to find a copy of his banned novel *The Rainbow.* He did not even own a copy of the book; fortunately news of the ban had clearly not reached Perth. Mrs Jenkins entertained them at her gracious home 'Strawberry Hill', lunched with them at the Savoy, and showed them around. Relaxed after the voyage which he'd enjoyed, Lawrence didn't mind being lionised, though he was relieved when Anna Jenkins found them a place of their own to stay at Darlington, forty miles from Perth.

'Leithdale', their home for the two weeks they spent in Western Australia, was a guesthouse run by two nurses. Mollie Skinner was one of them, but she was also a writer to whom Lawrence gave advice. The story she wrote at his encouragement would be sent back to him for editorial suggestions. Partly rewritten by Lawrence, and published under both their names as *The Boy in the Bush*, it is the only book DH Lawrence co-authored.

Perth newspapers announced his arrival, a local poet William Siebenhaar hurried to meet him, while Katherine Susannah Prichard was prevented from meeting him, much to her disappointment, because she was giving birth to her son.

---

2   DH Lawrence was literally a prize author, having won the James Tait Black award for fiction for his novel *The Lost Girl* just before leaving Europe.

3   This well-known Perth establishment in Hay Street had been founded in 1900 by Mrs Frances Zabel and was a popular meeting place for writers.

Lawrence had written little in the preceding months. His muse, he announced, had gone 'to a nunnery' and he felt no inspiration that might drag her back. But few writers have responded so intensely to place as did Lawrence and before he left the West, the Australian landscape had started to affect him. Like other literary travellers, he commented on the monotony of the bush. Darwin had disliked the lack of variety and seasonal change and the depressing droop of the eucalypts; Trollope had felt imprisoned by the endless gum trees; yet Agatha Christie had thought they were artistic. Only DH Lawrence looked more deeply. 'It is extraordinarily subtle, *unknown* country. The gum trees are greyish, with pale trunks—and so often the pale, pure silver dead trees with vivid limbs: then the extraordinary *delicacy* of the air and the blue sky, the weird bits of creek and marsh, dead trees, sand, and very blue hills . . . so apparently monotonous, yet when you look into it, such subtly different distances, in layers, and such exquisite forms.' It was, he felt, a land with a 'folded secret', a secret that would bring him the 'peace' he longed for if he could look into it hard enough. Most people look 'at' a landscape, but Lawrence very deliberately used the word 'into' to describe his way of looking at nature.

The 'spirit of the place' however did not fall on him immediately. At first the bush was frightening; he felt watched by some unseen presence, 'the hair on his scalp stirred and went icy cold with terror'. This 'something' that lurked could have 'reached a long black arm and gripped him', but it didn't. He stood there in the moonlight and stillness, intensely aware of the ghostly trees 'like corpses', the dark grey-green of the foliage, and the 'terror of the bush', and then he turned round and walked out of it. But something had gripped Lawrence—the intense sympathy with landscape that was always his greatest inspiration. The seeds were planted in this moment for *Kangaroo*, a novel about the power of an environment over those who live in it, about the alienation of people within landscapes. In writing this novel DH Lawrence would raise the lid on his suffocation and 'set [himself] free'. He had once remarked that 'one sheds one's sicknesses in books—repeats and presents again one's emotions, to be master of them'.

Although encouraged to stay in Western Australia by Anna Jenkins, and also by Frieda who was keen to settle in one place for a while, Lawrence wanted to move on to New South Wales. The ships for California left from Sydney and so they boarded the RMS *Malwa* and set off round the Great Australian Bight to eastern Australia. It was a nine-day journey that included a brief call at Adelaide and a night's stop in Melbourne. In both cities Lawrence visited the art galleries and was disappointed by what he found: 'nobody has *seen* Australia yet: can't be done. It isn't visible'. As he wandered around the galleries he may have got the idea of capturing Australia in words rather than with paint. By the end of the voyage that idea was certainly firmly in his mind. He visited those galleries as a little appreciated writer—few had yet recognised his genius. How surprised he'd have been at the thought that nearly a century later Australian galleries would bid large sums for art inspired by his life and writings.

They reached Sydney on 27 May 1922 and a rainbow—always an exquisite symbol of hope for

Lawrence—greeted their arrival. They stayed initially at Mrs Scott's private hotel on Macquarie Street, but it was too pricey for their modest means. Their walks in the 'handsome and well-kept' Botanic Gardens, past the Conservatorium of Music, along by Circular Quay and the Harbour, all appear in *Kangaroo* where Richard Lovatt Somers and his wife Harriet follow the footsteps of their creator.[4] The Lawrences enquired about houses to rent and travelled to Manly and Narrabeen. But Sydney wasn't right for either the Somers or for the Lawrences. Its Harbour, with its 'hidden and half hidden lobes intruding among the low dark-brown cliffs', might be 'one of the sights of the world', but Sydney was too much like other cities and was 'without any core' in Lawrence's opinion. The newspapers advertised accommodation at cheaper winter rates on the NSW south coast, so they caught a train heading that way, and got off in Thirroul.

Thirroul was a coalmining town, so there was much there to make a miner's son feel at home. Although moderately popular as a seaside resort, it was an unprepossessing little place with a population of about 2500. It did, however, provide a wonderful house for them; they settled into it on the very day of their arrival and for the next two and a half months rejoiced in its location. The wonderfully named 'Wyewurk' (there was a house called 'Wyewurrie' nearby), had been built by Thomas Irons in 1910, and was one of the first houses in Australia constructed in the Californian bungalow style, a style well suited to Australian conditions. A low

---

4   In some editions of *Kangaroo* Harriet's name is spelt as
    Harriett, but I have used the spelling of the Penguin
    edition of the novel.

roof, a deep verandah and lovely native timbers were part of its charm, but best of all was its position 'on the edge of the low cliff just above the Pacific Ocean'. A real estate advertisement for 3 Craig Street had boasted that its resident could 'tumble out of bed on its sheltered verandah, run down the path to the beachside, and in thirty seconds revel in the tumbling froth of the breakers'. That's exactly what these new residents did, swimming every day (though it was winter) in the 'very seaey' sea, walking the beach, and endlessly watching the ocean.

The Pacific crept into Lawrence's heart, and into the novel he wrote on that verandah: 'the sea talked and talked all the time, in its disintegrative, elemental language. And at last it talked its way into Somers' soul, and he forgot the world again, the babel. The simplicity came back, and with it the inward peace'. Lawrence delighted in the sea creatures: the leaping dolphins, and the washed-up bluebottles that he described so lyrically as 'fairy blue windbags, like bags of rainbow with long blue strings'.

Behind the house was the 'lonely lonely world' of the escarpment which he also explored with delight. Its

DH Lawrence sitting outside 'Wyewurk', the home in Thirroul where he wrote Kangaroo.

The rocks beneath 'Wyewurk', with the surf that DH Lawrence loved to swim in and listen to.

'saurian' ferns, its wild flowers 'stiff, sharp, like crystals of colour', its solitariness, all moved him deeply. The simplicity of the house and the beauty of its setting went into his marrow and made him feel drunk. In such a refuge his muse could safely re-emerge from her nunnery.

Also on the doorstep was the township of Thirroul, and township meant inhabitants. How did Lawrence respond to them and what did they make of this odd red-bearded man and his solid German wife? They were mutually unimpressed, but Lawrence had not gone there for the society. It pleased him that Thirroulians generally left them alone and, mercifully, asked few questions. Memories of Zennor interrogations were still fresh and raw. In *The Lost Girl* he had created a creepy, 'reptilian' doctor, Alexander Graham, who is most unpleasant; but since then he'd met nice Mrs Jenkins and two pleasant Australian couples on the boat, the Forresters and the Marchbanks.

Nevertheless, like Anthony Trollope, Lawrence

thought they 'blew': 'every man a little Pope of perfection', they were 'crude, raw and self-satisfied'. '"There's nothing better than me on earth", [the Australian] seems silently to proclaim . . . and not always silently'. They were too aggressively familiar and too democratic for his liking—'liberty gone senile' was how he described it. He found them shallow and lacking an inner life; 'barbarians' who lived 'in defiance, a sort of slovenly defiance of care of any sort', 'always vaguely and meaninglessly on the go'. 'The human life seems to me very barren', he concluded.

A painfully thin, weedy man himself, Lawrence developed an odd fascination for Australians' legs. His own were like white sticks, so the contrast with the sturdy bronzed pins of the Aussies was marked. The footballers he watched at Thirroul had 'hefty legs' and 'prominent round buttocks that worked madly inside the little white cotton shorts'; while a commercial traveller had 'big heavy legs, heavy thighs and calves that showed even in his trousers'. To Ben Cooley, the 'Kangaroo' character of his novel, he gave thighs that are very thick, powerful legs like those of the creature after whom he is nicknamed. 'They seem to run to leg, these people', Lawrence remarked.

He chatted to the local barber when he went once a week to have his beard trimmed. He and Frieda walked past the war memorial and argued about whether to spend money on tidying it up, 'to have four posts and an iron chain put round it' as Frieda wanted, or to leave it as it was, which was Lawrence's view. Frieda met the shopkeepers in town, though was puzzled that instead of the neat little basket she carried herself, other shoppers took suitcases with them. In *DH Lawrence in*

Australia, Robert Darroch argues that the author met important political activists while in the country, men who inspired the political content of *Kangaroo*. There is evidence for this, but 'socially nil' was how Lawrence himself described his time there.

In 1913 the Christmas edition of the *South Coast Times* had published 'Strike Pay', one of Lawrence's stories, but it had been incorrectly attributed to HD Lawrence, instead of to DH, so it would have been surprising if any of the locals had connected the story with the writer now in their midst. Thirroulians were not great readers—the School of Arts library had a good collection of Zane Greys (which Lawrence himself borrowed) and even a copy of his own *The Rainbow*, but literature was not a major part of local life. The Lawrences, wanting to be alone, must have seemed very unapproachable. A delivery boy approaching 'Wyewurk' heard the yells and plate-smashing that were an integral part of the Lawrence marriage, and raced off as fast as he could without completing his delivery. This incident exemplifies the socially uneasy relationship which existed between Thirroul and DH Lawrence (and which continues to this day). The coalmining township and the coalminer's son should have had a lot in common. But Lawrence did not want to connect with the people, only with the landscape. The locals sensed his rejection and resented it. When he portrayed their town and its people unflatteringly in his fiction, they found it hard to forgive.[5] Today, the town that ought to make so much of this important literary visitor virtually ignores him.

---

5   Thirroul is renamed Mullimbimby in *Kangaroo* but it is
    clearly recognisable as Thirroul.

While Frieda pottered in the house, Lawrence sat on the steps of 'Wyewurk' and wrote. He worked fast—*Kangaroo* was written in six weeks, at the rate of about three thousand words a day. At last, situated as far as he could get from England, Lawrence was finally able to deal with the trauma of the war and to 'shed his sickness'. 'These damned books... they are the crumpled wings of my soul. They get me free before I get myself free', and freedom is what *Kangaroo* gave him, or, more specifically, what one chapter of the book gave him.

'The Nightmare' hardly belongs to the rest of the novel, being more autobiography than fiction. In it Richard Somers, alias Lawrence, relives the wartime horror: 'Detail for detail he thought out his experiences with the authorities . . . it all came back, with a rush. It was like a volcanic eruption in his consciousness'. The Zeppelin raids, the naked humiliation of the medical examination with the jeering doctors, the spying 'invisible eyes' and the need to be 'watchful, guarded, furtive', the Christmas Eve visit of a 'burly police-sergeant', the expulsion and the revulsion—all of it came gushing onto the pages of his exercise book. 'A man culminates in intense moments', he wrote, and writing this chapter proved to be one of the most intense moments he ever experienced. His biographer Brenda Maddox calls the writing of 'The Nightmare' 'the turning point of his life and work'. No longer was he 'a sort of human bomb, all black inside, waiting to explode'. He underwent his 'volcanic eruption', shed 'the burden of intensive mental consciousness' and, like the phoenix which would become such an important symbol to him, he was born anew. 'Deep in his unconsciousness had lain this accumulation of black

fury and fear, like frenzied lava quiescent in his soul'
but, thanks to their refuge in Thirroul, the 'boomingly,
crashingly noisy' ocean below him, the 'remote gum
trees running their white nerves into the air' and the
'pale, white unwritten atmosphere of Australia' there
had been a 'strange falling-away' of that knotted fury.
Kangaroo is not a great novel, but writing it was a great
moment in the life of DH Lawrence.

Lawrence had the manuscript of *Kangaroo* typed
up in New York and then revised it. He changed the
ending, adding details of a dramatic storm that had
swept through Thirroul just before his departure, and
a picture of the boat leaving Sydney's shores, as well as
other details throughout the story. It was published in
October 1923, but as Australian booksellers apparently
turned it down, it was only read in Australia in early
1925 and its merits, or lack of them, have been debated
ever since. Three separate endings exist to the novel, all
stressing the importance of the solitary self as Somers
departs.

Kangaroo is uneven. At its best, it is lyrical
and evocative. The depiction of the natural world,
and Somers' intense response to it, is hauntingly
beautiful—there is the sea that was 'quiet as a purring
cat with white paws'; the kookaburra 'like a bunch of
old rag, with a small rag of a dark tail, and a fluffy pale
top like an owl, and a sort of frill round his neck'; the
bush at night 'raving with moonlight'; the emu, 'a very
remote, dirt-brown gentleman from the lost plains of
time'; the sun moving with 'a strong cat-like motion
through the heavens'; and 'tree-ferns standing on one
knobbly leg among the gums'. Lawrence captures the
'strange, as it were, *invisible* beauty of Australia, which is

undeniably there, but which seems to lurk just beyond...'
and makes it superbly visible to his readers' eyes. More
than almost any other novelist, he 'gets' the 'un-get-at-
able glamour' of the Australian landscape.

The novel also contains an intimate, very modern
analysis of the marriage of Harriet and Richard Somers,
clearly the marriage of Lawrence and Frieda (Harriet
is even given three of Frieda's own names). The pair
exist in a state of continual tension and change, with
him determined to be 'master', and her mocking such
pretensions. They sway back and forth in their emotional
struggle, each behavioural phase and nuance perceptively
documented. Sexually they are not very compatible and
have separate rooms at 'Coo-ee' (the fictional name
Lawrence gives to 'Wyewurk'), but Harriet does excite
her husband on one occasion as she rubs him dry after
a post-swim shower, and he enters her 'straight from
the sea, like another creature'. To add to the emotional
complexity, Somers is attracted to the character Ben
Cooley (Kangaroo) and the scenes where he resists this
homosexual temptation are powerful.

The novel is, in fact, far better on the politics of
marriage than it is on actual politics. The plot is confused,
contrived and unbelievable. Extensive research has been
done by Robert Darroch in *DH Lawrence in Australia*
into the possible and probable real-life models for Ben
Cooley, Willie Struthers and Jack Callcott. He argues
convincingly that Lawrence read about politics in the
papers while here, met men who were involved in plans
for a right-wing coup, and that by writing *Kangaroo* he
gave away their secrets in 'one of the most spectacularly
broken promises in literary history'. It's all interesting
detective work, but it doesn't actually improve those parts

of the novel which, whether based on fact or not, are long, dull, philosophising political rambles. Lawrence's letters from Australia reveal that his own sympathies were right-wing.[6] He worried, just like Rudyard Kipling, about Asian races waiting to drop into Australia 'like a ripe pear', he feared organised labour movements and strikes, and he disliked the robust sense of democracy within Australians. But sharing similar political views with his characters did not 'ignite' his novel, in the way his sympathy for the landscape did. After writing 'The Nightmare' chapter, he found it hard to get back to his plot, and no wonder—that chapter is true to the very core of Lawrence, while the political chapters hardly scratch his surface. In a novel that's more about place than it is about people, the political characters fail to come alive, either as Australians (though Lawrence sometimes gives them a bit of 'Strine' to make them sound more convincing) or as believable human beings.

Lawrence called *Kangaroo* a 'queer show'. Critics have found it chaotic, slapdash, 'a shocking mess' and incoherent; others have seen it as 'experimental, masterful, challenging', an exciting collage of Australian life, and a brilliant novel about Australia. All agree, that it is *not* DH Lawrence's greatest work. In the end, only the reader can decide if *Kangaroo* is a mess, a masterpiece or, like the curate's egg, very good in parts.

When Lawrence finished the novel he was ready to leave. There was some temptation to stay on because 'there is a great charm in Australia', but he had other

---

6 DH Lawrence wrote a total of forty-eight letters and postcards while at Thirroul.

battles to fight, other challenges he knew he needed to face in his development as a writer. 'If it weren't for fighting the world to the last gasp, I would stay here and lapse away from the world into the bush, into Australia'. On June 30 he and Frieda enjoyed a day in Wollongong (called Wolloona in *Kangaroo*), where they walked on the beach 'in a flat-icy wind' and noted the bare legs of the boys playing there. There were a few trips into Sydney to sort out sailing times and American visas and to visit Taronga Park Zoo. There was a ride through the bush in a sulky, memorable for the 'plumy many-balled wattle . . . the most delicate, feathery yellow of plumes and plumes and plumes and trees and bushes of wattle, as if angels had flown right down out of the softest gold regions of heaven to settle . . . in the Australian bush'. On the last weekend of July, the Lawrences' shipboard acquaintances, the Forresters and the Marchbanks, came to stay. Bill Marchbanks had earlier lent Lawrence money to tide him over until his next American payment reached him, but by late July Lawrence was flush again and splurged on hiring a car so he could drive his guests around the area. He loved showing them the scenery that had so delighted him. They went to the Loddon Falls and the photograph taken there shows Lawrence, perched on a rock, looking relaxed and happy.[7]

Lawrence didn't know it, but the area round 'Wyewurk' was rich in Aboriginal artefacts. In 1998 big storms unearthed from the sand dunes the six-

---

7   The Loddon Falls are hard to visit today as they are
part of the water catchment area for Sydney. They were
officially out of bounds to visitors in 1907, well before
Lawrence's visit, but for some years they remained a
popular picnic spot and were not fenced off until later.

DH Lawrence (seated, centre) and friends at the Loddon Falls near Thirroul.

thousand-year-old bones of an Aboriginal elder, just where Lawrence took regular walks. The Kuradji tribe has since fought against a planned development of this ancient burial site. Would Lawrence have cared, had he known this? Probably not. He is rare among the writers included in this book for recording no interest in the original Australians. A year later, in New Mexico, he would become fascinated by the Indian tribes, their customs, legends and symbols, and would write about them perceptively. But he wrote of Australia as a 'land that as yet has made no great mistakes, humanly', as if ignorant of the appalling treatment of Aboriginals by white settlers. And yet, DH Lawrence did pick up on their presence. In the bush at night, Somers in *Kangaroo* sees 'the tree-trunks like naked pale aborigines among the dark-soaked foliage, in the moonlight'. Perhaps this glimpse of an imagined Aboriginal, marginalised at the edge of the bush yet intimately connected to the natural world, there in the declining light of his own way of life, is the most perceptive comment made by any writer about the Australian native.

On August 9 the Lawrences left Thirroul. Frieda was more than ready to go; the place had not got under her skin as it had under Lawrence's. Their ship, the *Tahiti*, left Sydney on the Friday morning and a large crowd farewelled her from Walsh Bay. Lawrence watched from the deck as fellow passengers threw streamers down to friends 'in a glittering tangle of . . . colours connecting the departing with the remaining'. He'd arrived with the rain and left in the sunshine—an apt analogy for his state of mind on both occasions. But as the ship began to move, the streamers 'broke and fluttered loose and fell bright and dead on the water'.

Lawrence would travel many thousands of miles in the last years of his life. The *Tahiti* took him to New Zealand where he was prompted to send Katherine Mansfield a postcard, then on to Rarotonga and Tahiti, and the USA. Then it was back to England, to America again and Mexico, Italy, Germany, England again, and then France where his travels finally ended. Haemorrhaging and painfully thin and weak, Lawrence seemed to keep living by sheer force of will. HG Wells visited him in the sanatorium in Vence, in the south of France, and was devastated to see his friend in such a pitiable condition. But the traveller and the free spirit in Lawrence could not bear to die in an institution. He left it on 1 March 1930 and died the next day, with Frieda by his side. He was forty-four years old.

Lawrence fought against death to the bitter end and doctors were amazed he survived as long as he did given the state of his lungs. He also wrote to the very end, determined not to let illness get in the way of creativity. He showed tremendous courage in the last months of his life.

Even then, his journey was not done. Frieda had his ashes taken to New Mexico, or thought she did. Angelo Ravagli (the man who became her third husband) confessed after Frieda's death that he'd thrown the ashes away. So DH Lawrence is still travelling. But the streamers that connected his ship to Australia were broken only physically, not emotionally. The Australian novel he took with him would ensure a permanent connection.

⚓

'Australia is a weird country, and its national animal is beyond me', Somers tells Ben Cooley. Lawrence was determined that that national animal would not remain beyond his own reach and in Sydney he wrote a poem called 'Kangaroo' after visiting the zoo:

> In the northern hemisphere
> Life seems to leap at the air, or skim under the
>   wind
> Like stags on rocky ground, or pawing horses, or
>   springy scut-tailed rabbits.
>
> Or else rush horizontal to charge at the sky's
>   horizon,
> Like bulls or bisons or wild pigs.
>
> Or slip like water slippery towards its ends,
> As foxes, stoats, and wolves, and prairie dogs.
>
> Only mice, and moles, and rats, and badgers, and
>   beavers, and perhaps bears
> Seem belly-plumbed to the earth's mid-navel.

Or frogs that when they leap come flop, and flop to
the centre of the earth.

But the yellow antipodal Kangaroo, when she sits
up
Who can unseat her, like a liquid drop that is
heavy, and just touches earth.

The downward drip.
The down-urge.
So much denser than cold-blooded frogs.

Delicate mother Kangaroo
Sitting up there rabbit-wise, but huge, plumb-
weighted,
And lifting her beautiful slender face, oh! So much
more gently and finely-lined than a rabbit's, or
than a hare's,
Lifting her face to nibble at a round white
peppermint drop, which she loves, sensitive
mother Kangaroo.

Her sensitive, long, pure-bred face.
Her full antipodal eyes, so dark,
So big and quiet and remote, having watched so
many empty dawns in silent Australia.

Her little loose hands, and drooping Victorian
shoulders.
And then her great weight below the waist, her
vast pale belly
With a thin young yellow little paw hanging out,
and straggle of a long thin ear, like ribbon,

Like a funny trimming to the middle of her belly,
    thin little dangle of an immature paw, and one
thin
    ear.

Her belly, her big haunches
And in addition, the great muscular python-stretch
    of her tail.

There, she shan't have any more peppermint
    drops.
So she wistfully, sensitively sniffs the air, and then
    turns, goes off in slow sad leaps
On the long flat skis of her legs,
Steered and propelled by that steel-strong snake of
    a tail.

Stops again, half turns, inquisitive to look back.
While something stirs quickly in her belly, and a
    lean little face comes out, as from a window,
Peaked and a bit dismayed,
Only to quickly disappear again quickly away
    from the sight of the world, to snuggle down
    in the warmth,
Leaving the trail of a different paw hanging out.

Still she watches with eternal, cocked wistfulness!
How full her eyes are, like the full, fathomless,
    shining eyes of an Australian black-boy
Who has been lost so many centuries on the
    margins of existence!

She watches with insatiable wistfulness.

Untold centuries of watching for something to
    come,
For a new signal from life, in that silent lost land
    of the South.

Where nothing bites but insects and snakes and the
    sun, small life.
Where no bull roared, no cow ever lowed, no stag
    cried, no leopard screeched, no lion coughed,
    no
    dog barked,
But all was silent save for parrots occasionally, in
    the haunted blue bush.

Wistfully watching, with wonderful liquid eyes.
And all her weight, all her blood, dripping
    sack-wise down towards the earth's centre,
And the live little one taking in its paw at the door
    of her belly.

Leap then, and come down on the line that draws
    to the earth's deep, heavy centre.

No other literary tourist has captured the essence of this
unique creature as Lawrence has. His observations are
acute; his words show the animal's face so exactly—
'rabbit-wise', 'slender' and 'pure-bred', her eyes, full
and fathomless—the sloping shoulders like those in a
Victorian lady's portrait; the great downward pull to
the earth of the heavy belly, all out of proportion to the
delicate head; the muscular tail, strong like a massive
python; and finally, the legs, or, in Lawrence's words,
'the long flat skis'. There are in fact two kangaroos in the

The cover of The Boy in the Bush, *the Australian novel that Lawrence co-wrote with Mollie Skinner of Perth.*

poem, for she has a joey which makes furtive, frightened appearances into the world outside the warm pouch—a paw, an ear 'like ribbon', a 'lean little face', and then a different paw. The edge of the pouch is a window, a door from which it learns to view the world. The man who had written so brilliantly of the mother – son relationship in *Sons and Lovers* could also write superbly of a mother and infant in the animal world. Lawrence makes his reader see that the kangaroo belongs totally and solely to Australia. The animals of other countries move in their own individual ways, but the kangaroo seems to seep 'like a liquid drop' into the parched Australian earth.

❧

The Boy in the Bush by Mollie Skinner was originally *The House of Ellis* (the title change reflects Lawrence's far greater interest in the landscape than in society). With his encouragement, Mollie sent him her manuscript, and when he was in America in 1923 he revised it for her. He'd always been something of a magpie—the 'Bits' chapter of *Kangaroo*, where he borrows stories from newspapers and from other people proves that—and he found other people's ideas helpful in developing his own thought processes. As he revised, he turned Mollie Skinner's hero, Jack Grant, into the independent man he wanted to be himself, one who could take several wives if he wanted them, unquestioned and indulged. He added a twist to the final chapters by presenting this ideal of a man having two wives, and sent it off for publication with his name above, and Mollie's below. Mollie Skinner might have cried when she saw his changes, but the book gave her an immortality she would never have achieved on her own.

Inspired by DH Lawrence's visit to Australia, playwright David Allen wrote *Upside Down at the Bottom of the World* which premiered with the Queensland Theatre Company in 1981. In his play the famous writer and his wife spend twice as long in Australia as they did in reality, and that time is all spent in arguments, physical fights and reminiscing about England. In 1988 novelist Margaret Barbalet was inspired by a red-bearded surfer she saw on Thirroul Beach to write *Steel Beach*, in which she imagines that Lawrence fathered a son with a local woman. It is known that several pages were cut out of one of the exercise books into which Lawrence wrote *Kangaroo*, and Barbalet's novel provides the story she thought those missing pages contained.

Patrick White cited DH Lawrence and James Joyce as the two strongest influences on his writing. He made a pilgrimage to Taos, New Mexico, to see the Lawrence ranch and met Frieda there. Geoffrey Dutton, poet, publisher and critic, also made a Laurentian pilgrimage, but his was to the Villa Mirenda outside Florence in Italy. Dutton once made a most unusual claim to be 'the only person who [has] read the collected fiction of DH Lawrence while flying an aircraft'. During World War II flights, Dutton found he could balance a book above the controls and read whilst piloting the plane.

Many Australian poets have been undaunted by a comparison with Lawrence and have versified on Thirroul, 'Wyewurk' and Lawrence's life. 'Paraclete Pie' by CD Barron, 'Thirroul Evening Too' by Joseph Davis, 'DH Lawrence in Thirroul 1922' by Jeff Guess, 'DH Lawrence at Circular Quay' by John K. Ruffels, 'Visiting Wyewurk' by Thomas Shapcott and 'The Presence I, after Garry Shead' by Peter Skrzynecki are all poems that would never have been written had Lawrence not visited Australia.

DH Lawrence was a keen painter and held a London exhibition of his work which was raided by the police. It is therefore appropriate that Australian artists have found in Lawrence's art, written and visual, a source of inspiration. In 1937 photographer Max Dupain created 'Homage to DH Lawrence', in which a human arm reaches out to a volume of Lawrence's poems, but is endangered by a large flywheel while doing so. Sidney Nolan's 'Streamers' depicts Lawrence leaving New York Harbour and returning to England, with the streamers described at the end of *Kangaroo* still connecting him with those on shore.

*'Envoy III',
one of the series
of paintings
by Australian
artist Garry
Shead which
were inspired by
DH Lawrence's
novel*
Kangaroo.

Brett Whiteley knew Thirroul well as his family holidayed there. In 1973 he went back with his friend and fellow artist Garry Shead. The two men set up their easels on the verandah of 1 Craig Street (the owners of 'Wyewurk' next door having refused them entry) and painted a diptych, 'What DH Lawrence saw that afternoon on the beach at Thirroul when he walked on the beach and thought about the book he was writing, *Kangaroo*'. Whiteley's half of the picture is a strongly expressionistic portrayal of 'Wyewurk', looking storm-tossed and dark. He went on to capture the spirit of Thirroul in several more pictures.

Garry Shead, after finishing his half of the diptych, went on to paint a series featuring DH Lawrence at Thirroul. Shead first encountered Lawrence through his letters, and soon became obsessed; he read all his works and studied his art. Like Lawrence, Shead has suffered police raids on his artworks. In the early 1970s Shead painted his 'Thirroulia' series, landscapes imbued with the spirit of Lawrence and his writings, as well as with the spirit of Thirroul. In the 1990s Lawrence re-inspired him and he began a series relating to *Kangaroo*, comprising fifty paintings in total. In these paintings 'Kangaroo', not a man as in the novel but an animal, oppressively spies on the couple in 'Wyewurk'. Thirroul's main street, its bungalows, the escarpment and other physical features are all captured, but so too are less tangible aspects of the novel, such as mob mentality, marital conflict and the spirituality of the land. Shead credits Lawrence as a 'crucial impetus' on his work.

Australian sculptor Tom Bass also calls DH Lawrence his mentor and guide. During World War II he came across Catherine Carswell's book on Lawrence, *The Savage Pilgrimage*, and was so moved by it that he created a tooled leather jacket especially for it.[8] Bass's 1975 bronze sculpture 'Introspection', was inspired by the lines in the poem 'The Song of a Man who has Come Through':

> Like a fine, an exquisite chisel, a wedge-blade
> inserted;
> If only I am keen and hard like the sheer
> tip of a wedge
> Driven by invisible blows,
> The rock will split, we shall come at the wonder . . .

Paul Delprat, Principal of the Julian Ashton Art School in Sydney, identifies with the young artist Paul Morel in *Sons and Lovers*. He has done several studies of 'Wyewurk' and its surrounds in oils, and also watercolour illustrations for *Kangaroo*, including 'A frightening dip in the sandy foam' and a delightful picture of Lawrence watching that ragged kookaburra.

---

8 Catherine Carswell was a friend of Lawrence's, and corresponded with him while he was in Australia.

Lawrence also inspired Peter Sculthorpe's *The Fifth Continent*, composed in 1963 (later revised and retitled *Small Town*). It took 'its point of departure from a description of the NSW coastal township of Thirroul, given by DH Lawrence in his novel *Kangaroo*'. Sculthorpe wanted his music 'to sing of all small Australian towns', but states that Lawrence's influence on him has been 'more enduring than any other [writer]'. His *Irkanda IV* and *Sun Music I* are reflections on Lawrence's feelings about the sun from his short story *Sun*. *Sun Music I* was later turned into a successful ballet.

And finally, there are the creations of Australian filmmakers. Tim Burstall directed a 1987 film of *Kangaroo*. This starred Colin Friels as Somers and Judy Davis as Harriet but, disappointingly, was filmed south of Melbourne rather than in Thirroul. And there has been a miniseries production of *The Boy in the Bush*, directed by Rob Stewart, starring Kenneth Branagh and Sigrid Thornton.

As the physical source of such creative ferment, 'Wyewurk' should be regarded as a treasured part of Australian literary heritage, but it is not. Lawrence is a relative unknown in Thirroul and 'Wyewurk' has remained in private hands and had owners who have not encouraged Lawrence fans to trespass on the property. No plaque records his visit (though there is a plaque at Circular Quay in Sydney), no museum has been established, yet 'Wyewurk' (where he actually worked very hard indeed) is probably the only house in Australia known by name outside the country. In 1988 a two-storey extension, considerably altering the character of the house, was proposed by the owner but fortunately planning permission was refused and there is now a Conservation Order on the building. The DH Lawrence society of Australia has done much in this regard. In 2001 a park in Craig Street was named the DH Lawrence Reserve, and a memorial stone was erected there; and the Thirroul Seaside and Arts Festival has, in recent years, been keen to include Lawrence in its programmes.

Lawrence's reputation has gone up and down like the proverbial yoyo. Often vilified while alive, after death his works have come and gone from literary favour. Just before his life came to its tragically early end, DH Lawrence wrote a poem called 'The Ship of Death', in which he imagines fitting out a ship that will sail him into death. It closes with these lines:

> Oh build your ship of death, oh build it!
> for you will need it.
> For the voyage of oblivion awaits you.

Fortunately 'oblivion' was not to be the fate of DH Lawrence.

The DH Lawrence Reserve at Thirroul.

The memorial stone with the phoenix at the DH Lawrence Reserve at Thirroul.

The plaque for DH Lawrence at Sydney's Circular Quay.

CHAPTER ELEVEN

HG Wells

HG Wells had not planned to exchange angry words with the Prime Minister when he came to Australia, but somehow they both managed to insult each other.[1] Nor had he planned to upset the nation's Catholics, yet priests spoke out against him from pulpits around the country. He'd never heard of Robert Gordon Menzies before he reached Australian shores and certainly had no intention of embarrassing him, but he managed to do that as well. He insulted teachers around the country when he accused them of starving and crippling the minds of their pupils; he offended Jewish people by complaining that they kept themselves too much to themselves; and what he said about the leaders of the Germans and the Italians came close to causing an international incident. All this,

---

1   His name was Herbert George Wells, but his books
    were published under the name of HG Wells.

*HG Wells
in a 1939
photograph.*

within a month, from a man who said before he reached Australia that all he knew of the place was that it was home to kangaroos, koalas, the duck-billed platypus and some primitive black men. A photograph exists of HG Wells holding a very contented-looking platypus in his arms—it seems to have been one of the few creatures *not* stirred up by his visit to Australia.

Yet Australians had been eager to welcome this famous author and he was there by invitation, to address the Australia and New Zealand Association for the Advancement of Science (ANZAAS) conference, held in Canberra in January 1939. Australians loved his novels and books about science, and had bought them in large numbers. They were anxious to hear what he had to say. He was also the sort of man with whom many

*HG Wells with
a platypus.*

Australians could identify—he'd been born lower-class, the son of a servant and an unsuccessful tradesman; he'd fought against the odds to get formal education; he'd struggled to find work; he'd persisted doggedly to establish himself as a writer, and he'd known what it was to go hungry. Those who had lived through the recent depression in Australia could relate to those experiences, and admire a man who had succeeded in spite of so many disadvantages, a man who gave generously to the poor and whose political support was for the working classes. They flocked to hear his lectures, they tuned into his radio broadcasts, approached him in the streets for his autograph, and avidly read articles about him.

So what went wrong? Why did so many feel that he had abused Australian hospitality? Why did the *Courier-Mail* portray him unflatteringly in a cartoon and an ABC announcer state that it was a very good thing when this 'quarrelsome, bad-tempered old gentleman' finally left the country?

SLASH!

Cartoon from the Courier-Mail *depicting HG Wells' attacks on a host of issues while he was in Australia.*

When HG Wells (or HG as his friends called him) left Marseilles in France on a P&O liner, the *Comorin*, bound for Fremantle, he was looking forward to the challenges of addressing new audiences, and to speaking at the Canberra conference. The trip would provide a much-needed break from the many meetings he normally attended in London and might give him something to think about apart from his acute anxiety over the coming war. He'd felt flattered that a scientific convention had invited him as a speaker. But from the beginning, the visit to Australia disappointed him.

The *Comorin* was full of 'officials or business managers for India, or home-going Australians, or young women going out to be married in India'.[2] They appeared to him 'completely innocent of any religious, political or social questionings', happy to dance and play deck games and ignore the signs of impending war. The ship itself was far too nineteenth century for the taste of a man who, in his fiction, had invented time machines and invisibility

---

2   The ship called at Bombay en route to Australia.

potions: 'Her cabins are extremely small and you pay a considerable supplement for the private use of a small but historically interesting bathroom. The bath water is salt water'. There were no films shown and the telephones for use in port were so antiquated that HG felt he was enduring 'a complete relapse into Victorianism'. He renamed this 'steady, conservative vessel' the *Pukka Sahib* and spent the voyage growing daily more annoyed by the narrow-minded, self-satisfied empire-builders who were his fellow passengers. Getting sick didn't improve his temper. He was seventy-two years old—too old, he soon began to feel, for such an extended trip. By the time HG arrived in Western Australia, he regretted having set out at all.

His mood improved when he encountered a warm reception in Perth when the ship docked on 27 December 1938. A driver collected him from the wharf and took him on a scenic tour, past Monument Hill, along the Swan River, to the University of Western Australia. There he was guest of honour at an afternoon tea and met university senators, teachers and their wives, and was shown around the science building. His suggestion that a bust of Rutherford would vastly improve the cloisters was greeted with little enthusiasm. Had HG forgotten that Rutherford was a New Zealand scientist, not an Australian one?

That night he was honoured with a dinner in Perth's Palace Hotel with the Fellowship of Australian Writers. Katherine Susannah Prichard and Walter Murdoch gave welcoming addresses and HG responded, expressing his optimistic hopes that Australian literature would break away from the 'upper-middle-class tradition of English literature' and find exciting new ways to tell its own stories. He felt stimulated by the 'newness' of the country and, at this early stage of his visit, saw it as a land of exciting possibilities. 'I want to find out what Australia is thinking and to see how far Australian thought is turning towards America', he announced. Convinced already that Australia was 'coming from her comparative isolation', he hoped it would play an important part in the 'inter-relation of the great English-speaking countries', rather than remain just part of what he saw as the 'temporary political arrangement' of the British Empire.

After a day in Perth, HG left for Adelaide. Charles Darwin had landed in Western Australia in the *Beagle* over one hundred years before. His sea journey to get there had taken years and had kept him isolated from news of the rest of the world for months at a time. The idea of a machine that could whisk him into the air and then, a few hours later, deposit him in a place thousands of miles from his point of origin, is something Darwin could hardly have started to imagine. But such ideas had been at the heart of HG's early fiction, in which flying machines delivered Martians to Earth in frightening numbers. Yet in spite of his own imaginings, his passion for aeronautics and the hours he'd spent designing airships, HG still struggled to visualise air travel as a daily part of modern life. His 1901 *Anticipations of the Reaction of Mechanical and Scientific Progress upon Human Life and Thought* were sceptical that planes could ever be a serious and practicable form of transport. Yet only eleven years later he excitedly took his first flight and after that he rarely missed an opportunity to fly. So, unlike every other literary visitor, he could avoid long train trips across Australia or long sea voyages around its edges. On 28 December 1938, he flew to Adelaide.

His plane was met by the Director of the Tourist Bureau and he was escorted to the South Australian Hotel. HG had told the Perth press that he was seeing friends in Adelaide, but in his three days in the city there was little time for socialising, and there is no record of who his friends actually were. He visited the zoo and a koala park (it was presumably at one of these places that the undated photograph of him cuddling a platypus was taken), managed a trip to the museum, a scenic drive through the Adelaide Hills to admire the view from Windy Point and took tea with Sir John Langdon Bonython. Bonython, ninety at the time HG met him, had enjoyed an extremely successful career as a reporter, then as editor of the Adelaide *Advertiser*, a publication he turned into a prominent Australian paper and a mouthpiece for the middle classes. With the fortune he'd accumulated from mining speculation, he gave generously to public causes, supported educational reform, helped establish the Commonwealth Literary Fund and was one of the first Australian editors to recognise the power of advertising (HG Wells' 1909 novel *Tono-Bungay* portrays the growing importance of advertisements in the commercial world). The two men shared interests in journalism, education, commerce and philanthropy. Bonython's home, 'Carclew', on Montefiore Hill, was a fine example of the Australian Federation style at its most elaborate.

The first of HG Wells' Australian broadcasts was made from Adelaide. Entitled 'Fiction about the Future', it dealt with science fiction, the genre which he had pioneered, although HG described his own futuristic writings as 'ephemeral'. According to the Melbourne *Age* the radio talk 'delighted thousands'. So far, very few hackles had been raised. The occasional autograph hunter was annoyed to be told they must purchase his signature for 2/6, which would be given to the Diabetic Association of Australia (HG suffered from mild diabetes and was founder and president of the Diabetic Association in England). By now he'd begun to find things to criticise—six o'clock closing for pubs was a barbaric idea; interviewers who had not bothered to read his books made him cross; and he was unimpressed by the Australian mania for horseracing and by their wasting money betting because they couldn't think of anything better to do. But generally the visit had, so far, been relatively calm and happy.

It had also been hot. The Adelaide weather was extremely sultry and for an Englishman unused to heat, immaculately dressed in jacket, waistcoat and tie made from good English wool, it was a shock. As he sweltered in forty-seven degrees Celsius he grew 'very crotchety' indeed. It didn't help to be setting off on a two-and-a-half-day road trip to Melbourne in a car which heated up very quickly and which, of course, had no airconditioning. From the car, and during a night at a sheep station en route, he gazed sweatily out at the 'gum trees, sheep, drought and vast spaces' and was disappointed that 'kangaroos, wallabys, boiling the billy, black fellows and so on' were not a part of the landscape. The salt lakes were drying out, the creeks were empty and the bushes were stunted—he saw little beauty in the Australian landscape on this car journey. He was also starting to feel that Australians were too much like people from the English midlands or from his native Kent, when he'd hoped, after travelling halfway around the world, to find citizens of a brave new world. By the time he reached Melbourne on January 3 and booked into the Menzies Hotel, he was hot, frazzled, and in no mood to chat amiably to the crowd of journalists who awaited him.[3]

Several sources contributed to the geyser of wrath and insults which gushed from HG during January, sending the press into a feeding frenzy and intriguing Australians generally. The summer of 1938–1939 was one of the hottest ever, breaking records dating back to 1862. 'Inland Scorches', 'No Relief in Sight' and 'Half Continent Suffers' were headlines that month. There was scarcely a town in New South Wales that escaped the plus forty degree Celsius heat. Canberra, before and during the ANZAAS conference, broke all records and local scientists 'felt it was an unfair trick of fate to reserve weather of this variety' for British visitors. Bushfires raged around Victoria, townships in South Australia were wiped out by fire and the January death toll mounted to over a hundred. Dying animals and crops thirsted in vain for longed-for rain. With formal events being held in his honour, dignitaries to meet and banquets to attend, HG did not like to be informal and take off jacket and tie. 'White waistcoats for dinner and orders and medals' were expected dress, and even at garden parties, frock coats and Ascot toppers were worn. He sweated his way through the speeches and the handshaking, drank the hot cups of tea and ate the scones, all the while longing for a cool English breeze.

It added to his discomfort that he was starved for sex.

---

3   This was the same hotel in which Trollope and Mark Twain had stayed.

The Menzies Hotel in Melbourne, where HG Wells, Anthony Trollope and Mark Twain all stayed on their visits.

His sexual drive had always been strong and his persistent and urgent need for physical relations with women had caused controversy and disruption throughout his life. Married to his cousin in 1891, at the age of twenty-five, he seduced one of her friends within weeks of the wedding. Two years later he had an affair with a student, for whom he divorced his wife. He married her in 1895, but she soon had to get used to sharing him with other women. Amber Reeves had his illegitimate daughter in 1909, Rebecca West had his illegitimate son in 1914, and there were many others with whom he enjoyed affairs. By the time of his visit to Australia, his wife had died and a Russian Countess, Moura Budberg, had become his mistress. He offered to marry her, but she preferred to keep her independence, so they lived 'in open sin'. In his late sixties he told Charlie Chaplin, 'There comes a moment in the day when you have written your pages in the morning, attended to your correspondence in the afternoon, and have nothing further to do. Then comes that hour when you are bored; that's the time for sex'. But it was more than that—HG needed regular sex to keep him on an even keel. With Moura on the other side of the world, he had to sweat in bed all on his own, and he did *not* like it!

Then there were his problems with journalists, who were like flies in an Australian summer. Everywhere he went, they followed, pestering him for opinions on everything from surfing to the merits of Australian women, chronicling his every movement, waiting for him at every turn. He soon was fed up: 'This really is a lot of nonsense, this publicity', he told them.

Heat, age, diabetes, lack of sex and too much of the press were all contributing factors to his anger, but perhaps more than anything else was the growing realisation that he was bashing his head against a brick wall. For most of his life he had tried to change his fellow man, through political groups he'd joined, through pamphlets he'd written, by the education of his scientific books, and even through his novels. He could see war threatening, he had even predicted a nuclear bomb. But as he travelled around Australia, he felt that no one was listening to his warnings. Just as the English had ignored his message, so did the Australians. 'If the human race is not to go on slipping down towards a bottomless pit of wars, conquests and exterminations, it must be through the rapid and zealous expansion of the intellectual organisations of the English-speaking countries', he insisted. Yet in Australia he found the same old patriotism and love of Empire, the same tendency to herd with one's own, the same myopic vision of the world that he'd encountered back home. For him, it was a close-run race between drastic change and sweeping education on the one hand, and catastrophe on the other: 'catastrophe is well on its way . . . education seems still unable to get started, has indeed not even readjusted itself to start. The race may, after all, prove a walk-over for disaster'.

His worst moment of despondence came in Sydney, near the end of his trip. For an hour an impassioned HG poured forth 'all the reasons for believing that the human species was already staggering past the zenith of its ascendency and on its way through a succession of disasters'. Those present clapped politely and, led by Billy Hughes, 'shook off the disagreeable vision, and lifted up [their] voices in simple loyalty to things as they are' by singing 'God Save the King'. It was an ironic moment, but HG had not spent his life producing publications, joining committees and giving speeches to enjoy irony at this time of international crisis. Why would they not heed his warnings and do something to avert calamity? He felt his journey had not achieved its purpose, that it had been a waste of time. Feelings of despair, anger and impotence were intensified by the easygoing, relaxed attitudes he encountered in Australia. And so, in revenge, he hit out right and left, lambasting the very hosts who had welcomed him so warmly.

His first missile was in fact fired at Hitler and Mussolini. HG told reporters in early January that he regarded Herr Hitler as 'a certifiable lunatic' with his 'ravings and delusions', while Signor Mussolini was 'a fantastic renegade from the Socialist movement'. He added, just for good measure, 'those men are freaks'. He also insisted that Germany would have done better to have turned Communist in 1924. Every major paper in Australia printed these remarks and in Germany, the paper *Der Angriff* blasted his declaration as 'criminal' and accused him of short-sightedness. The German

Consul-General in Australia, Dr Aswin, was called on to intervene; he pressed the Prime Minister to publicly rebuke HG Wells. Prime Minister Joseph Lyons, from his home in Tasmania, did so on January 6, criticising the famous author for insulting 'a friendly Head of State', insisting that Germans and Italians must *not* think HG spoke for Australians, and suggesting that Wells should 'exercise his undoubted gifts for promotion of international understanding rather than international misunderstanding'. Joe Lyons knew that peace was walking a tightrope, and a breach with Germany had to be avoided at all costs. Of course, in the end HG was proved right—Hitler was a lunatic and Mussolini a renegade—but he failed to see that his remarks did nothing to help delicate political negotiations.

'Prime Minister Rebukes HG Wells' appeared on placards and in headlines. Pondering his next move, HG went quiet for a few days. Then he attended a dinner at Scott's Hotel in Melbourne, given in his honour by the newly formed PEN club of Australia. He was to be guest speaker, along with Attorney General Robert Menzies. PEN President and toastmaster was author Leonard Mann. One of the aims of PEN was the preservation of free speech and HG received a standing ovation before he uttered a word. Mann was sympathetic to HG's views and, in his welcoming address, remarked that Lyons' comments ought to be 'treated with true Australian ribaldry'. He then stepped back to allow the honoured guest to respond.

HG Wells gave a witty, courteous speech about PEN (he had been a founding member of the organisation), mentioned that there was a German branch of PEN that had been forced into exile in Paris because of Hitler's suppression of free speech, then moved on to the issue of free speech in general. Prime Minister Lyons, he insisted, had a right to express his opinions, but in his own view Australia was led by a man suffering 'delusions of sagacity', who wanted 'reality hushed up', who was fearful, resistant to change and acutely desirous of suppressing public opinion. Robert Menzies replied to the speech and did his best to support Lyons, insisting that the Prime Minister was not suppressing freedom of speech and that the audience there that evening warmly supported their own head of state. But Menzies' words did not go down well. Heckling from the audience and tepid applause left him embarrassed and uncomfortable. He had misread the situation.

Once again Lyons rebuked Wells in print for his 'needless affront to other nations', and Australians around the country waded into the argument. The Mayor of Newcastle backed HG Wells and said Lyons should 'mind his own business'; author Mary Gilmore wrote to thank Mr Lyons for his 'sane, dignified and necessary rebuke to Mr HG Wells'; and a Mr Vowles in South Australia wrote that HG Wells ought to be silenced as he was damaging Australian trade with Germany. He added, as an aside, that no lives had been lost by German persecution of the Jews! *The Sydney Morning Herald* devoted a long, balanced editorial to the argument, favouring HG's views but expressing concern that he'd resorted to name-calling. In the English House of Commons, Lord Winterton delivered a furious speech, denouncing Wells as an 'unamiable septuagenarian' who was never taken seriously by anyone, to which Wells replied, 'I have long been criticizing the education of the young men in England belonging to the so-called ruling classes. I note regretfully that Lord Winterton is an example of all that justifies my criticisms'. Also in England, the *News Chronicle* denounced Lyons as an 'ultra-Chamberlainite' who hampered his country and who had a serious problem with censorship (they had a point—only one week before HG reached Australia, a Labor Party radio station had been suspended for comments unfavourable to the Prime Minister). But Berlin newspapers praised Lyons for his 'pleasing adherence to the good traditions of civilized nations'.

HG wrote up his views on the argument and published them in *News Chronicle* in late January, and later in his *Travels of a Republican Radical in Search of Hot Water*: 'Mr Lyons had laid himself bare, artlessly and completely, as all that is most indecisive, disingenuous and dangerous in the present leadership of the British Communities'. But he had caused offence and diplomatic stress by his remarks in a period of intense political insecurity. One year later the whole of Australia could insult Hitler with impunity (and Joe Lyons, who died within months, was not there to hear it); but in January 1939 HG upset a nation and caused a diplomatic incident by calling Hitler names.

While in Melbourne HG managed some sightseeing. The blowing by Melburnians that had so irritated Trollope and Kipling had subsided somewhat, but HG found he was expected to do the praising of Melbourne for them. Everyone insisted he admire Collins Street and the layout of the city and praise the Yarra as a beautiful river. Like many other visitors, he found it tactful not to mention the glory of Sydney Harbour while he was in Melbourne. He was driven to Portsea and to Upper Macedon, but there was no relief from the heat in either place (it was over forty degrees Celsius every day during his time in Melbourne), or from the journalists. He gave a second radio broadcast on 'The World as I See It', an attack on the restriction and distortion of knowledge. 'In the modern world', he insisted, 'it is second only to murdering a child to starve and cripple its mind'. Children needed books, and books needed to be cheaper. His own childhood had been enriched by the library of the house where his mother was housekeeper and he felt every Australian child should have easy access to affordable books.

He was delighted to be able to fly to Canberra on January 10 in a private plane belonging to a WR Robinson. The flight took one and a half hours and, as HG wrote to his mistress, 'went high over solitary mountains with bushfires smoking everywhere and so cut out fourteen hours hardship in trains'. He arrived on the hottest day ever recorded in Canberra. 'Let me alone, I'm hot and tired and sweaty. You are a lot of nuisances', he gasped to the waiting reporters, and he was driven off to Government House.

The ANZAAS conference was a major scientific event, an attempt to provide an Australian/New Zealand scientific view of the world. Its theme was 'The Place of Science in World Affairs'. Visitors swarmed into town, over twelve hundred of them, filling every hotel (though at least one hotel hoped none of them would want anything to eat—with a temperature of forty-nine degrees in the kitchens, the chefs had refused to cook). Some were billeted to local homes, the more adventurous camped out at 'a miniature scientists' settlement' by the Molonglo River, but elite visitors such as HG stayed at Government House. A booklet was published to introduce the delegates to Canberra, its facilities and attractions. Its pull-out map did not, however, prevent visitors getting confused by the city's layout. As the *Canberra Times* noted, even geographers and astronomers managed to get lost. The *Handbook for Canberra* proudly gave information on the cost of engineering works for the city's construction, on its 'Law and Judiciary', on its climate (information which had, ironically, promised temperate weather), and on its local scientific and educational institutions. It advertised Canberra as 'Australia's Most Beautiful City'—'Stay a Day and You'll Want a Week' was its slogan. While the War Memorial was still under construction and not yet open to visitors, there were four cricket grounds available and three bowling greens, Parliament House

Government House in Canberra in the 1930s. HG Wells stayed here while attending the ANZAAS conference.

could be visited, the Cotter Dam Recreation Area and Commonwealth Offices could be seen. Canberra might be a new city, but the booklet announced that 'like the ship described by Kipling, [she] is "finding herself", and there is emerging a definite and characteristic Canberra spirit'.

The conference opened on January 11 at Telopea Park School. The speaker listened to with most interest was the weather forecaster, Inigo Jones, who promised relief from the broiling conditions. He was right; temporary relief came with some rain, but by next day the heat was as bad as ever. Governor-General Lord Gowrie welcomed everyone to the fourteenth ANZAAS conference, the presidency was formally passed from Sir David Rivett to historian Professor Ernest Scott, there was a 'scientific cricket game' between the economists and statisticians, and then the convention got down to business.

HG's first address on January 12, was read to the huge audience inside and outside the hall and transmitted by radio across Australia. George Bernard Shaw (his sometime friend, sometime enemy) had once said that HG's platform manner was like that of a shop assistant addressing a customer. HG had described himself as 'speaking haltingly on the verge of the inaudible, addressing my tie through a cascade moustache that was no help at all, correcting myself as though I were a manuscript under treatment'. Recordings of his voice exist—it is thin, high-pitched, Cockney. His blue eyes had penetration and power, but they were unseen by his radio listeners, who heard only his rather squeaky words.

The first address was titled 'The Role of English in the Development of the World Mind'. In it he encouraged his fellow man to 'abolish war through conscious co-operation' and to launch 'wilfully and intelligently upon a new and greater way of living'. He proposed education as the panacea for the ills of the species and insisted that what was needed was a world encyclopaedia. While not everyone agreed with him, others felt his vision was centuries ahead of its time.

But it was his January 16 talk, for the educational section of the conference, which really stirred things up. Entitled 'The Poison of History', it aimed to provoke, and it succeeded. It upset history teachers who did not like being told that they were blind to the present and indifferent to the future, that they over-stimulated patriotism in the young, and that 'school-made nationalism' was threatening the 'very existence of civilization'. 'History as it is taught today', HG told the nation, 'is by its very nature useless as a basis of a world peace ideology'. Why, he asked, did historians teach students about King Henry VIII and his six wives, and ignore human biology, the history of implements, the development of flying machines, environmental issues, and man's adaption to the modern world? Why did no one teach children to think about the future?

He also complained about the way history was taught as the history of localities, selected peoples and specific religious groups. In his view, teaching French history or Jewish history or the history of the British Empire was dangerously separatist and divisive, making man think he belonged more to a tribe or to a church than to the human race. Man needed to pull together, not break up into groups. Flags, religious schools and historical nationalism all exacerbated the problem.

The speech offended Australia's Jewish population. They were not pleased to hear HG announce that 'the greatest, most astounding story, masked and hidden beneath the misrepresentation of the old history, is the Judaeo–Christian mythology that has set the Jewish people apart from the rest of mankind. It was a poisonous history that arrested the amalgamation of the Aryan and Semitic cultures. It set up a division in the spirit of mankind'.

He also infuriated the Catholics by complaining that they too kept themselves apart. He disapproved of the Catholic treatment of women, of the claims of the Catholic Church to have a single truth, and of the way it dinned Hell, fear and submission into young minds. It was a church that frustrated 'the efforts of the scientific intelligence to bring about a final rational phase in the world of mankind', and for this he saw it as 'evil', a cancer eating away at the world. He'd been horrified at the power exerted by Catholics in Australia—never in his life had he been in such a Catholic-dominated country. In his last novel, *You Can't be Too Careful*, published two years after his visit to Australia, he wrote: 'Wherever the Catholic priest prevails, among the decadent pious [French] generals of the surrender . . . in Spain, in that spite-slum Eire, in Italy, in South America, in Australia, there you will find malicious mischief afoot against the enlightenment of mankind'. No wonder Australian Catholics didn't like him! They also strongly disapproved of his pro-abortion stance. HG had been Vice President of the Abortion Law Reform Society in England for some years, and he rarely lost an opportunity to push his view that abortion needed to be legalised. Bishops asked their priests to denounce him from their pulpits and so, on Sunday January 22, Catholics around the country prayed that HG either recant his sinful beliefs, or burn forever in the Hell he hadn't believed in since he was a schoolboy.

The Melbourne *Age* called his address 'a shock', the Melbourne *Leader* said it was 'aggressive', the Brisbane *Courier-Mail*, under the heading 'Mr Wells Tilts Another Lance', accused him of advocating book-burning. But the Communist Party praised him and the Tasmanian Minister for Education said he was quite right. The one thing upon which all were agreed was that with HG, there was certainly no danger of boredom.

Having started all these blazes at the conference, HG then went off to see the real fires roaring round the outskirts of Canberra: 'I went with the Governor-General, who was anxious to find out what help could be given to the threatened homesteads . . . My expectations were of the crudest sort; just as our imaginations of the coming war are of the crudest sort'. He and Lord Gowrie toured the devastated areas and spoke to the firefighters: 'blackened, sweaty men with a curious tough Cockney cheerfulness and brotherliness' equipped with water carts that were hopelessly inadequate:

> A bush fire is not an orderly invader, but a guerrilla. It advances by rushes, by little venomous tongues of fire in the grass; it spreads by sparks burning leaves and bark. Its front is miles deep. It is here, it is there, like a swarm of venomous wasps. It shams dead and stabs you in the back. It encircles you so that there is no sure line of flight for its threatened victims.

He found it exhilarating to drive through the fire zones, but he drew lessons from his own sense of excitement: 'The thing to note, in a war-threatened world, is that for Australians, as for people at home, this sort of thing exhilarates. Bush fires eliminate class and feuds . . . the only effective method of restraining bush fires is to locate their beginnings and go out to meet them. Here, as in most human affairs, aggressive prevention is the best defence'. Surely Australia could see that 'mental conflagration and devastation' needed to be dealt with just as urgently as the fires in the bush? And then, almost as he watched the fires, the wind turned and the temperature dropped—the terrible heatwave was over. If only his words could likewise avert the blazes, bombs and destruction of the ensuing war.

On the night of January 18 HG travelled to Sydney by train. The Wentworth Hotel was his base for the busy week he spent there. There were radio broadcasts on 'Utopias of the Future'—his plea for utopia to be achieved through science—and on 'The Way to World Unity'—his lament that the energy and talents of young men were being channelled into war. He lunched with the Institute of Journalists at the Blaxland Galleries, and with the Institute of Engineers, where he urged all present to cut themselves off from England's apron-strings. At a dinner given for him by the Fellowship of Australian Writers, at which he sat next to AB 'Banjo' Paterson, he threw one last missile on the issue of censorship. How could a country that provided free education then proceed to cut off free access to information, he wondered?

SYDNEY TOWN HALL

HENRY HAYWARD & D. D. O'CONNOR *announce*

THE ONLY

PUBLIC LECTURE

in Australia

by

Mr. H. G. WELLS

Celebrated Author

of

THE WAR OF THE WORLDS
THE SHAPE OF THINGS TO COME
THE INVISIBLE MAN
&c. &c.

Saturday, 21st January, 1939
at 8 p.m.

PREFERENTIAL BOOKING
A limited number at **10 -**
including tax
Forward remittance to Box Office
W. H. Paling & Co. Ltd

PLANS Open Wednesday, 11 a.m.
at W. H. Paling & Co Ltd
Reserved Seats **6 - & 8 -** (plus tax
Unreserved Seats **2 - & 4 -**

A.W.A. SOUND AMPLIFYING SYSTEM

Flyer for HG Wells' only public lecture in Australia.

I hear dreadful stories of illiterate people who interfere with your radio talks here. I hear dreadful stories of half-educated policemen who decide what is indecent in your books and who intercept books, speakers and writers at your ports. That kind of thing is an outrage against freedom. You are a half-Fascist country until you get rid of every form of censorship.

ANZAAS had paid HG £250 for travel. It was not nearly enough, so from the beginning he'd been anxious, like Mark Twain, to give a public lecture and make money from it. This finally happened on Saturday January 21, at 8 pm, in the Sydney Town Hall. The event was presided over by Billy Hughes. But HG was no Mark Twain—nobody laughed while listening to 'The Human Outlook', nor did he want them to. It would have been nice if they'd just sat up and taken notice. Certainly he was applauded and complimented, but 'the stimulant seemed to evaporate at once and the food was certainly not assimilated'. He felt there was a total avoidance of the issues he had raised: 'the discussion was over and nothing had come of it and things were still very agreeably as they had always been. Tea was served'. To him, Australians too much resembled the legendary man on the *Titanic* who ordered a drink in the bar and sat enjoying it because 'the damn ship hasn't gone down yet!'.

On January 26 HG left Sydney for Darwin, and from there he gave one last radio broadcast. He'd always been an avid reader of the works of Charles Darwin. Thomas Huxley, Darwin's close friend (nicknamed 'Darwin's Bulldog' for his dogged espousal of Darwinian theories), had been HG's own teacher in London. It's a nice thought that the place named after Australia's first literary visitor should, exactly one hundred years later, be visited by his ardent disciple; both Darwin and HG were writers and scientists; both were controversial and created considerable stir during their lives; both loved knowing how the world around them worked. Charles Darwin, had he ever got to the place named in his honour, could not have even posted a letter from there, but HG was able to speak to Australians on radio, sending his words out across the land on its airwaves. He could also fly away in a 'metallic bird' unlike any categorised by the great naturalist.

As HG climbed aboard the little Lockheed of the

A Royal Netherlands Indies Airways Lockheed aircraft—the plane in which HG Wells left Australia.

Royal Netherlands Indies Airways[4] and set off for Bali, Burma, India, Mesopotamia and Athens, Prime Minister Joseph Lyons formally warned his countrymen of the possibility of war. HG's dire predictions were on the verge of becoming terribly true.

⚜

HG Wells left Australia feeling sick—sick at heart and sick of body. He'd caught a bad cold when, one warm night, he'd fallen asleep with only a sheet on, then the temperature had suddenly and dramatically fallen. The cold woke him, but only after he had been chilled through. By the time of his departure from Darwin he felt tired and depressed rather than stimulated by his trip. His Fabian Society friend, Beatrice Webb, seeing him soon after his return, 'found him a physical wreck' and doubted he would live much longer.

---

4   HG flew 'Dutch' because it was the best organised air
    service in the world at the time. The English services
    lagged far behind. The Royal Netherlands Indies
    Airways later became KLM.

But she was wrong. HG had seven more years of fight still in him. Books, articles and journalism continued to pour from his pen until the end, and he battled, until the very outbreak of World War II, to do all he could to avert the threatening 'heart of darkness'. Words were his weapons, and his 'shrill jets of journalism' were sent out to fight on many fronts. Perhaps there were too many battles, too many causes. His readers grew unclear about which issues were most important to him, and where his priorities lay. Another problem was that his solutions were often too vague and impractical. Full of grand ideas, he was less certain about how they should be implemented. As war grew closer, and then became a reality, people stopped listening. HG had become a has-been, and he knew it: 'I am tired, I am old, I am ill. I have no gang, I have no party. My epitaph will be "He was clever, but not clever enough"'. Death had always been a strong presence in his books, but it grew even stronger; his novels became intense studies in frustration. Bravely, however, he fought on and continued writing until he died from cancer, a month before his eightieth birthday.

Only one of his books was written as a result of his travels, and it deals only in part with Australia. 'Radical' was one of HG's favourite words—'It suggests going to the root of things. It suggests digging and weeding'. And so his collection of articles and some of the addresses he gave in Australia were gathered together as *Travels of a Republican Radical in Search of Hot Water*, and published in 1939. 'Mr Lyons Protects Hitler, the Head of a Great Friendly Power, from my "Insults"' is an entertaining chapter, and 'Bush Fires' is of interest too; but the book ranges too widely. The Jewish question, the British ruling class in Burma, the American situation, and his fellow passengers on the *Comorin* are all jumbled together. The tone is argumentative, the writing hurried and slipshod, the scope too broad and vague. W. Somerset Maugham once said of HG that he had a fluent pen which too often ran away with him—he could well have been referring to *Travels of a Republican Radical*.

In 1942 HG Wells published *The Outlook for Homo Sapiens*. Cobbled together from two previous works, *The Fate of Homo Sapiens* (1939) and *The New World Order* (1940), the book was pessimistic in tone. Mankind, it stated, was rushing 'along the stream of fate to degradation, suffering and death'; it was on the fast track to extinction. His ANZAAS lectures in Canberra are recalled in the book, along with his disappointment that so few Australians took any heed of them.

⁂

If a time machine, like the one he invented in his fiction, were to whisk HG Wells into twenty-first-century-Australia, he'd make the pleasant discovery that the issues he'd raised while here are now being debated. Whose history should be taught in schools and how that history is taught, is very topical. The integration into society of various religious groups; whether different religions should be entitled to state-funded schooling; the pronouncements from leaders of religious 'sects' in Australia—all these issues frequently make headline news and are much discussed on radio and television. HG was ahead of his time in warning that man was abusing his environment—seventy years later, Australian politicians have caught up with his ideas and recognise that protecting the natural world and its resources must come high on the political agenda. HG advocated that Australia cut its 'apron-strings' with Britain and turn more towards America as a model. He'd have strongly supported Australia becoming a republic and would wonder why it had taken so long.

Before coming to Australia HG knew virtually nothing of its 'primitive black men', as he called the Aboriginals (although he had sympathetically mentioned the wiping out of Tasmanian Aboriginals in *The War of the Worlds*). While in the country, however, he read a book called *Winjan's People* by JE Hammond, and was so impressed with it he wrote to the author to tell him that the book had made him see Aboriginals as 'credible human people—instead of fantastic totem poles'. HG was always ready to learn and to admit he might have held a mistaken view of someone. Aboriginals, he felt, should be treated as every other Australian and integrated into the general community. Whether or not, and how, this should happen has remained a controversial issue.

While in Australia HG spoke out against censorship and in favour of freedom of speech. 'I am quite convinced', he said, 'that the most precious thing in life is to be able to express myself and I would rather be shot than stop expressing myself at the top of my voice to the best of my ability. I think that to not express oneself is suicide'. Censorship of art, film and literature, curbing public expression of extreme opinions, and censorship of sexual material are all areas of shifting boundaries and heated debate in Australia today. HG would have delighted in the internet and the way it has allowed the spread of information—it is, in many ways, the 'world encyclopaedia' he dreamed of. But he could not have imagined the complexities of the issues it has thrown up, many of those concerning censorship. However, he told Australians they must think carefully about censorship, and they are certainly doing so.

He came to Australia primarily to talk about peace and to encourage its citizens to work towards non-aggressive resolution in world affairs. Discovering that Australia has *not* ceased to participate in wars would send him rushing back to his time machine in despair. He knew it wasn't easy: 'Peace is not a foolish thing; it is not a retreating aspect of humanity. It is something more difficult than war, more exhausting of human energy. You have not only to arm and train for it; you have to educate for it'. That 'education for peace' has, sadly, not yet happened in Australia.

In his lifetime HG Wells was known as 'The Man who Invented Tomorrow' and was an influential writer of the early twentieth century. A powerful spokesman for the creative possibilities of science, a champion of mass education, a pioneer environmentalist and peace activist, he predicted World War II and a nuclear bomb; he foresaw the need for greater international cooperation, and he early recognised the problems of religious fundamentalism and separatism. George Orwell said of him: 'the minds of us all, and therefore the physical world, would be perceptibly different if Wells had never existed'. By stimulating discussion and thought on a range of vital issues, HG also changed the minds of Australians and contributed to debates still current and relevant today.

His ideas still have a place in Australian society, but what about his books? In his radio broadcast from Adelaide he suggested that his fiction should be short-lived and advised future generations to read 'fiction of their times and not read ours at all'. As it concerns his own books, that advice has been heeded. His scientific and political works are rarely read these days, except as historical curiosities by the occasional scholar. He wrote 120 books in his lifetime, but Australians would now be hard put to name more than a handful of them and *The War of the Worlds*, *The Time Machine*, *The Invisible Man*, *The First Men in the Moon* and *The History of Mr Polly* probably spring to the minds of many as films, or even musicals, rather than as novels (if they are thought of at all).

Nor will the literary tourist, following the Writers' Walk at Sydney's Circular Quay, find any memorial to him. HG Wells is the only male author discussed in this book for whom there is no plaque. No physical record exists to show that one of the most famous writers of his day came to Australia on a visit that was reported at length by every major newspaper in the country. The Writers' Walk does not show that he lectured at a prestigious scientific conference, that he met the Governor-General and other important politicians as well as writers and journalists, and that he raised national awareness on a range of vital issues. No plaque testifies to HG Wells nearly causing an international diplomatic incident and engaging in a very public fight with the Prime Minister of Australia. And so perhaps Joe Lyons can be said to have had his revenge after all.

POSTSCRIPT

It has been said that 'travel broadens the mind'. All the writers in this book certainly found their horizons extended by their visits to Australia. They learned there was far more to the place than leaping kangaroos, Aboriginals and men in chains. They discovered that Australians were not 'inferior British' stranded at the other end of the world, but an energetic people busy creating their unique cities and forging their own very personal national identity. Some loved the country they encountered; others were less impressed. But they all returned to their homes enlightened by the experience.

These literary travellers broadened not only their own minds but also the minds of Australians. Those who 'came, saw and wrote' encouraged Australians to look at themselves, to face unpalatable truths about their 'blowing', to see how outsiders viewed their national pastimes of enjoying picnics or having a flutter at the races, to read what others thought of their beaches and bush, their Outback, their animals, and even of their Aussie accent. It was not always pleasant to read what British and American visitors had to say, but these opinions had their effects. The physical shape of the land couldn't be changed in the manner proposed by Oscar Wilde, but literary talent gave each traveller a unique power—a power to influence the way in which Australia was regarded by other nations. Bestselling authors (as Trollope, Stevenson, Kipling, Twain, London, Christie and Wells were) sent out their written impressions of Australia to a vast readership. What they wrote influenced perceptions of Australia and its inhabitants for generations to come.

The journeys of these writers occurred a long time ago, but they can still teach Australians to see their country and its history afresh. While most everyone is aware there was once a White Australia policy, most have no idea of the extent and virulence of the racial hatred generated in 1908 by the Burns–Johnson fight. HG Wells ought to be given the credit he deserves for triggering the ongoing debate about how history should be taught in Australian schools; and it is a national disgrace that 'Wyewurk' has not been preserved as a museum, a lasting memorial to the great writer who 'found himself' there.

Mark Twain once commented that 'a classic is something that everybody wants to have read and nobody wants to read'. But the literary works of these eleven writers have endured for a reason—their creators knew how to write. Why not begin a journey yourself through the books of these literary travellers? For starters, try Stevenson's *Kidnapped*, not a book for children, but a book for all those with a love of adventure, history and memorable characters; Kipling's *The Elephant's Child*, with its haunting 'great, grey-green, greasy Limpopo river, all set about with fever trees' (surely one of the most wonderful phrases in all literature); Trollope's Barchester series, with Mrs Proudie terrorising the clergy and lovely Mr Harding playing his cello, or his brilliant

Palliser novels; Jack London's story *To Build a Fire*, about a solitary traveller in the Arctic who must light a fire or perish; or Conan Doyle's *The Hound of the Baskervilles* set on Dartmoor and pitting Sherlock Holmes against a giant murderous canine. Explore the childhood world of DH Lawrence as he depicts it in *Sons and Lovers*; travel with Conrad into the heart of Africa, with HG Wells to the moon, or drift with Mark Twain along the Mississippi. When you discover that, contrary to Twain's dictum, you *do* want to read the classics, then you will have started on a marvellous literary journey that will last a lifetime.

ACKNOWLEDGEMENTS

It has been quite a journey following eleven great writers around Australia, and many people have assisted along the way.

My first thanks are due to the Australia Council for the Arts. Without the generous grant from the Australian Government through this important arts funding and advisory body, this book would have taken far longer to write, and might not have been written at all.

Helen Malcher, dear friend and fellow Janeite, has been invaluable. She has sourced photographs, gained copyright permissions for me and been generous with her editorial advice for the early chapters. I am extremely grateful!

As reading every Agatha Christie novel to find Australian references, no matter how small, was a task I didn't have time for, I am also very grateful to those who read 'Agathas' with sharp eyes for me. Many thanks to Marlene Arditto, Nadia Cameron, Lynne Cairncross, Marie Doke, John Faulkner, Lorna Graham, Valerie Karolczuk, Joanna Penglase, Jean Porter, Jan Roberts, Lyn Stephenson and, especially, to Harriet Veitch, who read more than anyone else.

Tim Bell of 'Coochin Coochin', the beautiful homestead visited by Agatha Christie, has been most generous with photographs and family information.

My sincere thanks to Rodney Pyne for his photographs, to Jonathan Graham for his assistance and to the ever-helpful Paddington librarians. David and Adrienne Richards kindly gave permission for their Garry Shead painting to be reproduced. Bill Barnes of 'The Sydney Passengers' Sherlock Holmes Society assisted with Australian references, and members of the DH Lawrence Society of Australia, the Rudyard Kipling Society of Australia, the Anthony Trollope Appreciation Group of Australia and the Mark Twain Society of Australia have all helped in various ways.

Writing a book is a solitary experience and sometimes an author needs a refreshing break. I have been helped enormously by the convivial lunches, friendship and support of very dear friends Elizabeth Budge, Christine Humphreys, Amanda Jones, Brigitte Lucey, Josephine Newman and Anthea Scarlett. Gabrielle Black has assisted me with research and been warmly encouraging from the beginning of this project. Jon Spence should have been a 'literary psychologist'. His insights into writers' personalities and motivations have been incredibly helpful. I thank him for those and for his constant encouragement and friendship, which I value very highly.

I have been most fortunate to have Pippa Masson of Curtis Brown Ltd as my literary agent. Working with Rod Morrison, Kylie Mason and Belinda Lee of Picador has been fantastic. I thank them all.

My family has probably felt I've been living in the nineteenth century for the past year. Thanks to my husband Ian, who has had to hear far more about dead writers than he ever wanted to know; to my wonderful sons Kenneth and Carrick, who have encouraged and taken photographs; and to my gorgeous daughter Elinor, who has taken such loving interest in it all, in spite of also having to cope with the HSC.

I wish I could meet with and personally thank the ten men and one woman who travelled to Australia and are the subjects of this book. It's been a delight to be in their company and to share their brief encounters with Australia. My time with Charles, Anthony, Jozef, Rudyard, Louis, Sam, Jack, Arthur, Bert, Agatha and HG has been full of surprises and has proved constantly fascinating. I felt privileged to read their letters, journals, travel accounts, novels, stories and poems and to be in their company. I really fell in love with nine of the male writers (only one left me emotionally cold) and had great affection for the redoubtable Agatha. Writing about them all has been a joy.

Lastly I'd like to thank the reader of this book. Thank you for accompanying these writers on their Australian travels. If this book encourages you to go and read their works, then I've achieved my purpose.

BIBLIOGRAPHIES
AND REFERENCES

INTRODUCTION

Bibliography

Harman, Kaye, *Australia Brought to Book: Responses to Australia by Visiting Writers 1836-1939*, BooBook Publications Ltd, Australia, 1985

Morgan, Ted, *Somerset Maugham*, Jonathan Cape, UK, 1980

New York Tribune, 31 October 1882

References

'When I look at the map ... more beautiful form', *New York Tribune*, 31 October 1882

'No words can express ... unnamed drudgery', *Australia Brought to Book*, p.157

'wonderful country for Warrant Officers', ibid, p.168

'crude and monotonous', ibid, p.145 'the most gratifying enthusiasm' and 'the Mecca of the decrepit author', *Somerset Maugham*, p.249

'of beauty and wildness ... pen to delineate', *Australia Brought to Book*, p.212

DARWIN

Bibliography

Armstrong, Dr P., *Charles Darwin in Western Australia*, University of Western Australia Press, Nedlands, Australia, 1985

Bowlby, John, *Darwin: A New Life*, WW Norton & Co, New York, 1991

Bowler, Peter J., *Charles Darwin: The Man and his Influence*, Basil Blackwell, Oxford, 1990

Browne, Janet, *Charles Darwin—A Biography*, Knopf, New York, 1995

Darwin, Charles, *Charles Darwin's 'Beagle' Diary*, RD Keynes (ed.), Cambridge University Press, UK, 1988

Darwin, Charles, The Correspondence of Charles Darwin, Vol. I 1821-1836, Vol. II 1837-1843, Vol. IV 1847-1850, Vol. V 1851-1855, Vol. VI 1856-1857, Frederick Burkhardt and Sydney Smith (eds.), Cambridge University Press, UK, 1985

Darwin, Charles, *The Origin of Species*, Mentor, USA, 1958 (first published 1859)

Darwin, Francis, *The Autobiography of Charles Darwin and Selected Letters*, Dover Publications Inc, New York, 1958

Davis, Lloyd Spencer, *Looking for Darwin*, Longacre Press, New Zealand, 2007

Duffy & Snellgrove (no editor attributed), *Crossing the Blue Mountains: Journeys Through Two Centuries from Naturalist Charles Darwin to Novelist David Foster*, Australia, 1997

Keynes, Randal, Annie's Box: *Charles Darwin, His Daughter and Human Evolution*, Fourth Estate, London, 2001

Keynes, RD, *Fossils, Finches and Fuegians Adventures and Discoveries on the Beagle*, Oxford University Press, Oxford, 2003

Marshall, AJ, *Darwin and Huxley in Australia*, Hodder & Stoughton, Australia, 1970

Moorehead, Alan, *Darwin and the Beagle*, Hamish Hamilton, London, 1969

Nicholas, FW and Nicholas, JM, *Charles Darwin in Australia*, Cambridge University Press, Australia, 1989

Park, Ruth, *Ruth Park's Sydney*, Duffy & Snellgrove, Sydney, 1973

Smith, WH, *Great Writers*, Exclusive Books, UK, 1992

References

'on the strange character ... the rest of the World', 'An unbeliever in everything ... end is complete', 'of a Lion-Ant', 'the same genus ... European one', 'any two workmen ... a contrivance' and 'periods of Creation ... distinct and remote', ibid, pp.402–403

'I hate every wave of the ocean', *The Correspondence of Charles Darwin*, Vol. I, p.491

'Certainly I never was intended for a traveller', ibid, p.484

'I am looking forward ... part of the voyage', ibid, p.472

'Where Sydney Cove her lucid bosom swells ... her golden hair', 'broad streets and crescents', 'cities o'er the cultur'd land', 'solid roads', 'Embellish'd villas', *Charles Darwin in Australia*, pp.84–85

'the Natural History of T del Fuego', *Charles Darwin's 'Beagle' Diary*, p.405

'There never was a ship so full of home-sick heroes as the *Beagle*', *The Correspondence of Charles Darwin*, Vol. 1, p.490

'Early in the morning ... populous city' and 'the level country ... useless sterility', *Charles Darwin's 'Beagle' Diary*, p.395

'not a single letter', 'The same fate will follow ... last 18 months' and 'much inclined to sit down and have a good cry', *The Correspondence of Charles Darwin*, Vol. 1, p.482

'It is a most magnificent testimony ... born an Englishman' and 'everyone complains ... procuring a house', *Charles Darwin's 'Beagle' Diary*, p.396

'bent on acquiring wealth', *Charles Darwin in Australia*, p.78

'I know no finer field ... Sydney harbour', *Ruth Park's Sydney*, p.34

'Large towns ... can be perceived', *The Correspondence of Charles Darwin*, Vol. 1, p.482

'suddenly and without any preparation ... covered with forest', *Charles Darwin's 'Beagle' Diary*, p.399

'very comfortable' and 'a view of a similar ... stupendous character', ibid, p.400

'a long day's ride to Bathurst', ibid, p.403

'The trees ... peculiar light green tint', *Charles Darwin in Australia*, p.26

'the bark of some kinds ... arid sterility', *Charles Darwin's 'Beagle' Diary*, p.397

'The inhabitants ... the leafless tree', *Charles Darwin in Australia*, p.27

'nearly horizontal', ibid, p.26

'succeed on a very extended scale', ibid, p.79

'diving and playing in the water' and 'most extraordinary animal', ibid, p.52

'a great feat ... wonderful an animal', *The Correspondence of Charles Darwin*, Vol. 1, p.481

'animals are called ... they are Carnivorous', *Charles Darwin in Australia*, p.51

'the enormous amount of stone' and 'by the action of water', ibid, p.41

'The most Novel ... parties of Convicts', ibid, p.25

'hardened profligate men', 'the slaves from Africa' and 'claim for compassion', ibid, p.46

'good fortune', 'a score of Aboriginal Blacks ... other weapons' and 'good-humoured & pleasant', *Charles Darwin's 'Beagle' Diary*, p.398

'Van Diemen's Land ... a native population', *Charles Darwin in Australia*, p.97

'Wherever the European ... extirpating the weaker', ibid, p.30

'a place of exile', 'not very inviting', 'in the least danger', 'hideous' and 'most English-like house', *Charles Darwin's 'Beagle' Diary*, pp.403–405

'being surrounded ... be dreadful', *Charles Darwin in Australia*, p.78

'villainously dear', *The Correspondence of Charles Darwin*, Vol. 1, p.482

'of the ninety-two species ... previously unknown', *Charles Darwin in Australia*, p.90

'Nothing ... compel me to emigrate', *Charles Darwin's 'Beagle' Diary*, p.406

'On the whole I do not like New South Wales', *The Correspondence of Charles Darwin*, Vol. 1, p.485

'entered the mouth ... awful name', *Charles Darwin's 'Beagle' Diary*, p.408

'extensive Basaltic platforms ... of columns', *Charles Darwin in Australia*, p.94

'fine and broad', *Charles Darwin's 'Beagle' Diary*, p.408

'start for England ... inclination to bolt', *The Correspondence of Charles Darwin*, Vol. 1, p.490

'long pleasant walks', *Charles Darwin's 'Beagle' Diary*, p.408

'a small snake appeared from the disrupted egg', *Charles Darwin in Australia*, p.124

'most agreeable evening since leaving England', *Charles Darwin's 'Beagle' Diary*, p.409

'first rate Italian', *The Correspondence of Charles Darwin*, Vol. 1, p.490

'a good deal of Society' and 'much pleasanter than that of Sydney', *Charles Darwin in Australia*, p.112

'delightfully resemble England', *The Correspondence of Charles Darwin*, Vol. 1, p.490

'obliged to emigrate I should prefer this place', 'formed a very low opinion of the place' and 'not remember ... uninteresting time', *Charles Darwin's 'Beagle' Diary*, pp.409–411

'called the White Coccatoo men', 'were asked to hold ... dancing party', 'tubs of boiled rice and sugar' and 'As soon as it grew dark ... their wild cries', ibid, pp.411–412

'Farewell Australia ... sorrow or regret' ibid, p.413

'a most useful assistant', *The Correspondence of Charles Darwin*, Vol. 2, p.194

'a country ... if industrious', 'I have received a vast ... one locality' and 'One of the kinds ... thank you very sincerely', *The Correspondence of Charles Darwin*, Vol. 4, p.369

'any odd breeds of poultry, or pigeon, or duck', *The Correspondence of Charles Darwin*, Vol. 6, p.56

'afraid' and 'want to think ... toads and tadpoles', *Charles Darwin in Australia*, p.155

'with much interest', ibid, p.164

'sitting on booms', ibid, p.168

'I feel a great interest ... can get hold of' *The Correspondence of Charles Darwin*, Vol. 5, p.164

'drank some admirable Australian wine', 'fine country' and 'a very great one', *The Correspondence of Charles Darwin*, Vol. 6, p.345

'wide bay appearing between the two white cliffy heads', 'fine-grained sandstone', 'an appropriate opportunity ... and friend' and 'accordingly named this sheet of water Port Darwin', *Charles Darwin in Australia*, p.158

'In the Australian mammals ... stage of development', *The Origin of Species*, p.114

'in ancient times', ibid, p.334

'are either the same species or varieties of the same species', ibid, p.360

'I have always felt ... education of my mind', *The Autobiography of Charles Darwin and Selected Letters*, p.28

TROLLOPE

Bibliography

Edwards, PD, *Anthony Trollope's Son in Australia*, University of Queensland Press, Australia, 1982

Edwards, PD, *Anthony Trollope: His Art and Scope*, University of Queensland Press, Australia, 1977

Glendinning, Victoria, *Trollope*, Hutchinson, London, 1992

Handley, Graham (ed.), *Trollope the Traveller: Selections from Anthony Trollope's Travel Writings*, William Pickering, London, 1993

Harman, Kaye, *Australia Brought to Book: Responses to Australia by Visiting Writers 1836–1939*, BooBook Publications Ltd, Australia, 1985

Hennessey, James Pope, *Anthony Trollope*, Panther, UK, 1973

Jack, Ian, *Trollope and the Hawkesbury River,* New South Wales, The Anthony Trollope

Appreciation Group of Australia, Sydney, 2004

Terry, RC (ed.), *Oxford Reader's Companion to Trollope*, Oxford University Press, Oxford, 1999

Trollope, Anthony, *An Autobiography*, Oxford University Press, UK, 1883

Trollope, Anthony, *Australia and New Zealand*, The Trollope Society, London, 1873

Trollope, Anthony, *The Fixed Period*, The Folio Society, London, 1997

Trollope, Anthony, *Harry Heathcote of Gangoil: A Tale of Australian Bush Life*, Lansdowne Press, Melbourne, 1963

Trollope, Anthony, *John Caldigate*, Zodiac Press, London, 1978

Trollope, Anthony, *Lady Anna*, Oxford University Press, Oxford, 1990

References

'Of the further doings of Mr Daniel Thwaite ... live to tell', *Lady Anna*, p.513

'Nothing really frightens me ... enforced idleness', *The Fixed Period*, p.xvii

'I have attempted ... the most interesting', *Australia and New Zealand*, Vol. I, p.1

'Boys less than himself ... not liked it', *Harry Heathcote of Gangoil*, p.15

'many in England ... their children', *Australia Brought to Book*, p.64

'Colonists are usually fond ... they can do', *Australia and New Zealand*, Vol. I, p.117

'Now if I was sending a young man ... say to him', ibid, p.118

'on the strength of beef and through the inspiration of ale', *Oxford Reader's Companion to Trollope*, p.240

'bought some Australian preserved meat ... tasteless as meat', *Australia and New Zealand*, Vol. I, p.55

'felt as thought I were pervaded by meatiness for many hours' and 'palatable and nutritive', ibid, p.57

'stewed wallabi ... utmost with wine and spices', ibid, p.116

'such a world of loveliness of water ... Sydney Heads' and 'the beauty of Sydney Harbour', ibid, p.207

'I can say that it is lovely ... then again of land', ibid, p.211

'unrivalled by any that I have ever seen' and 'I had previously no idea ... their nature', ibid, pp.214-15

'not yet had time for success', ibid, p. 231

'Sydney is one of those places ... its loveliness', ibid, p.213

'I cannot say that as yet ... a stranger', ibid, p.249

'an apparent mixture of ... mind of a stranger', ibid, p. 247

'a look of scattered ... air of disappointment', ibid, p.249

'had she not found a husband ... in the bush', ibid, p.308

'I write for four hours a day ... brandy and water', *Trollope*, pp.437–438

'there arose at last ... never going anywhere', *Australia and New Zealand*, Vol. I, p.306

'simply goes out ... the nearest church', ibid, p.312

'the undoubted capital ... all Australia', ibid, p.383

'the best daily papers I have seen out of England', ibid, p.485

'We have taken away their land ... defended themselves', ibid, p.499

'Of the Australian black man ... in the matter', ibid, p.76

'troubled by ... remarkable a place' *Australia and New Zealand*, Vol II, p.23

'Tasmania ought to make jam for all the world', ibid, p.51

'not in the least doubt ... from her troubles' and 'were it my lot ... pitch my staff in Tasmania', ibid, p.76

'a very pretty little town', ibid, p.125

'No man perhaps ever ... moment becomes interesting', ibid, p.127

'the everlasting gum', ibid, p.323

'all the new people and all the new things', *Trollope*, p.414

'has the pertness ... good as you', *Australia and New Zealand*, Vol. I, p.475

'The barmaids ... remained at home', ibid, p.288

'to see my son among his sheep', *An Autobiography*, p.317

'had not at all succeeded in getting away from England', *Australia and New Zealand*, Vol. II, p.332

'His attitude was that of ... live there', *Australia Brought to Book*, p.63

'Of all the needs a book has ... be readable', 'the pages drag with me' and 'a thoroughly honest book ... trouble in listening', *An Autobiography*, pp.318–19

'should have been introduced into the arrangements of the world', *Harry Heathcote of Gangoil*, p.17

'very courteous, but full of wrath', *Australia Brought to Book*, p.68

'to be regarded as rather a bad man ... with indignation', ibid, p.67

'and at that age ... voyages round the world', *Trollope the Traveller*, p.xxviii

'the most hopelessly disappointing place', *Australia and New Zealand*, Vol. I, p.292

'eating a nauseous lump ... his pocket-knife', ibid, p.89

'there was gold being found ... his imagination', *John Caldigate,* p.15

'anything done in the wilds of Australia ... in England', ibid, p.306

'mining operations', ibid, p.108

'I hope my friends in the Sydney post-office ... quite unnecessary', *Oxford Reader's Companion to Trollope*, p.278

'bluffs and high banks', *Australia and New Zealand*, Vol. I, p.322

CONRAD

Bibliography

Allen, Jerry, *The Sea Years of Joseph Conrad*, Methuen & Co., London, 1967

Baines, Jocelyn, *Joseph Conrad: A Critical Biography*, Penguin, UK, 1960

Batchelor, John, *The Life of Joseph Conrad*, Blackwell, UK, 1994

Conrad, Joseph, *A Smile of Fortune* in *Twixt Land and Sea*, Penguin, UK, 1912

Conrad, Joseph, *Almayer's Folly*, Penguin, UK, 1936

Conrad, Joseph, *Because of the Dollars* in *Within the Tides*, Penguin, UK, 1978

Conrad, Joseph, *The Brute* in *The Works of Joseph Conrad*, Vol. II, John Grant, UK, 1925

Conrad, Joseph, *Chance*, Hogarth Press, London, 1984

Conrad, Joseph, *Lord Jim*, Penguin, UK, 1949

Conrad, Joseph, *Mirror of the Sea: Memories and Impressions* and *A Personal Record: Some Reminiscences*, JM Dent & Sons, London, 1946

Conrad, Joseph, *The Collected Letters of Joseph Conrad*, Vols. 1–9, Frederick R Karl and Laurence Davies (eds.), Cambridge University Press, UK, 1983

Conrad, Joseph, *The Planter of Malata* in *Within the Tides*, Penguin, UK, 1915

Conrad, Joseph, *The Shadow Line*, JM Dent & Sons, London, 1932

Conrad, Joseph, *The Torrens: A Personal Tribute* in *Tales of Hearsay and Last Essays*, JM Dent & Sons, London, 1928

Fletcher, Chris, *Joseph Conrad*, The British Library 'Writers' Lives Series', London, 1999

Gordan, John Dozier, *Joseph Conrad: The Making of a Novelist*, Russell & Russell Inc. New York, 1963

Jean-Aubry, G, *Joseph Conrad: Life and Letters*, Vol. I, William Heinemann Ltd, London, 1927

Knowles, Owen and Moore, Gene M, *Oxford Reader's Companion to Conrad*, Oxford University Press, UK, 2000

Knowles, Owen, *A Conrad Chronology*, Macmillan, UK, 1989

Meyers, Jeffrey, *Joseph Conrad: A Biography*, John Murray, London, 1991

Stape, John, *The Several Lives of Joseph Conrad*, William Heinemann, London, 2007

Tennant, Roger, *Joseph Conrad: A Biography*, Sheldon Press, London, 1981

References

'vanquished man', *The Several Lives of Joseph Conrad*, p.17

'the warmest regard for Australians ... Sydney especially', *The Collected Letters of Joseph Conrad*, Vol. 5, p.50

'imperfect oilskins which let water in a every seam', *Joseph Conrad*, p.26

'ships' crews had the trick ... those days', *Mirror of the Sea*, p.122

'I do not regret the experience ... incomprehensible propositions', 'On one occasion ... and operatic singers', 'impolite stories ... over the bulwarks', 'Sun-kum-on's was not bad' and 'monotony, the regularity ... own infamous wares', ibid, pp.122–23

'on Sundays and holidays ... visiting bent', 'engaging manners and a well-developed sense of fun' and 'one of the finest ... shone upon', ibid, p.121

'bent almost double ... off for meals', *Joseph Conrad: A Biography*, p.30

'one of the iron wool-clippers ... upon the world', *Mirror of the Sea*, p.38

'And the thought ... understand what I mean', *Chance*, p.28

'has the appearance ... port in capital order', *The Sea Years of Joseph Conrad*, p.116

'no sun, moon, or stars for something like seven days', *Joseph Conrad*, p.32

'harmonious creature ... string of cart-horses' and 'Directly my eyes had rested ... joyous emotion', *The Shadow Line*, p.71–72

'Captain Conrad Konkorzentowski', *The Sea Years of Joseph Conrad*, p.253

'Asses', *The Several Lives of Joseph Conrad*, p.53

'various knick-knacks, neither beautiful nor valuable', *Joseph Conrad*, p.45

'from an unparalleled drought', *A Smile of Fortune*, p.74

'the farmers around ... God-forsaken jetty', *The Collected Letters of Joseph Conrad*, Vol. 6, p.99

'Sailors and boys all swore by him', *Joseph Conrad*, p.64

'for apart from ... heavy weather', *The Torrens: A Personal Tribute*, pp.22–23

'launched in 1875 ... the Mediterranean', ibid, p.26

'Next day ... Very much', *A Personal Record: Some Reminiscences*, pp.16–17

'reminders of Africa', *The Collected Letters of Joseph Conrad*, p.125

'tales of ships and storms ... the Congo', *The Sea Years of Joseph Conrad*, p.290

'a capital chap ... fund of yarns', *Joseph Conrad: A Critical Biography*, p.165

'a great affection for ... memory itself', *Collected Letters of Joseph Conrad*, Vol. 8, p.335

'took a long look ... sea life altogether', *The Torrens: A Personal Tribute*, p.26

'the direction of the winds that brought you back', *Joseph Conrad*, p.26

'We have few travellers ... to Australia', *The Life of Joseph Conrad*, p.14

'knew the road to the Antipodes better than their own skippers', *Mirror of the Sea*, p.120

'honoured guests', ibid, p.121

'those bold spirits ... money and adventure', *Almayer's Folly*, pp.9–10

'He was a man with an immense ... hunting ground', *Lord Jim*, p.161

'making of Queensland!', ibid, p.164

'at some Australian port ... month or so afterwards', ibid, p.172

'superficial aspect of vapid sweetness' and 'small, red, pretty, ungenerous mouth', *Because of the Dollars*, p.154

'an abject sort of creature', ibid, p.157

'on that awful, blazing hot day ... idea where they had been', *The Brute*, p.120

'close with a dreadful hug', ibid, p.124

'the only literary newspaper in the Antipodes', *The Planter of Malata*, p.24

'a great colonial city', ibid, p.15

'evade the small complications of existence', ibid, p.57

STEVENSON

Bibliography

Aldington, Richard, *Portrait of a Rebel: The Life and Work of Robert Louis Stevenson*, Evans Bros Ltd, London, 1957

Bell, Ian, *Dreams of Exile: Robert Louis Stevenson: A Biography*, Henry Holt & Co., New York, 1992

Booth, Bradford and Mehew, Ernest (eds.), *The Letters of Robert Louis Stevenson*, Yale University Press, Yale, 1995

Butts, Dennis, *Robert Louis Stevenson*, The Bodley Head, UK, 1966

Cairney, John, *The Quest for Robert Louis Stevenson*, Luath Press, Edinburgh, 2004

Calder, Jenni, *RLS: A Life Study*, Hamish Hamilton, London, 1980

Daiches, David, *Robert Louis Stevenson and his World*, Thames & Hudson, London, 1973

Davies, Hunter, *The Teller of Tales: In Search of Robert Louis Stevenson*, Sinclair Stevenson, UK, 1994

Ellison, Joseph W, *Tusitala of the South Seas*, Hastings House, New York, 1953

Goddard, RH and Crivelli, RL, *The Union Club: A Historical Sketch*, Union Club, Sydney, 1990

Hammond, JR, *A Robert Louis Stevenson Companion*, Macmillan, New York, 1984

Hammond, JR, *A Robert Louis Stevenson Chronology*, Macmillan Press Ltd, UK, 1997

Harman, Kaye, *Australia Brought to Book: Responses to Australia by Visiting Writers 1836–1939*, BooBook Publications, Australia, 1985

Jolly, Roslyn (ed.), *The Cruise of the Janet Nicoll among the South Sea Islands: A Diary by Mrs Robert Louis Stevenson*, University of NSW Press, Sydney, 2004

Mackaness, George, *Robert Louis Stevenson: His Association with Australia*, DS Ford, Sydney, 1935

McLynn, Frank, *Robert Louis Stevenson: A Biography*, Hutchinson, London, 1993

Millar, David P, *Charles Kerry's Federation Australia*, David Ell Press, Sydney, 1981

Robinson, FO, *The Oxford Hotel*, Oxford Hotel publication, Sydney, 1908

Smith, WH, *Great Writers*, Exclusive Books, London, 1992

Stephenson, Pamela, *Treasure Islands: Sailing the South Seas in the wake of Fanny and Robert Louis Stevenson*, Headline, London, 2005

Stern, GB, *Robert Louis Stevenson*, Longman, UK, 1952

Stevenson, Robert Louis, *El Dorado* in *Virginibus Puerisque and Other Papers*, Chatto & Windus, London, 1907

Stevenson, Robert Louis, *Edinburgh: Picturesque Notes*, Pallas Athene, London, 2001

Stevenson, Robert Louis, *The Collected Poems of Robert Louis Stevenson*, Roger C. Lewis (ed.), University of Edinburgh Press, Scotland, 2003

Stevenson, Robert Louis and Osbourne, Lloyd, *The Wrecker*, Oxford University Press, UK, 1954

Stevenson, Robert Louis, *Travels with a Donkey in the Cevennes*, Folio Society, London, 1967

Stevenson, Mrs Robert Louis, *The Cruise of the Janet Nicholl among the South Sea Islands*, Roslyn Jolly (ed.), University of NSW Press, Sydney, 2004

References

'to travel hopefully is a better thing than to arrive', *El Dorado* in *Virginibus Puerisque and Other Papers*, p.120

'For my part, I travel … affair is to move', *Travels with a Donkey in the Cevennes*, p.50

'scowling town', 'To My Old Familiars' in *The Collected Poems of Robert Louis Stevenson*, p.189

'one of the vilest climates under heaven' *Edinburgh: Picturesque Notes*, p.7

'hundred, jingling, tingling, golden minted quid', *The Letters of Robert Louis Stevenson*, Letter 2214

'beautiful places, green forever … desire to go there', *The Quest For Robert Louis Stevenson*, p.xii

'had more fun and pleasure of my life … ten long years', *Great Writers,* p.233

'When I think of Melbourne … of the Yarra', *Robert Louis Stevenson in Australia*, p.12

'criminal stamp', *Robert Louis Stevenson: A Biography*, p.374

'unwashed loose dresses', *The Cruise of the Janet Nicholl among the South Sea Islands*, p.37

'laid myself out to be sociable' and 'several niceish people have turned up', *The Letters of Robert Louis Stevenson*, Letter 2214

'friends old and new … a lark', 'late Attorney General here, a handsome fellow' and 'evening after evening … old experiences', ibid, Letter 2218

'whirl of work and society', ibid, Letter 2214

'Lynch, of course' and 'I'm damned … cat's meat to me', *Tusitala of the South Seas*, p.131

'an ungainly structure with a tower', *Robert Louis Stevenson in Australia*, p.12

'not in the Pacific ... the same time', ibid, pp.9–10

'fame much grown', *The Quest for Robert Louis Stevenson*, p.177

'butt-ends of human beings', ibid, p.131

'I knew I was writing ... every insult heroic', *Robert Louis Stevenson in Australia*, p.15

'justified and righteous', ibid, p.12

'exposure, malaria, worry and over-work', *Robert Louis Stevenson: A Biography*, p.454

'a blooming prisoner' and 'This visit to Sydney ... in Scotland', *The Letters of Robert Louis Stevenson*, Letter 2215

'a most agreeable ship's company', ibid, Letter 2228

'at my old trade — bedridden', *Robert Louis Stevenson in Australia*, p.21

'Even here, which they call ... catch cold', *The Letters of Robert Louis Stevenson*, Letter 2239

'he spent a good deal ... went abroad', *Dreams of Exile*, p.225

'O Christ Jesus ... has dependents', The *Letters of Robert Louis Stevenson*, Letter 2248

'Kipling is too clever to live', ibid, Letter 2239

'a long life and more power to your elbow', ibid, Letter 2245

'If I haven't anything else to thank ... simply wonderful', *Robert Louis Stevenson in Australia,* p.21

'taking a moonlight promenade ... single handkerchief', *Robert Louis Stevenson: A Biography*, p.455

'laid on a bed ... foolish cough', The *Letters of Robert Louis Stevenson*, Letter 2300

'It is vastly annoying ... both ends, is it?', *Robert Louis Stevenson in Australia*, p.23

'in a terrific state of dentistry troubles', *The Letters of Robert Louis Stevenson*, Letter 2548

'the embodiment of a female Jekyll and Hyde', *Robert Louis Stevenson: A Biography*, p.444

'His physique is vastly improved ... Samoan climate', *The Quest for Robert Louis Stevenson*, p.174

'People all looked at me in the streets of Sydney', *Robert Louis Stevenson: A Biography*, p.455

'delightful and witty speech', *The Quest for Robert Louis Stevenson*, p.176

'rather too plain for publication' and 'The personality of a famous writer ... man of genius', ibid, p.174

'in an easy chair ... active figure, so sparse', ibid, p.175

'rang him up ... telephones even then', *Robert Louis Stevenson in Australia*, p.27

'the abiding impression ... when ill', ibid, p.29

'soft neck-wear and velvet jacket' and 'Your eyes sought joy ... critical faculty', *The Quest for Robert Louis Stevenson*, p.176

'chummed up with the cook ... quarters of the world', *Robert Louis Stevenson in Australia*, p.28

'thought by my family ... Mark Twain' and 'had very little time to do it', The *Letters of Robert Louis Stevenson*, Letter 2578

'splendid photos', 'Poor Fanny had very little fun ... maltine and slops' and 'rioting on oysters and mushrooms', ibid, Letter 2548

'lively sport', *The Quest for Robert Louis Stevenson*, p.177

'sudden and disastrous change', The *Letters of Robert Louis Stevenson*, Letter 2545

'seek safety in that inglorious spot, my bed', 'succession of genteel colds ... fine pleurisy' and 'no use for life without them', ibid, Letter 2549

'Stevenson used to say ... Circular Quay', *Robert Louis Stevenson in Australia*, p.29

'He was not to write ... tacitly withdrawn', *The Wrecker*, p.359

'now on a bench ... Larrikins of Sydney', 'dingy men', 'frowsy women', 'merciless', 'a new society of nursery-maids ... rich traps' and 'the round of night ... bawling for help', ibid, pp. 361–362

'When he came to ... wig and gown' and 'the best fare in Sydney', ibid, pp.368–369

'They're a dyngerous lot ... to imitate', ibid, p.363

'I was not born for age', *The Letters of Robert Louis Stevenson,* Letter 2816

'Books are good enough ... substitute for life', *An Apology for Idlers in Virginibus Puerisque*, Chatto & Windus, London, 1907, p.73

KIPLING

Bibliography

Birkenhead, Lord, *Rudyard Kipling*, Weidenfeld & Nicolson, UK, 1978

Carrington, Charles, *Rudyard Kipling: His Life and Work*, Macmillan & Co, London, 1955

Durbach, Renee, *Kipling's South Africa*, Chameleon Press, South Africa, 1988

Gilmour, David, *The Long Recessional: The Imperial Life of Rudyard Kipling*, Farrar, Straus & Giroux, New York, 2002

Gross, John (ed.), *The Age of Kipling: The Man, His Work, and His World*, Simon & Schuster, New York, 1972

Harman, Kaye, *Australia Brought to Book: Responses to Australia by Visiting Writers 1836–1939*, BooBook Publications Ltd, Australia, 1985

Kennedy, Rosalind and Pinney, Thomas, *Kipling Down Under: Rudyard Kipling's Visit to Australia, 1891: A Narrative with Documents*, XLibris, USA, 2000

Kipling, Rudyard, *Collected Stories*, Everyman's Library, USA, 1994

Kipling, Rudyard, *Something of Myself*, Penguin, UK, 1977

Laski, Marghanita, *From Palm to Pine: Rudyard Kipling Abroad and at Home*, Facts on File Publications, USA, 1987

Lycett, Andrew, *Rudyard Kipling*, Weidenfeld & Nicolson, UK, 1999

Nicolson, Adam, *The Hated Wife: Carrie Kipling 1862-1939*, Short Books, London, 2001

Ricketts, Harry, *Rudyard Kipling: A Life*, Carroll & Graf Inc, New York, 1999

Seymour-Smith, Martin, *Rudyard Kipling: A Biography*, St Martin's Press, New York, 1989

Wilson, Angus, *Rudyard Kipling: His Life and Works*, Secker & Warburg, London, 1977

References

'a good man spoiled', *Rudyard Kipling: A Life*, p.181

'uncertain moods' and 'difficult temperament', *Rudyard Kipling: A Biography*, p.199

'a hard devoted capable little person', *The Hated Wife: Carrie Kipling 1862–1939*, p.17

'poor concentrated Carrie', *Rudyard Kipling: A Biography*, p.195

'That woman is going to marry our Ruddy', *Rudyard Kipling: A Life*, p.181

'a small excursion to the other end of the world', *Rudyard Kipling*, A. Lycett, p.318

'get clean away and re-sort myself', *Something of Myself*, p.89

'bind chains round his heart', *Kipling's South Africa*, p.9

'sleepy unkempt little place', *Something of Myself*, p.89

'of all vile lands, South Africa was the worst', ibid, p.93

'the loveliest land in the world', *The Long Recessional: The Imperial Life of Rudyard Kipling*, p.99

'A small mare and a most taciturn ... a kiwi', 'soft and lovely in the sunshine' and 'a magic town', *Something of Myself*, pp.92–93

'a new land teeming with new stories', *Rudyard Kipling: A Life*, p.184

'caught something of the tone ... respectable occupation', *The Age*, 13 November 1891, pp.5–6

'he is rather below ... always on springs' and 'There were some Melbourne ... whole world', *The Age*, 7 November 1891, p.10 (from Otago Daily Times 20 October 1891)

'He lolls at ease ... matter of time', *The Argus*, 13 November 1891, p.6

'I can't say anything about the people ... pleasant interview', *The Age*, 13 November 1891, pp.5–6

'Could impudence go any further ... has provoked', *The Age*, 14 November 1891, p.10

'trains transferring me, at unholy hours ... seemed a bit on edge', and 'I went also to Sydney ... picnicking all the day', *Something of Myself*, p.91

'worldwide reputation', Sydney Mail, 21 November 1891, p.142

'Mr Rudyard Kipling has given ... in the world', *Bohemia*, 26 November 1891, p.16

'none but complimentary references to make to Australia', *Melbourne Punch*, 26 November 1891, p.353

'that having been nearly a week ... new constitution', *Table Talk*, 27 November 1891, p.3

'Rudyard Kipling landed ... Australian National Policy at 12.15', *Sydney Bulletin*, 21 November 1891, p.11

'long been Mr Kipling's worshippers', *The Argus*, 14 November 1891, p.13

'Wednesday 18 November: return to Melbourne ... in the afternoon', *Kipling Down Under*, pp.49–50

'Mr Rudyard Kipling's airy criticisms on Australia and Australians', *Table Talk*, 20 November 1891, p.1

'a hammock under the plane trees', *Kipling Down Under*, p.140

'resting and coquetting with an attack of influenza', *Bohemia*, 26 November 1891, p.16

'our distinguished visitor', 'great leap in the dark', 'unsupported by further evidence', 'a letter from a lady in England' and 'Florrie Garrard ... young author', *The Argus*, 21 November 1891, p.13

'had only a few minutes to stay here', *South Australian Register*, 26 November 1891, p.5

'Mr Kipling does not like being interviewed and says so', *Adelaide Advertiser*, 26 November 1891, p.5

'had a most delightful time in Australia', *South Australian Register*, 26 November 1891, p.5

'real home', *Kipling Down Under*, p.80

'return only when copper-fastened ... counts the days', *Rudyard Kipling: A Life*, p.180

'married tomorrow ... wrote the Naulakha', ibid, p.186

'a new land ... wonderful things some day', *Something of Myself*, p.91

'cleaner, simpler, saner, more adequate gang of men', *Rudyard Kipling: A Life*, p.266

'I put on my specs in Port Phillip ... Big Wide Earth', *Australia Brought to Book*, p.134

'Ustrelyahs ... as a sandhill drinks water', *Collected Stories*, p.538

'the most vindictive haters ... heavy meat diet', *Kipling Down Under*, p.65

TWAIN

Bibliography

Dimond, Jill and Kirkpatrick, Peter, *Literary Sydney*, University of Queensland Press, Australia, 2000

Harman, Kaye, *Australia Brought to Book: Responses to Australia by Visiting Writers 1836–1939*, BooBook Publications, Australia, 1985

Hoffman, Andrew, *Inventing Mark Twain: The Lives of Samuel Langhorne Clemens*, Weidenfeld & Nicolson, London, 1997

Jeffares, A. Norman and Gray, Martin (eds.), *Collins Dictionary of Quotations*, Harper Collins, Glasgow, 1995

Mort, Terry (ed.), *Mark Twain on Travel*, Lyons Press, USA, 2005

Powers, Ron, *Mark Twain: A Life*, Free Press, USA, 2005

Shillingsburg, Miriam Jones, *At Home Abroad: Mark Twain in Australasia*, University Press of Mississippi, USA, 1988

Stevens, Meic (ed.), *Collins Dictionary of Literary Quotations*, HarperCollins, Glasgow, 1991

Twain, Mark, *The Autobiography of Mark Twain*, Charles Neider (ed.), HarperPerennial, USA, 1959

Twain, Mark, *The Wayward Tourist: Mark Twain's Adventures in Australia*, introduced by Don Watson, Melbourne University Press, Australia, 2006

Ward, Geoffrey C. and Duncan, Dayton, *Mark Twain: An Illustrated Biography*, Alfred A. Knopf, New York, 2001

References

'I could remember everything whether it happened or not', *The Wayward Tourist*, p.xxviii 'began to pound his sides', *At Home Abroad: Mark Twain in Australasia*, p.95

'he could persuade a fish ... majestic liar', *Mark Twain: A Life*, p.545

'honour is a harder master than the law' and 'moral necessity', *At Home Abroad*, p.20

'Travel has no longer ... concerns one of those', *Mark Twain: A Life*, p.538

'our lecturing raid ... we captured it', *At Home Abroad*, p.14

'I could have done without it ... for jewelry', *Mark Twain: A Life*, pp.565–66

'the funniest man in America', *At Home Abroad*, p.79

'I'm going to write a book about Australia ... facts of things', *Australia Brought to Book*, p.138

'he has no heart ... is shoddy', *At Home Abroad*, p.32

'huge establishment ... shipment to England', *The Wayward Tourist*, p.23

'a step peculiar to myself—and the kangaroo', *Mark Twain: A Life*, p.143

'I reverence that man's hair ... been irresistible' and 'His head is like an amazed gum tree ... in the soup', *At Home Abroad*, p.47

'I'd love to run my fingers through Mark Twain's silky, grey hair', ibid, p.39

'It is shaped somewhat ... the general effect', *The Wayward Tourist*, p.6

'more spontaneous, heartier ... of welcome', *At Home Abroad*, p.42

'trembling all the time between tears and laughter', ibid, p.43

'the five-millionth of an inch', ibid, p.217

'high and delicate art', *Mark Twain: A Life*, p.155

'Father knew the full value ... be heard', ibid, p.568

'mount(ing) a balloon ... and spontaneous ... observation', *At Home Abroad*, p.47

'In France a cat is a male ... of uncertainty' and 'a deceased fishwife ... to herself', ibid, p.211

'A dog is *der* Hund ... borrowed dog that way', *Mark Twain: A Life*, p.418

'a verb has ... those Germans do', *Collins Dictionary of Literary Quotations*, p.96

'decline two drinks than one German verb', *Mark Twain: A Life*, p.418

'Whenever a literary German ... verb in his mouth', *Collins Dictionary of Literary Quotations*, p.136

'Wagner's music is better than it sounds', *Collins Dictionary of Quotations*, p.716

'reminds me of its company ... possession I have', *At Home Abroad*, p.70

'an acute attack of rheumatism', ibid, p.54

'Think of the paralysis of intellect that gave that idea birth', *The Wayward Tourist*, p.47

'the owner of these hands ... of humour', *At Home Abroad*, p.57

'people were packed like sandwiches ... eager faces', ibid, p.67

'If I am going to write a book ... and began' and 'for if you get the sense ... no sense in it', ibid, p.45

'Your gum trees ... grave and serious', ibid, p.58

'assertive, aggressive green', ibid, p.73

'fountain-sprays of delicate feathery foliage', *The Wayward Tourist*, p.123

'they are of a blueness ... with spirituality' *At Home Abroad*, p.58

'with the necessary stock in trade, i.e. religion', *Mark Twain: A Life*, p.156

'about 64 roads to the other world' and 'You see how healthy the religious ... can live in it', *The Wayward Tourist*, p.81

'the interviewed has nothing to say ... say it', *At Home Abroad*, p.75

'musical and gurgly', ibid, p.187

'Lo there is Geelong ... don't give a __', ibid, p.190

'feeling the market before visiting a barber', ibid, p.123

'hens laid fried eggs', *The Wayward Tourist*, p.7

'to get a glimpse of any convicts ... the island', *At Home Abroad*, p.125

'Indeed, it is so curious ... beautiful lies', *The Wayward Tourist*, p.65

'It was like ... and wrinkles' and 'Too healthy. 70 is old enough for me', ibid, pp.181–82

'the neatest town that the sun shines on', ibid, p.179

'There are many humorous ... other savages', ibid, p.110

'The Whites always ... chicken coop', ibid,
p.162

'the England of the far south', *At Home
Abroad*, p.131

'flowing and graceful', ibid, p.136

'gruesome', ibid, p.185

'to enable one to realise ... Christian devils',
*Inventing Mark Twain: The Lives of
Samuel Langhorne Clemens,* p.407

'I caught one myself ... let go', *At Home
Abroad*, p.185

'English friendliness ... left out', *The
Wayward Tourist*, p.24

'good and kind to us everywhere', *At Home
Abroad*, p.124

'the cordial nation', ibid, p.xiii

'two people and a half ... 6th floor', ibid,
p.62

'In America if your uncle ... advertise it',
The Wayward Tourist, p.22

'it was positively thrilling', ibid, p.121

'The tyble is set ... the breakfast', ibid, p.24

'These reports came ... ceased to come' and
'It was wonderful ... I can remember',
ibid, pp.147–49

'Good breeding consists ... other persons',
Collins Dictionary of Quotations, p.717

'The truth is that ... critical things said' *At
Home Abroad,* p.127

'desolate-looking', ibid, p.196

'Susy was peacefully released today', *Mark
Twain: A Life*, p.578

'serious to the point of madness', ibid, p.89

'lying cheerfulness', *At Home Abroad,* p.230

'an old man ... trying to joke', ibid, p.225

'unalloyed pleasure' and 'stunning reading',
ibid, p.227

'She was my life ... a pauper', *The
Autobiography of Mark Twain*, p.288

LONDON

Bibliography

The Australian Star, Australia, 28 December
1908

The Australian Star, Australia, 7 January 1909

The Australian Star, Australia, 14 January
1909

Barltrop, Robert, *Jack London: The Man, the
Writer*, the Rebel, Pluto Press, London,
1976

Conrad, Joseph, *The Collected Letters of
Joseph Conrad*, Frederick Karl (ed.),
Cambridge University Press, UK, 1996

Day, A. Grove, *Jack London in the South
Seas*, Four Winds Press, New York,
1971

Harman, Kaye, *Australia Brought to Book*:
*Responses to Australia by Visiting Writers
1836–1939*, BooBook Publications,
Australia, 1985

Kershaw, Alex, *Jack London: A Life,*
HarperCollins, London, 1997

London, Jack, *The Best Short Stories of Jack
London*, Doubleday & Co. Inc., USA,
1945

London, Jack, *The Complete Short Stories
of Jack London*, Vol. I, Vol. II, Vol. III,
Earle Labor, Robert C. Leitz and I. Milo
Shepard (eds.), Stanford University
Press, California, 1993

London, Jack, *The Cruise of the Snark*, Mills
& Boon Ltd, London, 1926

London, Jack, *John Barleycorn*, Western
Tanager Press, Santa Cruz, 1981

London, Jack, *The Letters of Jack London,*
Vol. I 1896–1905, Vol. II 1906–1912,
Vol. III 1913–1916, Earle Labor, Robert
C. Leitz, I. Milo Shepard (eds.), Stanford
University Press, California, 1988

London, Jack, *The Sheriff of Kona in Tales of
the Pacific*, Penguin, UK, 1989

The Lone Hand, Australia, 1 February 1909

Sinclair, Andrew, *Jack: A Biography of
Jack London*, Weidenfeld & Nicolson,
London, 1978

Smith, Terry, *The Old Tin Shed: Sydney
Stadium 1908–1970*, Eric Spilsted Publications, Australia, 1999

Wells, Jeff, *Boxing Day: The Fight that
Changed the World*, Harper Sports,
Australia, 1998

References

'Citizens who have never prayed ... coon
into oblivion' and 'black bastard', *The
Old Tin Shed*, p.32

'big buck nigger', Boxing Day, p.121

'I would never have possibly written ...
Kipling never been', *Jack London: A Life*,
p.79

'No writer of prominence ... around the

world', *Jack London in the South Seas*, p.144

'noseless, lipless', *The Sheriff of Kona*, p.133

'I wouldn't have gone ... man in the world', *Jack London: A Life*, p.198

'The biggest specialist in Australia ... medical libraries', *The Letters of Jack London*, Vol. II, p.775

'unable to cut a piece of cold meat with a knife and fork', ibid, p.776

'No case like it ... thick as they were long', *The Cruise of the Snark*, p.305

'own climate of California' and 'weak and wabbly', *The Letters of Jack London*, Vol. II, p.779

'the greatest open-air stadium in the world', *The Old Tin Shed*, p.23

'dusky Cyclops', *Boxing Day*, p.127

'a symbol of a racial ideal to be upheld', ibid, p.94

'worse negro-haters even than the Americans', *Australia Brought to Book*, p.163

'Fight like a white man', *The Old Tin Shed*, p.34

'a great black cat', *Boxing Day*, p.165

'A dew drop would ... colossus and apygmy', *The Australian Star*, 28 December 1908, p.1

'sunlight had found darkness and lost' and 'whether the spectre ... of Sydney', *The Old Tin Shed*, p.34

'Johnson has shown ... pure nigger', *Boxing Day*, p.198

'grant that the defeat ... dark-skinned people', ibid, p.208

'There was no fraction ... preposterous heroic', 'All hail to Johnson ... accounts to the contrary' and 'Personally I was with Burns ... white skin', *The Australian Star*, 28 December 1908, p.1

'Whenever a traveller ... potsherds at him', 'It is only the reckless ... facts are irrefragable', 'managed by Barbarians', 'three able-bodied night porters', 'hold a conference', 'Siamese twins', 'And I got no more candles ... the rules', 'sleepless the rest of the night', 'Between midnight and 1 ... re-echoing sound' and 'I know now the license ... remain unscathed', *The Australian Star*, 7 January 1909, p.1

'blowing up water-mains and wrecking railroad tracks', *The Australian Star*, 14 January 1909, p.1

'the whole history of mankind ... the exploited', *Jack London: A Life*, p.40

'too willing to honour the exalted', *The Letters of Jack London*, Vol. II, p.796

'well-phrased, clear-cut, aggressive eloquence' and 'nothing of the air of the great author about him', *The Lone Hand*, p.367

'in a place where there was nothing to drink' and 'soaked in the cool air, rode horseback', *John Barleycorn*, p.294

'a couple of beautiful black eyes' and 'a gum-boil ... four inches', *The Letters of Jack London*, Vol. II, p.800

'With the last morsel ... buy the bread', *A Piece of Steak* in *The Best Short Stories of Jack London*, p.73

'Blimey, but couldn't I ... he muttered aloud', 'Tom King grunted ... the tradesmen' and 'It was a drought year ... difficult to find', ibid, p.75

'heavyweight champion of New South Wales' and 'Tommy Burns and that Yankee Jack Johnson', ibid, p.76

'Stowsher Bill had cried afterward in the dressing room' and 'grizzled old chopping block', ibid, pp.77–78

'Always were these youngsters ... bodies of the old uns', ibid, p.79

'policy of economy', ibid, p.81

'a superfluous movement', ibid, p.83

'He had not had sufficient ... thirty quid to him' and 'one stiff punch would do it', ibid, pp.85–86

'And Tom King ... must deliver' and 'like the surf at Bondi Beach', ibid, p.87

'tottering on the hairline ... piece of steak', 'Unnerved by the thought of the missus sitting up for him' and 'an unwonted moisture', ibid, p.88

'I was carrying a beautiful alcoholic ... a drink', *John Barleycorn*, p.298

'immensely touched' and 'a grateful and cordial handgrasp', *The Collected Letters of Joseph Conrad*, Vol. V, p.508

'I would rather be ashes ... my time', Sydney Writers' Walk, Australia

CONAN DOYLE

Bibliography

Booth, Martin, *The Doctor and the Detective: A Biography of Sir Arthur Conan Doyle*, Thomas Dunne Books, New York, 1997

Brown, Ivor, *Conan Doyle*, Hamish Hamilton, London, 1972

Carr, John Dickson, *The Life of Sir Arthur Conan Doyle*, John Murray, London, 1949

Dimond, Jill and Kirkpatrick, Peter, *Literary Sydney: A Walking Guide*, University of Queensland Press, Australia, 2000

Doyle, Sir Arthur Conan, *The Original Illustrated 'Strand' Sherlock Holmes,* Wordsworth Editions Ltd, UK, 1989

Doyle, Sir Arthur Conan, *The Wanderings of a Spiritualist*, Hodder & Stoughton, London, 1922

Doyle, Sir Arthur Conan, *'The Guards Came Through' and Other Poems,* John Murray, London, 1919

Doyle, Sir Arthur Conan, *Letters to the Press*, JM Gibson and RL Green (eds.), University of Iowa Press, USA, 1986

Edwards, Owen Dudley, *The Quest for Sherlock Holmes: A Biographical Study*, Mainstream Publishing, Edinburgh, 1983

Fido, Martin, *The World of Sherlock Holmes: The Facts and Fiction behind the World's Greatest Detective,* Carlton, UK, 1998

Harman, Kaye, *Australia Brought to Book: Responses to Australia by Visiting Writers 1836–1939*, BooBook Publications Ltd, Australia, 1985

Higham, Charles, *The Adventures of Conan Doyle: The Life of the Creator of Sherlock Holmes*, Hamish Hamilton, London, 1976

Jones, Kelvin I., *Conan Doyle and the Spirits: The Spiritualist Career of Sir Arthur Conan Doyle*, Aquarian Press, UK, 1989

Lellenberg, Jon L. (ed.), *The Quest for Sir Arthur Conan Doyle: Thirteen Biographers in Search of a Life,* Southern Illinois University Press, USA, 1987

Library Council of Victoria, *Holmes Away from Home: An Exhibition at the State Library of Victoria to celebrate 100 Years of Sherlock Holmes in Print and featuring the visit to Australia by Sir Arthur Conan Doyle*, 7 December 1987–31 January 1988, Australia, 1988

Lycett, Andrew, *Conan Doyle: The Man who Created Sherlock Holmes,* Weidenfeld & Nicolson, London, 2007

Pearsall, Ronald, *Conan Doyle: A Biographical Solution*, Weidenfeld & Nicolson, London, 1977

Pearson, Hesketh, *Conan Doyle,* Unwin Paperbacks, Methuen & Co., UK, 1943

Stashower, Daniel, *Teller of Tales: The Life of Arthur Conan Doyle*, Henry Holt & Co., New York, 1999

Symons, Julian, *Portrait of an Artist: Conan Doyle*, Whizzard Press, London, 1979

Wynne, Catherine, *The Colonial Conan Doyle*, Greenwood Press, USA, 1971

References

'one of the most unscrupulous … finished types', *The Original Illustrated 'Strand' Sherlock Holmes*, p.819

'governor of one of the Australian colonies', ibid, p.554

'the taking of which by the Australians was one of the feats of the war', 'The reckless dare-devilry … Imperial ranks' and 'the perfect equality of the Australian … he might', *Australia Brought to Book*, p.174

'I seemed suddenly … between two worlds', *The Colonial Conan Doyle*, p.155

'When I heard thy well-known voice … a sign', 'Fate', *'The Guards Came Through' and Other Poems*, pp.77–78

'All other work … nothing compared to this', *The Wanderings of a Spiritualist*, p.11

'I had spent … in the common cause', ibid p.13

'that smouldering glow … more lively flame', *Australia Brought to Book*, p. 175

'the lectures … Australia at last', *The Wanderings of a Spiritualist*, p.56

'Those poor black fellows! Their fate is a dark stain upon Australia', ibid, p.57

'But the noble Maori … with its neighbours', ibid, p.58

'so pretty, so orderly and so self-sufficing', ibid, p.62

'Many of the intellectual leaders ... an attraction', ibid, pp.69–70

'I feel sure that many mothers ... have given' and 'May you be struck dead before you leave this Commonwealth', ibid, p.77

'hideous lizard with open mouth', ibid, p.81

'black evil ... be purely evil', ibid, pp.69–70

'The Five Fruits ... and Futility', *Holmes away from Home,* p.42

'Never in any British town have I found such reactionary intolerance', *The Wanderings of a Spiritualist*, p.89

'a tendency to divide and to run into vulgarities', ibid, p.91

'a troop of mounted police... the pavilion' and 'Ah! Here it is', ibid, p.93

'the most beautiful place I have ever seen', ibid, p. 147

'We shall always ... real Australia', *Australia Brought to Book*, p.176

'He seemed surprised ... to think about', *Holmes away from Home*, p.41

'no idea it was so great a place', *Australia Brought to Book*, p.177

'It seems a weak point ... best in the world', *The Wanderings of a Spiritualist*, p.153

'Wherever I go ... looked into it', *The Life of Sir Arthur Conan Doyle*, p.327

'If Spiritualism had been a popular cult ... my visit', *Teller of Tales: The Life of Arthur Conan Doyle*, p.369

'a real romp with Nature' and 'told that there were men competent to ride them', *The Wanderings of a Spiritualist*, p.160

'enough hot water without seeking a geyser', ibid, p.192

'clearly had these powers ... impaired them', *Conan Doyle: The Man who Created Sherlock Holmes*, p.386

'Every man looks on his own country ... reasons than most', *The Wanderings of a Spiritualist*, p.221

'that we should never see ... old material form', ibid, p.226

'It is a terrible thing ... these absurd conflicts', ibid, p.227

'who work with us ... the enterprise through', ibid, p.241

'the highest general level of any sensitive in Australia', ibid, p.259

'The one thing clear ... complete failure', ibid, p.273

'Long after you leave us your message will linger', ibid, p.280

'It is the unliveliness ... on my nerves', *Letters to the Press*, p.290

'the failure of State control', *The Wanderings of a Spiritualist*, p.267

'less disciplined', *Australia Brought to Book*, p.179

'that little fringe of people ... handle it', *The Wanderings of a Spiritualist*, p.116

'History abhors a vacuum ... fill it up' and 'like an enormous machine ... drive it', *Australia Brought to Book*, p.178

'A fine handsome body ... solid and capable', ibid, p.177

'We like the people ... in speech and dealings' and 'more English than the English', ibid, p.178

'They are dear folk ... out of their groves', ibid, p.179

'Should the reader ... put the book down', *The Wanderings of a Spiritualist*, p.8

'meddling in the occult', abc.net.au, *Reconciliation, faith prominent in Archbishop's Easter messages*, posted Friday 21 March 2008 http://www.abc.net.au/news/stories/2008/03/21/2196227.htm?section=justin

'I had often endeavoured ... turning them over', *The Original Illustrated 'Strand' Sherlock Holmes*, p.342

CHRISTIE

Bibliography

Christie, Agatha, *Agatha Christie: An Autobiography*, Fontana/Collins, UK, 1977

Christie, Agatha, *Partners in Crime,* Collins, London, 1929

Christie, Agatha, *Peril at End House,* Fontana/Collins, UK, 1932

Christie, Agatha, *Sparkling Cyanide,* Fontana/Collins, UK, 1944

Christie, Agatha, *The Golden Ball and Other Stories*, GK Hall & Co, Boston, 1990

Christie, Agatha, *The Mystery of the Blue Train*, Lansdowne Press, London, 1970

Christie, Agatha, *The Secret Adversary*, HarperCollins, London, 1922

Christie, Agatha, *The Sittaford Mystery*, Collins, London, 1931

Christie, Agatha, *They Came to Baghdad*, GK Hall & Co, Boston, 1991

Christie, Agatha, *Why Didn't They Ask Evans?*, Collins, UK, 1934

Keating, HRF (ed.), *Agatha Christie: First Lady of Crime*, Weidenfeld & Nicolson, London, 1977

Morgan, Janet, *Agatha Christie: A Biography*, Fontana/Collins, UK, 1984

Sanders, Denis and Lovallo, Len, *The Agatha Christie Companion: The Complete Guide to Agatha Christie's Life and Work*, WH Allen, London, 1985

Thompson, Laura, *Agatha Christie: An English Mystery*, Headline, UK, 2007

Wagstaff, Vanessa and Poole, Stephen, *Agatha Christie: A Reader's Companion*, Aurum Press, London, 2004

References

'in the development ... Dependencies overseas', *The Oxford History of the British Empire*, Judith M. Brown and William Roger Louis, Oxford University Press, 1988, p.214

'Whether the shortage ... hear it' and 'I didn't know a thing ... there you are,' *Agatha Christie: A Biography*, p.87

'the appearance of a villain in a melodrama' and 'sinister aspect', *Agatha Christie: An Autobiography*, p.298

'very wonderful', *Agatha Christie: A Biography*, p.93

'From Australia we went to Tasmania', *Agatha Christie: An Autobiography*, p.306

'incredibly beautiful Hobart ... trees and shrubs', ibid, p.306

'death casts of several of the Aboriginals' and 'sketches and water colours ... perfectly lovely', *Agatha Christie: A Biography*, p.95

'Trees are always the first ... the landscape', *Agatha Christie: An Autobiography*, p.302

'All Australian scenery ... never be caught', 'We are resisting to the last ditch', 'He really does think he is a King' and 'Australians will not stand ... down well', *Agatha Christie: A Biography*, pp.95–96

'If you are buying canned ... are good', ibid, p.97

'I was so astonished to find ... a luscious fruit', 'busy putting forth the claims ... so forth' and 'the most delicious things you can imagine', *Agatha Christie: An Autobiography*, p.303

'It always seems to me ... deal of desert', 'the extraordinary aspect of the trees' and 'blue and red ... flying jewels', ibid, p.302

'a green grassy desert', ibid, p.304

'enormous stretches of flat ... periodic windmills' and 'We seemed always to be eating ... or turkey', ibid, p.303

'a plate with ... jugs of cream' and 'dried milk places', *Agatha Christie: A Biography*, p.96

'having heard of Sydney ... I suppose', 'the Bell family numbered ... of sons', 'a wonderful flirt' and 'who rode splendidly', *Agatha Christie: An Autobiography*, p.304

'of stale commercial traveller', *Agatha Christie: An English Mystery*, p.145

'was always treated ... royalty', *Agatha Christie: An Autobiography*, p.305

'really like the royal family ... their own', *Agatha Christie: A Biography*, p.97

'like energetic young fillies', *Agatha Christie: An Autobiography*, p.304

'Among the various servants ... her show' and 'I was entranced by landscape ... paint box', ibid, pp.305–306

'the sanitary arrangements ... no privacy', ibid, p.303

'I still think New Zealand ... is extraordinary', ibid, p.307

'Finis Iterum', 'R.I.P.' and '1st class! Good oh! Right, here!', *Agatha Christie: A Biography*, p.103

'To our enormous surprise ... liked Belcher', *Agatha Christie: An Autobiography*, p.316

'criminals are invariably ... another name', *The Mystery of the Blue Train*, p.147

'Fellows that go off to the Colonies ... that reason', *The Sittaford Mystery*, p.144

'a bit too sociable', 'a bit too hospitable for English ideas' and 'over friendly ... like Colonials are', ibid, p.37

'bonza detective', *Peril at End House*, p.51

'they were, perhaps ... too thoroughly', ibid, p.55

'jackaroos to an Australian station', *Sparkling Cyanide*, p.31

'a lady ... to Australia', *They Came to Baghdad*, p.45

'Which colony ... at any rate', *The Golden Ball and Other Stories*, pp.34–35

'I shouldn't like the colonies ... like me', *The Secret Adversary*, p.18

'who go to Australia and come back again', *Why Didn't They ask Evans?*, p.22

'Australian voice', *Agatha Christie: An English Mystery*, p.145

'simply one of the most ...', 'game for anything' and 'not terribly clever', *The Unbreakable Alibi in Partners in Crime*, pp.134–35

'drive very recklessly', ibid, p.140

'very nice young lady ... kangaroos', ibid, p.143

'gambling family', ibid, p.136

LAWRENCE

Bibliography

Darroch, Robert, *DH Lawrence in Australia*, Macmillan, Australia, 1981

Davis, Joseph, *DH Lawrence at Thirroul*, Collins Ltd, Sydney, 1989

DH Lawrence Society of Australia, *Rananim*, Vol. 12, No. 1, Sydney, February 2004

Grishin, Sasha, *Garry Shead: The DH Lawrence Paintings*, G & B Arts International, Australia, 1993

Hamalian, Leo (ed.), *DH Lawrence*, McGraw-Hill Book Co., USA, 1973

Harman, Kaye, *Australia Brought to Book: Responses to Australia by Visiting Writers 1836–1939*, BooBook Publications Ltd, Australia, 1985

Hope, AD, *DH Lawrence's 'Kangaroo'. 'How it Looks to an Australian'*, in *The Australian Experience*, Australian National University Press, Canberra, 1974

Lawrence, DH, *The Letters of DH Lawrence*, Vol. IV, June 1921–March 1924, Cambridge University Press, UK, 1987

Lawrence, DH, *Kangaroo*, Penguin, UK, 1950

Lawrence, DH, *Selected Poems*, Keith Sagar (ed.), Penguin, UK, 1972

Maddox, Brenda, *The Married Man: A Life of DH Lawrence*, Sinclair-Stevenson, UK, 1994

Moore, Harry T., *The Priest of Love*, Penguin, UK, 1974

Niven, Alastair, *DH Lawrence: The Writer and His Work*, Longman, UK, 1980

Russell, Roslyn, *Literary Links: Celebrating the Literary Relationship between Australia and Britain*, Allen & Unwin, Australia, 1997

Worthen, John, *DH Lawrence: The Life of an Outsider*, Counterpoint, UK, 2005

References

'something that brings me peace', *The Letters of DH Lawrence*, p.255

'wrestling with the void', *DH Lawrence: The Life of an Outsider*, p.175

'terrible, terrible war ... his own integrity', *Kangaroo*, p.236

'obsolete, hideous stupidity', *The Letters of DH Lawrence*, Vol. I, p.291

'The war is just hell ... you can't move' and 'War finished me ... sorrows and hopes', *DH Lawrence: The Life of an Outsider*, p.150

'menace to our public health', ibid, p.164

'curse ... body and soul ... eternal damnation', ibid, p.165

'the spirit of the war ... so far yet', *Kangaroo*, p.241

'awful years', ibid, p.237

'The tales began ... stone fences', ibid, p.251

'He had come to the end of his own tether', ibid, p.166

'broken apart', ibid, p.287

'I've got to come unstuck from the old life and Europe' and 'half-cajoled', *DH Lawrence: The Life of an Outsider*, p.258

'that tension and pressure', *The Letters of DH Lawrence*, p.213

'out of it all', *DH Lawrence: The Life of an Outsider*, p.259

'like a prison', *The Letters of DH Lawrence*, p.231

'Oh I wish he'd stand up', *DH Lawrence: The Life of an Outsider*, p.264

'too boneless and negative', *The Letters of DH Lawrence*, p.231

'a lid down over everything' and 'I thought ... presses tighter here', ibid, p.227

'One may as well move on, once one has started', ibid, p.220

'to a nunnery', *The Letters of DH Lawrence*, p.243

'It is extraordinarily subtle ... exquisite forms', ibid p.265

'folded secret', *Kangaroo*, p.266

'spirit of the place', 'the hair on his scalp with terror', 'reached a long black arm and gripped him', 'like corpses' and 'terror of the bush', ibid, pp.18–19

'one sheds one's sicknesses ... master of them', *DH Lawrence: The Life of an Outsider*, p.65

'nobody has *seen* Australia yet ... isn't visible', *The Letters of DH Lawrence*, p.273

'handsome and well-kept' and 'hidden and half-hidden lobes ... dark-brown cliffs', *Kangaroo*, pp.24–25

'one of the sights of the world', *The Letters of DH Lawrence*, p.250

'without any core', *Kangaroo*, p.33

'on the edge of the low cliff just above the Pacific ocean', *The Letters of DH Lawrence*, p.249

'tumble out of bed ... froth of the breakers', *DH Lawrence at Thirroul*, p.20

'very seaey', *Kangaroo*, p.303

'the sea talked ... inward peace', ibid, p.172

'fairy blue windbags ... long blue strings', ibid, p.363

'lonely lonely world' and 'saurian', ibid, p.197

'stiff, sharp, like crystals of colour', ibid, pp.390–91

'every man a little Pope of perfection', *The Letters of DH Lawrence*, p.247

'crude, raw and self-satisfied' and 'There's nothing ... not always silently', ibid, p.250

'liberty gone senile', ibid, p.246

'in defiance ... of any sort', *Kangaroo*, p. 72

'always vaguely and meaninglessly on the go', *The Letters of DH Lawrence*, p.263

'The human life seems to me very barren', ibid, p.246

'hefty legs' and 'prominent round buttocks ... cotton shorts', *Kangaroo*, p.200

'big heavy ... his trousers', ibid, p.304

'They seem to run to leg, these people', ibid, p.32

'to have four posts and an iron chain put round it', ibid, p.212

'socially nil', *The Letters of DH Lawrence*, p.271

'These damned books ... myself free', *DH Lawrence: The Life of an Outsider*, p.281

'Detail for detail ... his consciousness', *Kangaroo*, pp.286–87

'invisible eyes' and 'watchful, guarded, furtive', ibid, p.252

'burly police-sergeant' and 'A man culminates in intense moments', ibid, pp.249–50

'the turning point of his life and work', *The Married Man*, p.316

'a sort of human bomb ... to explode', *Kangaroo*, p.184

'the burden of intensive mental consciousness' and 'Deep in his unconsciousness ... his soul', ibid, p.264

'boomingly, crashingly noisy', *The Letters of DH Lawrence*, p.271

'remote gum trees ... into the air', *Kangaroo*, p.380

'pale, white unwritten atmosphere of Australia' and 'strange falling away', ibid, p.365

'quiet as a purring cat with white paws', ibid, p.202

'like a bunch of old rag ... his neck', ibid, p.198

'raving with moonlight', ibid, p.20

'a very remote, dirt-brown ... of time', *Kangaroo*, p. 227

'a strong cat-like motion through the heavens', ibid, p.367

'tree-ferns standing on one knobbly leg among the gums' and 'strange, as it were ... range', ibid, p.87

'un-get-at-able glamour', *The Letters of DH Lawrence*, p.282

'straight from the sea, like another creature', ibid, p.164

'one of the most spectacularly broken promises in literary history', *DH Lawrence in Australia*, p.125

'like a ripe pear', *The Married Man*, p.314

'queer show', *The Letters of DH Lawrence*, p.261

'a shocking mess' and 'experimental, masterful, challenging', *DH Lawrence at Thirroul*, pp.184–85

'there is a great charm in Australia' and 'If it weren't for fighting … into Australia', *The Letters of DH Lawrence*, p.277

'in a flat-icy wind', *Kangaroo*, p.302

'plumy many-balled wattle … Australian bush', ibid, pp.389–90

'land that as yet has made no great mistakes, humanly', ibid, p.381

'the tree trunks like naked … the moonlight', ibid, p.19

'in a glittering tangle … with the remaining' and 'broke and fluttered loose … the water', ibid, pp.392–93

'Australia is a weird country, and its national animal is beyond me', *Kangaroo*, p.129

'the only person … an aircraft', *Rananim*, p.15

'crucial impetus', ibid, p.7

'to sing of all small Australian towns' and 'more enduring than any other', ibid, p.13

WELLS

Bibliography

Australia and New Zealand Association for the Advancement of Science, *Handbook for Canberra: Prepared for the Members of the Australian and New Zealand Association for the Advancement of Science on the occasion of its Meeting held in Canberra, January, 1939*, Kenneth Binns (ed.), Canberra, 1938

Coren, Michael, *The Invisible Man: The Life and Liberties of HG Wells*, Atheneum, New York, 1993

Foot, Michael, *HG: The History of Mr Wells*, Black Swan, UK, 1996

Hammond, JR, *An HG Wells Companion: A Guide to the Novels, Romances and Short Stories*, Macmillan Press, UK, 1979

Hammond, JR, *HG Wells: Interviews and Recollections*, Macmillan, UK, 1980

Harman, Kaye, *Australia Brought to Book: Responses to Australia by Visiting Writers 1836–1939*, BooBook Publications, Australia, 1985

Lyons, Dame Enid, *So We Take Comfort*, Heinemann, London, 1965

Mackenzie, Norman and Jeanne, *The Time Traveller: The Life of HG Wells*, Weidenfeld & Nicolson, London, 1973

Murray, Brian, *HG Wells*, Continuum, New York, 1990

Smith, David C., *HG Wells: Desperately Mortal*, Yale University Press, New Haven, 1986

The Sydney Morning Herald, 28 December 1938–30 January 1939, Sydney

Vallentin, Antonine, *HG Wells: Prophet of our Day*, trans. Daphne Woodward, The John Day Co., New York, 1950

Wells, HG, *The Correspondence of HG Wells*, Vol. I, 1880–1903, Vol. II, 1904–1918, Vol. III, 1919–1934, Vol. IV, 1935–1946, David Clayton Smith (ed.), Pickering & Chatto, London, 1998

Wells, HG, *Travels of a Republican Radical in Search of Hot Water*, Penguin, London, 1939

West, Anthony, *HG Wells: Aspects of a Life*, Hutchinson, London, 1984

References

'quarrelsome, bad-tempered old gentleman', *HG Wells: Desperately Mortal*, p.350

'officials or business managers … married in India', 'complete innocence of any religious, political or social questionings', 'Her cabins … is salt water', 'a complete relapse into Victorianism' and 'steady, conservative vessel', *Travels of a Republican Radical in Search of Hot Water*, pp.11–12

'upper-middle-class tradition of English literature', *Australia Brought to Book*, p.220

'I want to find out what Australia … towards America', 'coming from her comparative isolation ... English-speaking countries' and 'temporary political arrangement', *The Sydney Morning Herald*, 21 December 1938

'ephemeral' and 'delighted thousands' and 'very crotchety', *The Age*, 6 January 1939

'gum trees, sheep, drought and vast spaces' and 'kangaroos, wallabys, boiling the billy, black fellows and so on', *The Correspondence of H.G. Wells*, p.215

'Inland Scorches', 'No Relief in Sight' and 'Half Continent Suffers', *The Sydney Morning Herald*, 7 January 1939 and 9 January 1939

'felt it was an unfair trick ... this variety', *The Sydney Morning Herald*, 10 January 1939

'White waistcoats for dinner and orders and medals', *The Correspondence of HG Wells*, p.218

'in open sin' and 'There comes a moment ... time for sex', *The Time Traveller*, p.388

'This really is a lot of nonsense, this publicity', *HG Wells: Desperately Mortal*, p.342

'If the human race ... English-speaking countries', *The Time Traveller*, p.414

'catastrophe is well on its way ... walk-over for disaster', ibid, p.416

'all the reasons for believing ... of disasters' and 'shook off the disagreeable vision ... as they are', *Australia Brought to Book*, p.224

'a certifiable lunatic', *The Time Traveller*, p.415

'ravings and delusions', *Travels of a Republican Radical in Search of Hot Water*, p.42

'a fantastic renegade from the Socialist movement' and 'those men are freaks', *The Sydney Morning Herald*, 5 January 1939

'a friendly Head of State', *The Time Traveller*, p.415

'exercise his undoubted ... international misunderstanding', *The Sydney Morning Herald*, 6 January 1939

'treated with true Australian ribaldry', *HG Wells: Desperately Mortal*, p.343

'delusions of sagacity' and 'reality hushed up', *Travels of a Republican Radical in Search of Hot Water*, p.44

'needless affront to other nations', *Australia Brought to Book*, p.221

'mind his own business', *HG Wells: Desperately Mortal*, p.344

'sane, dignified and necessary rebuke to Mr HG Wells', *So We Take Comfort*, p.266

'unamiable septuagenarian' and 'I have long been ... my criticisms', *HG Wells: Desperately Mortal*, pp.344–45

'ultra-Chamberlainite', *Travels of a Republican Radical in Search of Hot Water*, p.39

'pleasing adherence to the good traditions of civilized nations', *Australia Brought to Book*, p.221

'Mr Lyons had laid himself ... British communities', *Travels of a Republican Radical in Search of Hot Water*, p.39

'In the modern world ... its mind', *HG Wells: Desperately Mortal*, pp.345–6

'went high over solitary mountains ... in trains', *The Correspondence of HG Wells*, p.217

'Let me alone...You are a lot of nuisances', *The Sydney Morning Herald*, 12 January 1939

'Australia's Most Beautiful City' and 'Stay a Day and You'll Want a Week', *Handbook for Canberra*, inside cover

'like the ship described by Kipling ... Canberra spirit', ibid, p.62

'speaking haltingly ... manuscript under treatment', *The Time Traveller*, p.185

'abolish war through conscious co-operation' and 'wilfully and intelligently ... way of living', *HG Wells: Desperately Mortal*, p.346

'school-made nationalism' and 'very existence of civilization', ibid, p.347

'History as it is taught ... world peace-ideology' and 'the greatest, most astounding ... of mankind', *The Sydney Morning Herald*, 17 January 1939

'the efforts of the scientific ... of mankind' and 'Wherever the Catholic priest ... of mankind', *The Time Traveller*, p.428

'I went with the Governor-General ... crudest sort', *Travels of a Republican Radical in Search of Hot Water*, p.46

'blackened, sweaty men ... brotherliness' and 'A bush fire ... threatened victims', ibid, p.47

'The thing to note ... best defence', ibid, p.49

'mental conflagration and devastation',ibid, p.51

'I hear dreadful stories ... form of censorship' and 'the stimulant seemed ... not assimilated' and 'the discussion was over ... Tea was served', *Australia Brought to Book*, p.224

'the damn ship hasn't gone down yet!', *The Time Traveller*, p.416

'found him a physical wreck', ibid, p.419

'shrill jets of journalism', ibid, p.299

'I am tired, I am old ... clever enough', ibid, p.413

'It suggests going to the root ... digging and weeding', HG: *The History of Mr Wells*, p.256

'along the stream of fate ... and death', *The Time Traveller*, p.439

'credible human people ... totem poles', *The Correspondence of HG Wells*, p.217

'I am quite convinced ... is suicide', *HG Wells: Desperately Mortal*, p.141

'Peace is not a foolish ... educate for it', ibid, p.140

'the minds of us all ... never existed', *The Time Traveller*, p.430

'fiction of their times and not read ours at all', *HG Wells: Desperately Mortal*, p.142

PICTURE CREDITS

INDEX